VOICES FROM AMSTERDAM

THE SOCIETY OF BIBLICAL LITERATURE
SEMEIA STUDIES
Edward L. Greenstein, Editor

VOICES FROM AMSTERDAM
A Modern Tradition of
Reading Biblical Narrative

Selected, translated, and edited by
Martin Kessler

Scholars Press
Atlanta, Georgia

VOICES FROM AMSTERDAM

Library of Congress Cataloging in Publication Data
Voices from Amsterdam: a modern tradition of reading biblical
    narrative/ selected, translated, and edited by Martin Kessler.
        p. cm. — (Society of Biblical Literature Semeia studies)
    Collection of articles originally published in Dutch.
    Includes bibliographical references.
    ISBN 1–55540–896–6 (alk. paper). —ISBN 1–55540–897–4 (pbk.:
alk. paper)
    1. Bible. O.T.—Criticism, interpretation, etc. 2. Bible. O.T.—
Criticism, interpretation, etc.—Netherlands—Amsterdam—History—
20th century.   I. Kessler, Martin, 1927–   . II. Series:
Semeia studies.
BS1172.2.V64   1993
221.6—dc20
                                        93–5716
                                        CIP

Printed in the United States of America
on acid-free paper

Contents

C   Other Hebrew Bible Studies

Preface

From beginning to end (the beginning being a modest proposal by the editor to translate a few of the articles authored by Amsterdam scholars) this has been a labor of love. The idea that these scholars' method and their work might deserve a wider reading was supported by the enthusiasm displayed by the authors whose work appears in this volume.

The "Amsterdam combination" has come up with a unique, balanced style of exegesis, which takes seriously the text in its ultimate form (meaning for them: synchronics and a translation along the lines of Buber and Rosenzweig), with a theological orientation directed toward a biblical theology rooted deeply in the text itself. Each of these points is amply clarified in what follows. The perceptive reader will discover many familiar things. However, this is assuredly not a carbon copy of anything done elsewhere.

The editor is grateful to each of the authors of these articles and the publishers for permitting to have their work published in this form. In the case of Palache and Beek (may their memory be a blessing), permission was granted, respectively, by the publisher (Brill, Leiden) and the family. It is hoped that the other authors find the publication of some of their work in English dress a distinct pleasure.

Special acknowledgements are due to Professor Karel Deurloo, Professor of Old Testament at the University of Amsterdam, and Drs. F. J. Hoogewoud of the Bibliotheca Rosenthaliana of the same university. Together with the editor, they have shown constant concern for this work, preventing the translator from making too many mistakes. I am grateful, too, to Dr. Frank Polak, of Tel Aviv University, for improvements in the translation of chapters 1 and 2. Now we may rejoice together that the work is ready for the critical and, one would hope, appreciative eyes of students of the Hebrew Bible.

Last but not least, a special word of thanks goes to Professor Edward L. Greenstein, Editor of Semeia Studies, for agreeing to include this little book in *SBL Semeia Studies,* and for the conscientious manner in which he did what was necessary to ready the work for publication.

Introduction

Martin Kessler

"We are going to find ourselves like Ruths [sic] agleaning in strange and alien fields, in places we have not seen before, among companions we have not met before, but with gains we have not known before," wrote John Dominic Crossan in 1982 for a gathering of invited scholars who had come to engage in creative dialog on exegetical methods at Carleton University (Ottawa, Canada, in 1977).[1]

All of the articles in this volume were originally published in Dutch, in The Netherlands. Accordingly, to an overwhelming majority of North American scholars they have been among "strange and alien fields." However, that in itself is insufficient reason to expend the energy and expense required to put them before an English speaking public!

Those who know the *Fachliteratur* in the field of Hebrew Bible are likely to be familiar with the Dutch series *Oudtestamentische Studiën* published by Brill in Leiden by the Oudtestamentisch Werkgezelschap (Old Testament Workgroup) in The Netherlands. However, the annual in which some of the essays in this volume were first published, *Amsterdamse Cahiers voor Exegese en Bijbelse Theologie* is probably not very well known in the English speaking world, partly because virtually all its

---

[1] *The Biblical Mosaic. Changing Perspectives*, eds. R. Polzin and E. Rothmann (SBL Semeia Studies; Philadelphia: Fortress, Chico: Scholars, 1982) 209.

articles are written in Dutch. It is expected that in the near future articles published in this annual will be listed in *Old Testament Abstracts*.

Let the reader glean from the fare offered here and judge; hopefully, some refreshing insights may be gained.

Genesis of this Work

For the editor who selected and translated these articles this work goes back to 1968, when Professor Beek published an article (the second in this collection) in the Dutch journal *Vox Theologica*.[2] In this article he sounded a clarion call for a new type of biblical exegesis; for many Dutch readers it served to clarify the stance of what has been called the "Amsterdam school." In the Netherlands at any rate, the scholarly world was made aware of how exegesis was being done in Amsterdam.

Introductory Articles

Since some of these articles were first published some time ago, the conclusion may suggest itself that they are therefore "out of date." That might be particularly the case with the first article in this collection, by Professor Juda Palache, which represents a transcript of the inaugural address of his professorate at Amsterdam in 1925. Professor Palache's address seems to be in a class by itself, as someone said recently: "It looks as if it were written yesterday!" This essay makes a number of important points that deal with significant literary issues. In a time when virtually every reputable scholar followed the bandwagon of Graf-Wellhausen-Kuenen, Palache reminded his colleagues that narratives, apart from their history of origin, also have a significant history of existence: the question of diachronic and synchronic criticism. Acknowledging ancient "piety toward tradition," he stressed the pragmatic character of Israel's historiography and its freedom to change materials which had been handed down. In many of these points Palache represented a fresh voice that, in retrospect, may be seen as a forerunner of what came to be called the "Amsterdam tradition."

When Palache taught at the University of Amsterdam, there was no conscious exegetical tradition in Amsterdam. Palache's scholarship was not fully appreciated till after World War II, when a volume of his representative work was published (*Sinai en Paran*; Leiden: Brill, 1950). Palache's was a significant voice from Amsterdam. Others built on his

---

[2] "Verzadigingspunten en onvoltooide lijnen in het onderzoek van de oudtestamentische literatuur," *Vox Theologica* 38 (1968) 2–14.

work and gave it the shape which eventually came to be characterized as a "school" in its own right. Frits Hoogewoud of the Bibliotheca Rosenthaliana in Amsterdam claims that the Amsterdam school was created by the combined contributions of Beek, Buber, Breukelman, and Miskotte, and presently personified in Karel Deurloo.

The second and third articles, by Palache's successors, Professors Beek and Deurloo, are programmatic in nature and discuss methodological questions. Professor Smelik's lecture (presented as a memorial address for Professor Beek) surveys the "official side" of the Amsterdam school: the professors and their students, while Zuurmond's essay on what Amsterdam hermeneutics might look like, completes the methodological section.

Comparison to the American Scene

American readers may wonder whether the Amsterdam school may be comparable to (American) rhetorical (or synchronic) criticism. A connecting link with the American scene may indeed be suggested by the fact that in the same year Beek's article, "Saturation Points..." was published, James Muilenburg gave his oft-quoted SBL presidential address "Form Criticism and Beyond" which appeared in print the following year.[3] Superficially considered, one might be tempted to conclude that the "Amsterdam school" simply represents a Dutch version of synchronic criticism, and that it is therefore comparable to "rhetorical criticism," (Muilenburg's label), "(French) structural criticism," a biblical application of "new criticism" or "literary criticism" (in the synchronic sense).

The picture is far more complex, however. Admittedly, when Professor Muilenburg spoke of historical criticism having come "to an impasse" and when he mentioned "the excesses of source analysis"[4] he said things that also have been said in various ways by scholars of the Amsterdam school (particularly Beek in his first essay in this collection). But there are also many differences. Muilenburg's proposed method which he called "rhetorical criticism" was presented as supplemental to form criticism; he spoke at a time when form criticism still enjoyed high favor. Beek, on the other hand, reacted more negatively toward form criticism. Overall, Amsterdam scholars are clearly more consistently syn-

---

3 Published in *JBL* 88 (1969) 1–18.
4 Ibid., 1.

chronic in their approach; they tend to be critical of diachronic methods even though they do not usually get involved in polemics on the subject.

By contrast, Muilenburg never came out rejecting the Graf-Wellhausen documentary hypothesis any more than Gunkel did in his day. In both cases there is the sustained effort to somehow reconcile the older literary criticism with newer methods: form criticism for Gunkel and rhetorical criticism for Muilenburg.

Comparing the American scene with the Amsterdam tradition, the following provisional conclusions may be suggested, which the reader may want to bear in mind in reading the articles in this collection.

1. The Amsterdam school's methodological concerns go well beyond strictly analytical methods. As such it moves beyond typical synchronic studies as illustrated, for example, by Fokkelman's work,[5] in that it is consciously theologically oriented (though in varying ways among its practitioners). In North America, synchronic criticism tends to remove itself from explicit theological concerns, or at least, tries to practice literary criticism without taking a theological stand. In Amsterdam, as illustrated particularly in Deurloo's essay on Cain and Abel, and further explicated in Uwe Bauer's dissertation (see note 14), Amsterdam literary criticism is founded on a distinct theological basis. Yet, the Amsterdam tradition has not shied away from creative dialogue. The fact that Palache was Jewish raised some eyebrows in the Netherlands (in the twenties, a time when the liberal-fundamentalist controversy raged in the United States!), but Palache acquitted himself well of his task. After World War II, with the Dutch Jewish community decimated by the Nazi occupation, a Christian was appointed to the chair. However, Beek had almost from the beginning of his career been deeply interested in the Jewish input into biblical interpretation. His interest in the writings of Martin Buber and in the Bible translation principles advocated both by Buber and Franz Rosenzweig points in the same direction. Karel Deurloo, the present occupant of the chair, has continued the same emphasis. Another factor, discussed below, is the role of Kornelis Miskotte (Professor of Theology at Leiden) and the extent to which he provided a theological foundation for the Amsterdam school. The end result is that the Amsterdam school, in line with much Christian thinking in the Netherlands, has been influenced by its study of Judaism. The "neutral" ideology found in much American scholarship is foreign to

---

5 J. P. Fokkelman, *Narrative Art in Genesis* (Assen: Van Gorcum, 1975), to mention just one example of his work.

Amsterdam. Biblical exegesis in the Amsterdam tradition is for proclamation, and the church is called to awareness of her roots; that means,
among other things, cultivating and maintaining constructive relationships with Judaism.

2. The Amsterdam school has developed in various areas, not only in
biblical exegesis, but also in (systematic) theology,[6] biblical theology,[7]
dogmatics,[8] politics,[9] liturgy and pastoral practice,[10] and the translation
of biblical texts (see below).

3. Contrary to some critical claims,[11] scholarship of the Amsterdam
school[12] is concerned with historical questions (especially the work of
Smelik and Deurloo). Amsterdam scholars, however, spend considerably
less time on dating the literature than has often been customary among
biblical scholars.

4. Though it does not speak with one voice, the Amsterdam school
shows remarkable homogeneity. There is a clear continuity in its scholar-

---

[6] See *De Bijbel maakt school. Een Amsterdamse weg in de exegese* (The Bible Goes
Academic. An Amsterdam Way in Exegesis), eds. Karel Deurloo and Rochus Zuurmond (Baarn: Ten Have, 1984).

[7] Particularly the work of F. H. Breukelman: *Bijbelse Theologie, I, 1. Schriftlezing*
(Reading of Scripture; Kampen: Kok, 1980), and 2, *III, De theologie van de evangelist
Mattheus, 1. De ouverture van het evangelie* (Kampen: Kok, 1984). Other works in this
series (on Genesis) are in progress.

[8] As inspired and informed by biblical exegesis; see N. T. Bakker, "Dogmatiek en
exegese," in *De Bijbel maakt school*, 92–107.

[9] Particularly the work of D. Boer. See W. van der Spek, "Exegese en politiek," in
De Bijbel maakt school, 108–14.

[10] See B. P. M. Hemelsoet, "Commune martyrum," and Th. J. M. Naastepad, "In de
praktijk," in *De Bijbel maakt school*, 121–36. See also: *Voor de achtste dag. Het oude testament in de eredienst. Een bundel opstellen voor Prof. Dr. J. P. Boendermaker* (For the Eighth
Day. The Old Testament in Worship. A Volume of Essays for Prof. Dr. J. P. Boendermaker), eds. K. van der Horst et al. (Kampen: Kok, 1990).

[11] Roel Oost, *Omstreden Bijbeluitleg. Aspecten en achtergronden van de hermeneutische
discussie rondom de exegese van het Oude Testament in Nederland. Een bijdrage tot gesprek,*
(Controversial Biblical Interpretation. Aspects and Backgrounds of the Hermeneutical Discussion Surrounding the Exegesis of the Old Testament in the Netherlands. A
Contribution to Conversation; Dissertation, University of Groningen; Kampen: Kok,
1986) passim.

[12] See especially K. A. D. Smelik, *Saul. De voorstelling van Israels eerste koning in de
Masoretische tekst van het Oude Testament* (Saul. The Presentation of Israel's First King
in the Masoretic Text of the Old Testament; Dissertation, University of Amsterdam;
Amsterdam: PET, 1977); and more popularly, K. A. Deurloo, *Waar gebeurd. Over het
onhistorisch karakter van bijbelse verhalen* (Truly Happened. Concerning the Unhistorical Character of Biblical Narratives; Baarn: Ten Have, 1981).

ship. Its emphases set it apart from the canons of the type of biblical scholarship that originated chiefly in Germany.

5. The Amsterdam school's work is being discovered by individuals abroad, particularly in Germany.[13] Some German students are year after year attracted by way of the Old Testament to study theology at the University of Amsterdam. One of them, Uwe Bauer, received his doctorate December 1991.[14] The methods of the Amsterdam school enjoy a vitality as well as a committed following. *Amsterdamse Cahiers*[15] features articles from a goodly number of authors who who are in various ways committed to the Amsterdam methods.

Amsterdam Beginnings: Palache

The original impetus for the kind of Old Testament study described and illustrated in this volume must be credited to Juda L. Palache. Born in Amsterdam in 1886, his father was chief rabbi of the Portuguese Jewish congregation. The young Palache studied classical and Semitic languges, particularly Hebrew, Aramaic, and Arabic. He became an eminent philologist with a particular interest in etymological questions. In 1924 he was appointed not only to the philological/philosophical faculty, but also to the theological faculty at the University of Amsterdam, where he served with distinction till the Germans removed him in November 1940, when all Jewish personnel were dismissed from public

---

[13] Among the books in (or related to) the Amsterdam tradition, translated in German, are: K. H. Miskotte, *Wenn die Götter schweigen* (3rd ed.; Munich: Kaiser, 1966); M. A. Beek, *An Babels Strömen. Hauptereignisse aus der Kulturgeschichte Mesopotamiens in der alttestamentlichen Zeit* (Munich: Kaiser, 1959); N. Bouhuijs, K. A. Deurloo, *Zur Bedeutung biblischen Redens und Erzählens*, ed. Raimer Henne (Offenbach: Laetare, 1988); idem, *Näher zum Anfang. Die Bedeutung der ersten Erzählungen der Bibel* (Offenbach: Laetare, 1989). Among the titles translated in English are: M. A. Beek, *Atlas of Mesopotamia* (London/Edinburgh: Nelson, 1962); idem, *A Journey through the Old Testament* (London: Hodder & Stoughton; New York: Harper, 1959); idem, *A Short History of Israel from Abraham to the Bar Cochba Rebellion* (London: Hodder & Stoughton, 1963). The last two titles were also translated in German and Portuguese. Also: K. H. Miskotte, *When the Gods are Silent* (New York/Evanston: Harper & Row, 1967).

[14] *Kol haddebarim ha'elleh. All diese Worte: Impulse zur Schriftauslegung aus Amsterdam; expliziert an der Schilfmeererzählung in Exodus 13,17–14,31* (Dissertation, University of Amsterdam; Frankfurt a/M: Lang, 1992).

[15] Kampen: Kok, 1980–. The editors of this annual, most of whom have served since its inception, are: Prof. Deurloo (University of Amsterdam), Prof. Hemelsoet (Catholic Theological University, Amsterdam), Drs. Hoogewoud (Bibliotheca Rosenthaliana, Amsterdam), Prof. Smelik (Protestant Theological Faculty, Brussels) and Prof. Zuurmond (University of Amsterdam).

service. Samples of his scholarship were published in *Sinai en Paran.
Opera Minora*.[16] Of particular interest for Hebrew Bible scholarship and
for the characteristic development of the Amsterdam school (among
them its continuing openness to Jewish approaches) is his article "Het
karakter van het Oud-Testamentisch verhaal" (The Nature of Old Testament Narrative) to which reference has already been made and which is
published in this volume. One of his major theses, and one which has
profoundly influenced Amsterdam scholars, is: "the most ancient writers
of the Old Testament ... must have behaved much more independently
toward tradition, and must have composed far more than is usually
assumed."[17] He illustrates this thesis with references both to biblical and
Arabic literature. Far from being "scissors and paste" artists, biblical
writers were composers to a far greater degree than we might imagine.

M. A. Beek

After World War II, M. A. Beek took the vacated chair (1946), which
he occupied till his retirement in 1974. Beek had studied in Leiden with
B. D. Eerdmans,[18] who charted an independent course vis-à-vis Graf-
Kuenen-Wellhausen's regnant *Urkundenhypothese* (though Eerdmans was
not taken very seriously). Beek also studied in Germany, with Professors
Alt and Von Rad among others.[19]

At some point quite early in his career he became interested in the
Jewish approach to the Bible. His most significant Jewish impetus came
from Martin Buber, who had been busily engaged with what has been
called a "concordant" translation of the Hebrew Bible in German in
which task he was joined by Franz Rosenzweig until that scholar's
premature death.[20] As Beek indicates in "Saturation Points...," he was
also impressed by modern literary methods.[21] He believed that they
offered valuable contributions in the practice of biblical criticism.

Beek's influence on his students is cogently traced by Professor
Smelik in his memorial address "Narrative in the Hebrew Bible." Three

[16] Leiden: Brill, 1959.
[17] Ibid., 35.
[18] Author of *Alttestamentliche Studien, I, II* (Giessen: Töpelmann, 1908–1910).
[19] "Vier leermeesters," in *De Bijbel maakt school*, 76–82.
[20] See M. A. Beek, "The Meditator and his Task" (addressed to Martin Buber on
the occasion of the Paemium Erasmianum ceremony in Amsterdam, 1963), in *Leo
Baeck Institute Yearbook* 7 (1964) 258–59.
[21] Among the scholars named in Beek's article are: Emil Staiger, Wolfgang Kayser
(both of the German *Werkschule*), L. Alonso Schökel and Meir Weiss ("Saturation
Points...," passim).

articles by Beek's doctoral students appear in translation in this volume: in addition to Smelik, also Van Daalen and Deurloo.

Methodological Reflections: Oost and Bauer

However, the history of the Amsterdam school is not only traceable institutionally, by observing the occupant of the Old Testament chair and the doctorates awarded by it. The school's intellectual history may also be profitably studied. Two attempts have been made in the Netherlands to describe this history. Roel Oost, whose dissertation has been referred to above,[22] focusses chiefly on Beek and three of his students, with an excursus on Miskotte.[23] The second chapter (first part) offers a description of "stylistic and structural analysis" with emphasis on Staiger, Wellek and Warren, and Kayser.[24] The author expresses his hope that proponents of both diachronic and synchronic methods may be encouraged to enter into fruitful dialogue. Another dissertation that offers a history of the Amsterdam school together with an in-depth exegetical piece in the Amsterdam style, has been written by Uwe Bauer.[25] Both dissertations were very helpful in the research for this introduction.

Intellectual and Theological Antecedents

Various factors may be discerned in the history of the Amsterdam school. They represent trends of thought and academic disciplines, but they are ultimately embodied in individuals who then in turn add their own unique contribution to a living tradition. In what follows I shall accordingly name certain key individuals.

1. As is the case in most places where the Hebrew Bible is taken seriously, Dutch scholars typically involve themselves in the study of the *ancient Near East*. This involvement is quite evident in Palache and continues in Beek, who wrote a history of ancient Israel (translated in three languages) as well as an atlas of Mesopotamia (see note 13). Hebrew Bible training in Amsterdam usually includes a solid grounding in the languages, cultures, literatures, and history of the *Umwelt*.

2. Among Christian theologians who influenced the Amsterdam tradition, one of the most significant is probably *K. H. Miskotte*. Uwe

---

[22] See n. 11 supra.
[23] Oost, *Omstreden Bijbeluitleg*, 18–21.
[24] Ibid., 31–44.
[25] See n. 14 supra.

Bauer has traced the lines of influence with some completeness, beginning with John Calvin and the Bible translation produced by the
Reformed Church in the Netherlands in 1637.[26] Karl Barth, read and
studied diligently[27] there, had his most influential interpreter in
Miskotte, who began as a parish pastor and later served on the faculty at
Leiden University, becoming, in the words of Bauer, "one of the most
significant Dutch theologians of this century."[28] He protested against
what he termed the "fatal dualism" of pulpit versus classroom, of church
and university, of science and faith. He felt strongly that this chasm
should be bridged.[29] This theme has found a home in the thinking of the
Amsterdam school. Beek's lecture on David and Absalom illustrates his
conviction that the biblical narrative in itself can be proclamation for the
general public. Other exponents of the Amsterdam school have also written books for an audience beyond the scholarly community.

Quite early in his career (in 1928) Miskotte discovered Franz Rosen-
zweig's *Stern der Erlösung*,[30] which sparked his interest in Judaism.[31]
When National Socialism reigned supreme in Germany in the thirties,
Miskotte published a critical study attacking Nazism: *Edda en Thora*.[32]

G. H. ter Schegget has written enthusiastically about Miskotte in *De
Bijbel maakt school* (The Bible Goes Academic)[33] in which he called
Miskotte the great inspiration of the Amsterdam school: "not the founding father, but the silent strength behind it."[34] Disturbed about the care-
lessness of Christendom, Miskotte became a renewer, going back to the
sources that he knew had not dried up but were still abundantly flowing.
He began with a small circle whom he taught, out of which experience
came his book *Bijbels ABC*.[35] Miskotte's comments on biblical exegesis

---

[26] Bauer, *All Diese Worte*, 20–34.
[27] Ibid., 35–49. See especially: Karl Barth, *The Doctrine of the Word of God* (Church
Dogmatics, I, 1, 2; Edinburgh: Clark, 1967 and 1969).
[28] Bauer, *All Diese Worte*, 50.
[29] R. Zuurmond, "Theologia Theologorum," *Summa. Theologische Faculteit*
(Amsterdam: Universiteit van Amsterdam, December, 1985) 29–31.
[30] Frankfurt: Suhrkamp, 1988.
[31] Bauer, *All Diese Worte*, 51.
[32] (Edda and Torah: A Comparison of Germanic and Israelite Religion) 2nd ed.
(Nijkerk: Callenbach, 1970). The first edition was published in 1939, when its anti-
Nazi polemic was highly relevant.
[33] "Miskotte, inspirator, voortrekker," 83–91.
[34] Schegget, *De Bijbel maakte school*, 83.
[35] Baarn: Ten Have. This book was first published in 1941 but it has been reprinted
seven times (most recently in 1992). It was translated in German as *Biblisches ABC:
Wider das unbiblische Bibellesen* (Neukirchen/Vluyn: Neukirchener Verlag, 1976).

are found in *Om het levende woord. Opstellen over de praktijk der exegese* (About the Living Word. Essays on the Practice of Exegesis).[36] While literary-historical and phenomenological exegesis remain secular, theological exegesis concerns itself with kerygmatic content. Miskotte invokes the *pars-pro-toto* principle: "Every part of Scripture is not only part of the whole, but it also itself contains the whole."[37]

3. *Martin Buber (1878–1965) and Franz Rosenzweig (1886–1929)*. The influence of Buber on the Amsterdam school is profound.[38] Beek and Deurloo quote Buber and Rosenzweig in the opening articles of this volume. Miskotte and Breukelman have likewise expressed their indebtedness to Buber.

One may get some clues to Buber's thought through his well known work *I and Thou*. The Hebrew Bible was not written down for reading (silently) but for reading aloud, or rather, for "calling out": *miqrāʾ*—the traditional Jewish name for the Bible. The spoken word is therefore decisively important because it addresses the hearer and calls him into living dialogue with the *erhörenden* God.[39] For Buber, the spoken word enters the sphere between persons. Conversation is more than the sum total of what is said. This is the practical application of his *I and Thou*.[40]

Because of these characteristics the Bible is truly one, regardless of the reliability of sources or witnesses. Rosenzweig was keenly concerned with the composition of the Bible as suggested by his famous statement that R is not *Redaktor* but *Rabbenu*, "our teacher."

---

36 The Hague: Daamen, 1948. See also *Wenn die Götter schweigen* (Munich: Kaiser, 1963), translated in English as *When the Gods are Silent*. See also Ray S. Anderson, ed., "Preaching as the Narrating of the Acts of God," *Theological Foundations for Ministry* (Grand Rapids /Edinburgh: Eerdmans, 1979) 648–88.

37 Bauer, *All Diese Worte*, 53, on whom the information in this paragraph relies.

38 Though the names of these two scholars are quite familiar, they seem to be only superficially known in our hemisphere. Several works of Buber remain in print in English translation: *Moses. The Revelation and the Covenant* (Atlantic Highlands: Humanities, 1988); *Pointing the Way. Collected Essays* (Atlantic Highlands: Humanities, 1990); *The Knowledge of Man. Selected Essays* (Atlantic Highlands: Humanities, 1988); *The Way of Response*, ed. N. N. Glatzer (New York: Schocken, 1988); *On Judaism*, ed. N. N. Glatzer (New York: Schocken, 1972). Rosenzweig's major work, *Der Stern der Erlösung* (Berlin: Schocken, 1930) was translated into English by William W. Hallo with the title *The Star of Redemption* (Notre Dame: University of Notre Dame Press, 1985).

39 F. Rosenzweig, "Das Formgeheimnis der biblischen Erzählung," in *Die Schrift: Aufsätze, Uberträgungen und Briefe,* ed. K. Thieme (Königstein: Athenaum, 1984) 26.

40 Bauer, *All Diese Worte*, 66.

Though scholars of the Amsterdam school have always made appreciative use of the Buber-Rosenzweig translation, they do not always agree in every detail. Beek, for example, criticized the translation's consistent rendering of the divine name as "*ER.*" However, the Amsterdam school unequivocally agrees with Buber and Rosenzweig in their opposition to dynamic-equivalent translations of the Bible (such as the Good News Bible and parallels in other languages). The Amsterdam school prefers the designation "idiolect" to "concordant." In the words of Bauer: "only an idiolect translation can guarantee that Scripture remains functional as subject of critique."[41]

When the Dutch (Protestant) Bible Society (NBG) published a new translation of the Bible in 1951, critical voices were heard, none more eloquent and persistent than Breukelman's.

4. *F. H. Breukelman* is probably named as frequently as any other person in connection with the development of the Amsterdam school.[42] Strictly speaking, he should not be listed among "antecedents" but rather as an eloquent and influential exponent of the Amsterdam tradition. Like Miskotte, he started his career as a small town church pastor when people began to beat a path to his door to be taught. In 1968 students finally prevailed with the authorities at the University of Amsterdam to give him a post. Rochus Zuurmond, his successor in Amsterdam (promoted to professor in 1991) said of Breukelman in 1986 that he judged him to be one of the most, if not the most, significant contemporary Dutch theologian: "creative like few others, original and profound."[43]

As suggested above, Breukelman became well known by a series of critical articles on the recently published new Dutch translation of the

---

[41] Ibid., 186. For the Amsterdam scholars, "concordant" is too mechanical (translating each word precisely the same way) whereas "idiolect" is concerned with the stylistic peculiarity (*to idion*) of the text; the idiolect translation seeks to reflect the moulding of the original text, its sphere, style, power of statement (*Aussagekraft*) and dynamic as faithfully as possible in translation (ibid., 112, n. 23).

[42] In addition to Breukelman's article translated in this volume, one may refer to *Vox Theologica* 36 (1966) 106–11.

[43] Bauer, *All Diese Worte*, 77. Oost comments that Breukelman's work often functions like an "infra-text" in Dutch Hebrew Bible scholarship (*Omstreden Bijbeluitleg*, 12).

Bible (1951).[44] These articles were perhaps the first signal of the fact that the Bible was going to "become academic in a particular manner."[45]

In his article on the brief but difficult pericope Gen 6:1–4 in this volume, he prefaces his exegesis with a brief outline of his view of the structure of Genesis. His exegesis is typical of the Amsterdam school: the text can only be understood if we pay attention to its context, not narrowly but broadly conceived. The *pars pro toto* principle is fully operative in his exegesis. His major publication project is his *Bijbelse Theologie*. Only a small portion has been commercially published (see note 7, above). The first part of his study of Genesis was published in 1992.

The Present Scene: Deurloo

Returning to the University of Amsterdam, the present occupant of the Old Testament chair is Karel A. Deurloo. The third article in this collection (the introduction to his dissertation on Cain and Abel) describes his version of the Amsterdam methodology. Similarities to Beek's approach are immediately apparent: he dialogues with historical criticism (diachronics versus synchronics) and speaks appreciatively of German *Werkinterpretation*. But he goes beyond Beek in building theological foundations; he not only refers to Buber and modern biblical exegetes (as did Beek) but also disputes von Rad, interprets Barth, and quotes Miskotte. Abstracting his article "Scope of a Small Literary Unit," he quotes with approval what Bauer considers an appropriate motto of Breukelman's work: *scriptura scripturae interpres*.

Among members of the Amsterdam school, Deurloo is unquestionably the standard-bearer.[46] He is a prolific writer and some of his books (sometimes co-authored with colleagues) have seen many printings. While he has written about several aspects of the Old Testament, his most insistent focus is on Genesis.[47] Two of his articles dealing with

---

44 Some articles have been reprinted in *Amsterdamse Cahiers* 3 (1982) 8–37; 4 (1983) 8–27; 5 (1984) 9–26.

45 *De Bijbel maakt school*, 10.

46 Oost distinguishes various "contours" in the Amsterdam tradition: first, Old Testament interpretation, inspired and supported by Jewish scholarship (chiefly Buber), next, by modern literary critical scholarship. This "contour" is represented by Beek. The second contour, originating with Breukelman, was driven by biblical/ theological and hermeneutical concerns: Barth and Miskotte (as well as by Buber and Rosenzweig). Oost claims that Deurloo is the connecting link between these two "contours" (*Omstreden Bijbeluitleg*, 13).

47 *De mens als raadsel en geheim. Verhalende antropologie in Genesis 2–4* (Man as Riddle and Secret. Narrative Anthropology in Genesis 2–4; Baarn: Ten Have, 1988);

themes in Genesis are included in the present collection. The article "The Ways of Abraham" was specifically written for this book. Those who want more of the same may be referred to his "Narrative Geography in the Abraham Cycle," *OTS* 26 (1990), 48–62.[48]

Deurloo's exegetical results are clearly related to his focus on what von Rad calls the *Jetzgestalt* or the *Letztgestalt* (in the article "Narrative in the Hebrew Bible"). He adopts Alonso Schökel's term *Sitz in der Literatur*,[49] which of course indicates a parting company with the canons of form criticism and its *Sitz im Leben*. According to Bauer's analysis, in Deurloo the dogmatic-hermeneutic and biblical-theological strand of the Amsterdam school joins with the literary-scientific strand in Hebrew biblical exegesis. "While Deurloo accomplished this connection, he has rendered the 'Amsterdam school' an important, directional [*richtungsweisenden*] service."[50]

Deurloo, as a churchman, is also engaged in liturgical concerns, often in connection with the Dutch Professor Dr. G. van der Leeuw Stichting. He has written a book of what would be called in North America "junior sermons"—well interpreted, engagingly told biblical stories for youth: *Een kind mag in het midden staan. Exegetische vertelsels voor kleine oren* (A Child May Stand in the Midst. Exegetical Stories for Little Ears.)[51] A more recent publication in the liturgical area is "Van Pasen naar Pinksteren" (From Easter to Pentecost) in the Boendermaker *Festschrift*.[52]

Bible Translation

Inspired by the translation of Buber-Rosenzweig, and convinced of the need to render the text in a manner which faithfully reflects the verbal thrust of the original, several representatives of the Amsterdam

---

and *De dagen van Noach* (The Days of Noah; co-authored by R. Zuurmond and A. M. Van Apeldoorn; Baarn: Ten Have, 1991) and more popularly, with K. Bouhuijs, *Dichter bij Genesis* (Closer to Genesis; 5th printing; Baarn: Ten Have, 1980). This little book has also been translated in German: *Näher zum Anfang: Die Bedeutung der ersten Erzählungen der Bibel* (Offenbach: Laetare, 1988).

[48] Among the work of Deurloo's students, see: A. Dicou, *Jacob en Esau. Israel tegenover de volken in de verhalen over Jakob en Esau en in de grote profetiëen over Edom* (Jacob and Esau. Israel vis-à-vis the Nations in the Jacob and Esau Narratives in the Great Prophecies against Edom; Dissertation, University of Amsterdam, 1990); and J. Siebert-Hommes, "Twelve Women in Exodus 1 and 2. The Role of Daughters and Sons in the Stories concerning Moses," *Amsterdamse Cahiers* 9 (1988) 47–58.

[49] Oost, *Omstreden Bijbeluitleg*, 20–21.

[50] Bauer, *All Diese Worte*, 119.

[51] 2d printing; Baarn: Ten Have, 1984.

[52] *Voor de achtste dag*, (see n.10 supra) 35–44.

school have diligently worked to produce idiolect renderings of the Hebrew text. In 1961 Beek founded the Societas Hebraica Amstelodamensis, which has done much to promote the study of the Hebrew Bible in Amsterdam and its environs.[53] As mentioned above, when a new Dutch translation of the Bible was published in 1951, Breukelman in particular raised strong protests against the dynamic-equivalent tendencies of that text. The upshot of his critical articles was a series of attempts at idiolect translations: of Ruth, Jonah, Judges, Amos, Obadaiah, and Micah, as well as parts of Genesis.[54]

The Essays: An Overview

The methods and ideas embodied in the various personalities who have passed us in review, find their expression in the collection of essays that follow. As indicated above, the introductory section is intended to give the reader some impressions of what the Amsterdam school stands for. The statements by Palache, Beek, and Deurloo are fundamental. Palache boldly tackled a crucial subject with great insight. Beek also wrote for a wider public, while Deurloo's essay illustrates a deeper involvement in the theological aspects of exegesis.

Zuurmond's contribution is hermeneutical in its thrust, as its title suggests.

Deurloo's chapter, "The Way of Abraham," illustrates some fundamental exegetical points: the need for close reading and reading in context, attention to keywords, and an endeavor to discern themes—in this case, the gift of the land. He also sketches the interrelation of places and themes, demonstrating once again the proclaiming function of this literature. The same exegetical principles are applied in his paper on the "Binding of Isaac," Genesis 22. The "going" (as in Genesis 12) is a leading

---

53 See *Een vertaling om voor te lezen* (A Translation for Reading Aloud; Haarlem: Nederlands Bijbelgenootschap; Boxtel: Katholieke Bijbelstichting, 1986–1991). This includes translations of Amos, Obadiah, Jonah, Judges, Ruth, and Micah.

54 K. A. Deurloo, F. J. Hoogewoud, "Communi ardore ad litteras hebraicas inflammati. Bij het vijfentwentigjarig jubileum van SHA" (Amsterdam: Juda Palache Instituut, 1986) 91–105. The article includes summaries of all lectures. See also F. J. Hoogewoud, "Stap voor stap. Een kroniek bij 'Een vertaling om voor te lezen' (NBG/KBS)" (Step by Step. A Chronicle of 'A Translation for Reading Aloud', *Amsterdamse Cahiers* 1 (1980) 102–15; and by the same author, "Bij een nieuwe vertaling van Richteren" (With a New Translation of Judges), in Hanna Blok et al., *Geen koning in die dagen. Over het boek Richteren als profetische geschiedschrijving* (Baarn: Ten Have, 1982) 159–80. There are also plans afoot for a complete Bible translation along indicated lines ("De vertaling 2000") to be published by the Dutch Bible Society (NBG).

theme, as is Abraham's "hearing" (God—and his wife, 16:2!). The word-play is subtle: *yr'* and *r'h*: the "God-fearer" gets "to see."

Breukelman has tackled a story that has puzzled many interpreters of the Bible. Making the point that this story (and any biblical story) must be read within its context, he proceeds to sketch that context. Let the reader be patient! Breukelman's conclusion is that Israel is firstborn, blessed, and representative of humankind—in contrast to the story of Genesis 6, which points to the mythology of the (pagan) nations.

Van Daalen's exegesis of part of Exodus 3 also underscores the pro-claiming function of a pericope, illustrating several features of Hebrew narrative technique and showing how they function to support a keryg-matic thrust.

Two more articles by Beek conclude the collection. His study of the role of Joshua in the Bible (first published in an Albright *Festschrift*) is not historical, but literary. Joshua (whose historicity is widely questioned, apart from Beek's article) is seen as the "ideal savior"—an idea that is supported by the way he is referred to in other biblical books—who assembled *"all* the people...in *one* country...around *one* Torah." An echo of Palache's address may be heard in this article.

Beek's final article shows him at his best in "story-telling." The reader may not be surprised that one of Beek's best-selling publications is a "story Bible" (for adults): *Wegen en Voetsporen van het Oude Testament* (Ways and Footprints of the Old Testament).[55] It reflects the Amsterdam tradition well. If the Bible has, as Beek never tired of saying, a "proclaim-ing function," then the persons who have the requisite skills to interpret it intelligently and engagingly should communicate their findings to the widest possible public. Not surprisingly, Amsterdam scholars are quite visible in the Netherlands, for communication is high on their agenda. Professor Beek's anniversary lecture is not for entertainment (as he said)—anymore than the text he expounds! Even in the David and Absalom story there is proclamation: a tragic story in narrative dress, illustrating the nexus between actions and experiences by portraying the fate of the *dramatis personae.*

A NOTE ON TRANSLATION: No consistent pattern has been followed in quotations from the Bible. Frequently, an English translation has been made from the rendering in the original

---

[55] 6th printing; Baarn: Wereldvenster, 1969; translated in English as *A Journey through the Old Testament* (London/New York: 1959).

Dutch text of the article translated. The Dutch text is virtually always translated, as are bibliographical items, which does not mean, of course, that such articles or books are available in English translation.

A

Methodological Essays

—⤙ **1** ⤚—

THE NATURE OF
OLD TESTAMENT NARRATIVE

*J. L. Palache**

ABSTRACT

The Renaissance forms the border between the orthodox-dogmatic view of the Bible as superhuman revelation and the independent, humanistic exegesis that eventually led to the critical-scientific method. However, criticism has been taken to extremes with the result that the larger view has been pushed into the background.

Scholarship has greatly occupied itself with the role of the redactor(s). Gunkel wrote that the source sigla were not single authors but schools of narrators, whereas Lods has claimed that redactors, in spite of their great piety toward the past, have imprinted something of their personality on their work.

Narrative is a preferred means for framing thoughts or to persuade. It provides (often unhistorical) answers to all sorts of questions, not only in the Bible, but also in the *Haggadah* (as in the Arabic *Hadith*). These stories incline toward visualization and concrete representation. They are often poetic and are not bound to reality or to older traditions.

---

* This chapter is a slightly edited translation of "Het karakter van het Oud-Testamentishe verhaal," the inaugural address at the University of Amsterdam (1925), published in Amsterdam in 1925 and reprinted in *Sinai en Paran. Opera Minora van wijlen Dr. J. L. Palache* (Leiden : Brill, 1959) 15–16.

The truth question must be reversed from the usual perception. The story is not told because it happened, but becomes real by the telling. The telling creates tradition in generations that follow, supported by the belief of the pious. When there are two recensions, they are never identical. Moreover, in the Bible at least, there is little concern to remove incongruencies and inconsistencies. In all, biblical writers have related far more independently toward the material and the tradition than is commonly assumed. They likely composed materials themselves.

The question, where might there be the dwelling place of Wisdom, that mysterious key of the riddles of life and the world, preoccupied the ancients. The form in which it is asked already points clearly in the direction of where the answer might be expected, and it does not surprise us that the solutions of the problem that the literatures of Egyptians and Babylonians, of Greeks, Indians, and Persians have preserved, bear the seal of mythology. Either the high heavens or a far distant land or the depths of the Nether World or Ocean—that is where the seat of Wisdom is sought.

But even when those mythological ideas have long since been superseded and have disappeared from people's faith, their traces remain in imagery or simile in literature—vague reminders of what once was a representation of reality. In the Old Testament we also have such allusions. "Not inaccessible and not far off is the commandment that I give you today; not in heaven that you should say: who will ascend for us into heaven; and not on the other side of the ocean, that you should say: who will cross the ocean for us to bring it to us and to proclaim it to us, that we might accomplish it?"[1]

In the Book of Job the problem is treated in poetic verse: "Wisdom: where may she be found, and where is the dwelling of understanding? The deep says: she is not with me; the ocean says: she is not with me...She is hidden to all that lives, and to the birds of the sky she is hidden. The netherworld and the realm of the dead say: with our ears we have perceived a rumor about her."[2]

We are not gullible enough to expect or to accept a concrete answer to such questions. But the question itself with respect to its meaning and content, that is to say, the question of the paths along which knowledge

---

[1] A free translation of Deut 30:11–13, closely corresponding to the author's rendering. See H. Gunkel, *Das Märchen im Alten Testament* (Tübingen: Mohr, 1917) 53. (English translation: *The Folktale in the Old Testament*, trans. M. D. Rutter [Sheffield: Almond Press, 1987].)

[2] Job 28:12,14.

and wisdom and truth must be sought, has remained ever relevant. Particularly in those fields where, beside knowledge, religion lets its light shine, it has often enough become a burning question which has already led to much conflict. To these fields belongs also the ancient Hebrew literature, the Old Testament.

It is not my intention to treat this point exhaustively at present. I would then have to relate the long and tortuous history of the exegesis of the Old Testament. Instead I propose to invite your attention to some considerations concerning the character of Old Testament narrative. But first I should like to say a word about the two main streams that may be observed in the area of exegesis, and the related study of the canon and text of the Old Testament.

The history of the exegesis of the Old Testament may be handily divided into two parts between which the Renaissance forms the natural border. Antiquity and the Middle Ages are—apart from some independent and passing expositions—virtually dominated by the thesis, that the origin at least of that wisdom which is given us in the Bible is in heaven, and that that heavenly wisdom has found a medium to express itself in that Book of Revelation, that book of superhuman character, which is inspired from beginning to end by the Deity. Even as directions and methods differ and the grammatical-historical interpretation compete for priority with the allegorical (soon also with the mystical), the starting point is always the infallibility of the divine word revealed therein and the conviction that all wisdom, indeed every truth of whichever character, and wherever and whenever it might be found, must be in harmony with it. It was precisely allegory with its unlimited possibilities—*aliud verbis aliud sensu* [one thing is said, something else is meant]—and the theory of the multiple meaning of the scriptural word, often defended by Jews and Christians, which offered as much room as necessary for this. The boundaries between the different conceptions of the biblical text came to run parallel with the boundaries between religions and dogmatic trends, wherever it touches the problems of religion directly or indirectly.

The Renaissance introduced a totally different course. The enthusiasm for ancient culture that comprises the essence of humanism brought in its wake scholarly interest in ancient Hebrew language and literature. Study of the classics and the exact philological methods that were followed in the interpretation of those ancient authors could not but cross-fertilize the interpretation of the Bible. With that came the striving of humanists to liberate scholarship in general, and thus also in this special field, from the belief in authority, from dogma and tradition, and to give free play to individual judgment. Presently the Reformation demanded more attention (also among Christian theologians) for the Old Testament. It is quite evident how strongly the humanistic view has influenced the views of the first Reformers. With more or less emphasis the demand is voiced among them to seek the meaning of the biblical word based solely on the original, which for the Old Testament is the Hebrew text, and so-called multiple sense and allegory are rejected as contrary to sound exegesis. Even critical utterances, for which antiquity had already offered some leads, appear among them, albeit hesitantly.

Naturally there followed a counterreaction. However, these paths, once chosen, were too attractive to scholarship to be ever abandoned. Thus, since the beginning of the seventeenth century these two streams increasingly diverge: the one, which might be called orthodox-dogmatic, oriented to faith and tradition, the other, the liberal-critical. According to the first stream, biblical writers are above criticism and their theory of inspiration excludes all human judgment. As a matter of course, within this stream remain different views, mostly in accord with different religious conceptions. In the critical-scientific stream those boundaries could not but disappear. Men of the seventeenth century with such varying outlooks as Hugo Grotius, Cappellus, the philosophers Hobbes and especially Spinoza, and the Catholic theologian Richard Simon, are among the leading exponents of this scholarship. They paved the way for the newer school, which is characterized by names such as Astruc, Semler, Eichhorn, Graf, Kuenen, and Wellhausen, to mention but a few, with their countless students and followers up to our time. The critical-scientific method had also important representatives in our country, and it has become authoritative in our universities.

The principles and results of modern Old Testament scholarship have been set down in a very extensive literature: in the so-called introductions, in exegetical handbooks, in descriptions of the religion of Israel, in historical monographs concerning those parts of the history which deal with the Old Testament, etc. Let me only mention, that the common principle is that the Bible must be read and understood like other books of high antiquity and that the religion of Israel is a historic entity which, by analogy with every other historic event, must be understood in its development and its dependence on temporal and local, as well as foreign, influences. Compared to traditional views, the joint result is a totally altered conception of the character and the origin of the

Old Testament writings and, consequently, also of the course of the historic process that they describe.

As a matter of course, in all areas numerous nuances and variations in concept and outlook appear, all sorts of extreme and moderate points of view find their representatives, and in all details there exist many differences of opinion. This cannot be adduced as an objection against the method any more than it can in any other branch of scholarship.

But the question may be asked—and has been asked—whether a certain onesidedness has not come to prevail and whether that has not led to exaggeration, as it does always and everywhere. It might sometimes be of great importance to establish that v. 10aα was written in the eighth and v. 10aβ in the seventh century or that a certain part of the sentence is a gloss from a later period. But, apart from the subjectivity that is often entailed, one time and again asks oneself whether such criticism, if carried to extremes, really brings us that much closer to a deep insight into the *soul* of the narrative, which, apart from the history of its *coming into being*, also has a significant history of *existence*.[3]

It was particularly Hermann Gunkel who complained repeatedly that vis-à-vis the pedantic literary criticism of the older, and of the religio-historical criticism of the newer, school, the larger view of that literature and of literary historical problems has been pushed too much into the background. We still do not have a history of the literature of the Old Testament, though a few modern scholars have made a beginning, particularly in the field of poetry. Gunkel himself has provided a sketch of Old Testament literature according to its different genres,[4] but the main work still remains undone.

"Narrative materials are particularly international in character," says Gunkel,[5] and he insists that all narratives that have something in common with Israelite narratives, including those of distant peoples, be collected and compared with them. "One then becomes aware of the strangest relationships, but on the other hand, it is precisely in these materials that one actually recognizes what is characteristic of the Israelite spirit." He himself has worked in that direction, *inter alia*, in his

---

3 The Dutch word *ontstaan* (German: *Entstehung*) is here rendered "come into being." Dutch *bestaan* (German: *Bestehen*) is translated "existence." The author is juxtaposing what is called in our time "diachronics" and "synchronics" (translator).

4 *Die orientalischen Literaturen* (Kultur der Gegenwart, herausg. von Paul Hinneberg, I. VII; Berlin/Leipzig: Teubner, 1906) 51–102.

5 *Reden und Aufsätze* (Göttingen: Vandenhoeck & Ruprecht, 1913) 37.

book concerning *das Märchen im Alten Testament*,[6] in which he systematically treats references to and parallels with the "fairy tale motifs" that exist elsewhere and are found in the Old Testament, too. Shortly thereafter came the large work by Frazer, *Folklore in the Old Testament*,[7] in which the author compares countless ethnic traditions from all parts of the world with Old Testament narratives, and attempts to reconstruct the latter on the basis of the former. His book is a masterwork of ethnological method in Old Testament scholarship.

However, in order to apply that method fruitfully and, on the other hand, to escape the dangers of generalization and levelling which may lie hidden in it, one needs to go a few steps further. Not only the motif and the content of the story, but also its form, its shaping, and its tenor, that is to say, the entire narrative as such, as a phenomenon, must be examined psychologically and treated systematically and comparatively, separately for each people symptomatically or every group. For a complete understanding we must study not only what is described, but also the form in which it takes shape and the intentions and the thought world of the writer.

In our case, in addition to the material we have in the Old Testament, narrative in related Semitic literatures is, as a matter of course, especially relevant. The manner of thought and representation of the Semitic peoples, which is in many respects similar, points the way for us. It appears to me that the interpretation of the Old Testament stands much to gain from that side, as well as much that may correct the results obtained by the literary-critical method.

Analysis of the historical books of the Old Testament has revealed in them a reservoir into which many streams have flowed. The material that has been incorporated in these books originated in different sources and has undergone numerous redactions, revisions, expansions, elaborations, and editorial shapings. Research, in which many concatenated and overlapping generations of scholars have participated, have each traced those different streams for itself, in an attempt to determine the individual characteristics as well as the often divergent characters of each, trying to make intelligible the complicated and lengthy process of their gradual coalescence into the form in which we now have them.

There is no unanimity at all concerning the nature of those successive redactors of the biblical books and documents. Were they writers who

---

6 See note 1, p.15.
7 London: Macmillan, 1919.

composed independently while using oral and written materials,[8] or were they compilers who concerned themselves exclusively or almost exclusively with the editing of what they found in that tradition? At the moment, the latter opinion is by far the most dominant. Let me cite Gunkel concerning J and E of the Hexateuch.[9] After a lengthy argument, in which he concludes, "thus J and E are not single authors but schools of narrators," he continues: "These collectors are therefore not masters but servants of their material. We may think of them as filled with piety toward the beautiful ancient narratives and concerned to hand them down as faithfully and as well as they could. Faithfulness was their first quality; for that reason they have taken over much that they only partly understood and what was far from their own experience." But according to Gunkel they have not reproduced the traditional material without any change. That is proved, e.g., by the uniform linguistic usage in the various collections. In an essay of recent date Lods, who takes the same position, says: "In spite of their great piety for the past, they have imprinted something of their personality on their work."[10]

The question is of fundamental importance, for that piety and that faithfulness, that conservative and conscientious attitude toward the hypothetical original on the part of the collectors, particularly the first and the last, not only offers an important advantage for critical work, but really forms a primary condition. Only thereby does it become possible to recognize the sources and to separate them. An independent, renewed treatment of the material, would likely have smoothed out the contradictions and would not have preserved the different recordings of names, numbers, and other details, all those repetitions and doublets, whereas they now serve as the starting point and a criterion for source division.

To a certain extent one has, without further ado, to acknowledge that piety toward tradition. It is due precisely to that, that so much historic material of great age and of high value has been preserved for us, unchanged and unadulterated. Archeological investigation of the last decades has provided much new proof for this. No one familiar with the

---

8 Thus, e.g., Dillmann and concerning J in particular, Bernhard Luther, *apud* Ed. Meyer, *Die Israeliten und ihre Nachbarstämme* (Halle: Niemeyer, 1906) 105–173 (English translation: "The Novella of Judah and Tamar and Other Israelite Novellas," in David M. Gunn, ed., David E. Orton, trans., *Narrative and Novella in Samuel: Studies by Hugo Gressmann and Other Scholars 1906–1923* (JSOT Sup 116; Sheffield: Almond, 1991) 89–118.).

9 In his commentary on Genesis (HKAT; Göttingen: Vandenhoeck & Ruprecht, 1902, 2. Aufl.), LXXV. Also in *Kultur der Gegenwart*, 19, n.1.

10 *Revue de l'Histoire des Religions* 88 (1923) 58.

ancient Near East will find it surprising that many stories, historical and non-historical, which circulated orally for centuries almost without change, were preserved in the same form. On the other hand, the pragmatic character of Israel's historiography (taken in the broadest possible sense) has long been underscored. History is always viewed from the perspective of a certain idea, and the alternation in dominant ideas is reflected in the historical representation.[11] However, this actually presupposes a freer and more independent treatment of the data at hand. Moreover, the person of the final redactor is always difficult to fathom psychologically. Apparently he wanted to unify all those smaller collections. Did he not notice all those contradictions? How else could he include them all in his single work? Also, how is it possible that for so many generations of diligent readers and students of the Bible, all those heterogeneous components could coalesce into a single unit until the strong light of the critical lamp was directed toward it? All such questions need to be reckoned with.

To this end it is of great importance to view the Old Testament narrative in its literary-historic context and in the larger framework of the entire genre, especially in the Semitic literatures; it is particularly significant to pay attention to those types that by virtue of their sacred tradition are related to the biblical story.

In the first place, anyone who is familiar with these literatures will notice the important position of narrative. This is not only due to the large number of historical works that they contain; neither is it only due to the joy the Oriental has always experienced in narrative as a means of recreation, to which we owe the many collections of fairy tales and legends, as in Arabic literature. It is also due to the important role which narrative had and still has with Oriental peoples as a didactic and parenetic vehicle. Narrative makes up for a person's impotence vis-à-vis the abstract and one's need for visualization, by providing a means to learn all sorts of things and to answer all kinds of questions.[12] Already in the Pentateuch memories from the past must always serve as an admonition for the future. "Remember, do not forget, how you angered God at Horeb"[13]; then follows a resumé of what happened then and afterwards.

---

[11] See J. Wellhausen, *Prolegomena zur Geschichte Israels* (3. Auflage; Berlin: Reimer, 1883), 175; English tr., *Prolegomena to the History of Israel* (Edinburgh: Black, 1885; reprinted 1957).

[12] Even at present. See H. Schmidt & P. Kahle, *Volkserzählungen aus Palästina* (FRLANT 17; Göttingen: Vandenhoeck & Ruprecht, 1918) 35*–38.*

[13] Deut 9:7.

The Koran contains many of such historic and quasi-historic tales. But a true or, more frequently, imaginary tale also serves to answer all sorts of questions, which confront a person or which are submitted to one by others, questions of a religious, ethical, or philosophical nature, that we today would answer with abstract explanations. The Talmudic *Haggadah*—a word that means nothing else but "narrative"—is almost entirely of that character. A sage is asked for proofs for God's omnipotence, his wisdom, or his government of the world; or the Talmud raises such questions as: Why is the prophecy of Balaam indicated by a term different from that of Moses? Why did the animals, too, have to be destroyed when humans had sinned? Why does God, who has the whole world at his disposal, demand that sacrifices be brought to him—and a thousand additional more or less profound questions. Normally such questions are answered with a story, a parable (*māšāl*) that is based on either reality or imagination. This use of parables is also well known from the New Testament. The number of Haggadic tales runs in the hundreds. The preferred form is that of the dialogue. A division between different viewpoints or moods, pro and con, feelings of internal conflict, doubt or hesitation concerning two or more persons, makes for a more vivid impression and facilitates visualization. Conversations between God and Moses, between God and the angels, between a Jewish sage and a pagan, between a philosopher and a child, etc., are very numerous. By the same token, the "histories" play a dominant role in the later literature of Judaism, particularly in works with an ethical-didactic tendency, and even philosophers make ample use of this form of framing a thought.[14] One naturally thinks here of the contrived speeches and conversations that, e.g., classical authors weave into their historical descriptions.

Somewhat different in character, yet in the same category, is the Arabic *Hadith*, once again a word that means "story," but which is understood in Islam as a particularly sacred tradition in the form of information about what Muhammad or authoritative men around him had said or commanded or permitted and which serves as guide for religious practice alongside the Koran. The so-called *isnād*, or tradition-chain, ties all such stories and sayings to the authority of Muhammad or one of his companions, but scholarship, particularly that of the great Islamicist Ignaz Goldziher, has definitely established that the *Hadith* is in reality a collection of the theses and opinions of succeeding generations,

---

[14] See A. S. Yahuda in his prolegomena to Bachja, *Al-Hidaja ila farāʾid al-qulūb* (Leiden: Brill, 1912) 110–12.

which, incidentally, often enough contradict each other. Here, too, the outer shape in which the theses are dressed is no more than a form for presenting them as sound and incontestable. Modern readers are not likely to judge this approach favorably. We shall shortly return to this point.

The unhistorical character of the *Hadith*-narratives appears particularly strong in such stories where theological and philosophical arguments are put in the mouths of persons who might be least likely to make such comments. From many similar traditions let me offer a single characteristic example in abbreviated form.

Abu Sofyān, leader of the Koraišites and a fierce opponent of Muhammad, tells that when he was once in Syria with members of his tribe during the truce of Hodaibiya, he was summoned by Emperor Heraclius. "Which of you," the emperor asked, "is the closest relative of the man who claims to be a prophet?"—"I am," said Abu Sofyan. "Well then," he had his interpreter say, "I wish to interrogate this man and command the others, to inform me, when he does not speak the truth." Then he asked: "What do you think of his pedigree ?"—"He is of a noble family," said Abu Sofyān.—"Has anyone else among you learned the same things as he?"—"No."—"Has any of his ancestors ruled over you?"—"No."—"Are his supporters among the noble or the common people?"—"Among the common."—"Does their number increase or decrease?"—"It increases constantly."—"And are there among them people who eventually reject his teaching and fall away?"—"No."— "Have you formerly suspected him of speaking falsely?"—"No."—"Is he ever unfaithful to his word?"—"No."—"Did you ever fight him?"— "Yes."—"And what was the outcome of the battle?"—"Variable; sometimes he won, other times we did."—"And what does he enjoin for you?"—"He commands us to pray to Allah only and to no one besides him and to leave the faith of our fathers; he further enjoins us to do the ṣalāt, to be righteous, clean of morals and of one mind among ourselves."—After having asked all these questions, Heraclius said: "I have asked you about his origin, and you said that he is of noble birth. Well, God's ambassadors are always chosen from the noblest of their people. I have asked you whether anyone before him had proclaimed his teaching, and you said: No. For I thought: maybe, he imitates former teachers. I asked you whether one of his ancestors had ruled among you, and you said: No. I thought that he might have desired the throne of his ancestors. I asked you whether you have regarded him as a liar, and you said: No. I conclude from this that he is not the kind of man to speak falsehood to his fellow men and that he surely does not do it toward God. I asked you about the circle from which his supporters come, and you said: From the common people. Well, they are precisely the supporters of true prophets. And they increase constantly, you said. That is the nature of faith, that it increases till its complete development. And none of his supporters fall away later. Thus the truth of the faith penetrates the inner man. Thus, all the other things that you said to me about him are proof of the truth of his mission. This man will surely conquer even the place on which my feet are standing. Mind you, I knew that such a divine messenger would soon appear, but I did not know that he would come from you. If I could, I would visit him immediately and not rest till I had washed the dust of his feet."

How out and out unhistorical this story is, in all its features, hardly needs any argument at all. It is impossible. In any case, one notes, that here, too, the long, drawn out dialogue has been chosen as the form of representation.

Those who wish to treat in detail the subject which I have discussed, will find an abundance of material in Arabic literature of this type, but I had to confine myself to one small example.

That Syriac literature also has a great preference for this sort of formulation, is proven by the relatively well-represented genre of the saints' legend, in Syriac tešʿītā, "tale." Also typical, to mention something else, is the curious form in which Syriac writers express in the introductions of their books the hesitation which they had to overcome to write their work. We typically read, e.g., a letter directed to a friend, of which the contents is roughly thus: repeatedly you have requested me, dear brother, and attempted to persuade me to publish my work. Many years I have not been able to decide to do that, though you pressed me whether in living voice, or in long letters. Sometimes I hid behind the slight competence of my pen, other times behind the excuse that there was no need for my work. What would my feeble attempts mean compared to all the books that learned and holy men have composed? Your longing did not decrease, however, and finally you came yourself to the cloister where I reside, accompanied by another great and wise man, to persuade me, and you have made my heart and my spirit soft with the noble water of your power of persuasion, and I have therefore, out of sheer necessity, decided to undertake the work with God's help, etc.[15] As appears from the sustained and unified course of these stories and their

---

[15] Thus, e.g., Thomas v. Marga, *Book of Governors*; Joshua the Stylite, et al.

cliché-ridden character, one is able to see embodied in them only a stereotyped expression of modesty.

Let these examples from different parts of the Semitic literatures be sufficient proof that narrative, indeed the historical, the semi-historical, the quasi-historical, or the fictitious tale—is the preferred means for expressing a theory or thought and for making it persuasive.

Upon further consideration of stories in Semitic literature, particularly of those which are akin to the stories in the Bible or the Koran, we are struck by the great *freedom* that is displayed in them, both vis-à-vis reality and the traditions laid down in those sacred books. We have here tangible proof that later generations, not satisfied with the information given in those books, have the inclination to constantly augment it, to make it more beautiful and precise, and to develop it further. Thus is formed a kind of popular tradition, which gradually grows together with the original and in which the most differing elements have been conjoined. Stories of very diverse provenance are tied to familiar persons, in the *Haggadah*, in the *Hadith*, and in the *Thousand and One Nights*.

Let us return to the Talmudic *Haggadah*. The entire biblical history appears to us there in an augmented edition. Distinguished persons and important events, such as the birth of Moses, the exodus from Egypt, the giving of the Law at Sinai, and the building of the Temple by Solomon, became the core of detailed explanations in which the data of the biblical text are used roughly as the writer of a novel takes a historical motif as the foundation for his story. The *Haggadah* knows all the details which the original report leaves aside. A fugitive comes to tell Abraham that his nephew was taken captive; who was that fugitive? One of the ten brothers of Joseph opens his food bag on the way to Canaan; which of the ten? Moses sees two Hebrew men fighting; who were they? The *Haggadah* names them all. The *Haggadah* knows the cause of the dispute between Cain and Abel and why Cain's sacrifice was not acceptable to God. It knows the name of the daughter of Pharaoh who has mercy on Moses as well as the family relations of Hagar, "the Egyptian slave woman." It describes in detail which religious questions the people came to submit to David and which proofs of great wisdom made the queen of Sheba admire Solomon so much. Time and again one recognizes the same motif: the need for concrete representation. One thinks inadvertently of a child who is not content to see the pictures in his books but asks: Who is that? What is his name, and what is he doing? He wants an answer but is satisfied with any answer. It will probably be no problem if, after a few days, when you have forgotten your answer, you mention another name.

It must be possible to *play*, as it were, the pictured story. What is told must clearly appear to the eyes with precise names, numbers, forms, and colors.

Some of these Haggadic expansions have their origin in ancient popular traditions whose origin is lost in the mists of time but which likely have precisely the same history; most are undoubtedly—and so it is usually rightly assumed—a free poetic elaboration of the original. We are mostly dealing not with the spontaneous formation of legends but with literary composition. However, as it is not obvious from a psychological point of view, it is worthwhile to assert that such a free treatment of the authentic "word of God" and of authentic tradition is permitted. It appears that the respect one undoubtedly had for a tradition dictated by God himself, did not mean that one felt compelled to hand it down forever unchanged, neither augmented nor abridged. Often enough the emotional and intellectual content of the biblical story are also not insignificantly changed by the *Haggadah*. A figure like David is glorified to one's heart's content. The image of the warrior takes a backseat to the pious servant of God, proficient in all details of religious law. He most assuredly has not sinned. The biblical story about this must be understood differently. The courtesies of Esau at his meeting with Jacob and the blessings of a Balaam receive a bitter taste in the Haggadic presentation or are even changed into their opposite. Such types of goodness or evil must be made into a well-rounded image.

It would not be difficult to show the further development of that process in later medieval Jewish literature, too, in liturgical poetry, for example. Rather than following through on this, I wish to point out that the same free method of the *Haggadah* vis-à-vis the Old Testament, which constantly develops toward the concrete and the visual, plays just as large a role in Muslim literature relating to the Koran and the history revealed by Allah. Here, too, Abraham's stay in Mecca and his building of the Kaaba with his son Ishmael, or Muhammad's life in all particulars, are painted for us almost in the style of a diary. However, after what I have said about the *Haggadah* and the instances which I cited, I do not need to cite additional examples from Islamic books. They would be of entirely the same kind. Goldziher has furnished interesting information concerning the interpretation of the Koran in his recent work on the subject.[16]

---

[16] *Die Richtungen der islamischen Koranauslegung* (Leiden: Brill, 1920) 90–92, 289–91.

For this curious freedom in dealing with handed down material we have still older witnesses for Judaism than those mentioned. We may cite some products of apocryphal literature such as the Book of Jubilees; and further, the familiar additions to the book of Esther in the Septuagint in which decrees, letters, and edicts that are only mentioned in the Hebrew text, are given *in extenso* entirely in the spirit of the later *Haggadah;* prayers of Mordecai and Esther before the latter appears in the king's presence are related along with some additional particulars, all products of free rhetorical composition. But we need to point particularly to Flavius Josephus, the Jewish historiographer of the first century A.D. Judgments concerning the work of Josephus vary greatly, and the problem of the sources which he utilized is complicated and still not completely clarified. However, this much is certain: that Josephus, too, does not at all retell the Old Testament accurately whether according to the Hebrew or the Greek; his story shows many deviations from the text, also in the specifications of numbers and names, and many expansions, which partly agree with the Haggadic tales that were incorporated several centuries later in the Talmudic literature. Thus, he apparently borrowed them from the same source, the repositories of popular tradition and popular exegesis of which others may be found in the works of Hellenistic Jewish writers. Still, much remains whose provenance we do not know at all and in which the writers' fantasy apparently had the lion's share. Nor can Josephus be adduced as witness to the anxious piety that holds fast to written tradition.

We learn something else, however, from this example. Josephus intended to write *history* and was conscious of doing so. The legendary expansions had apparently already become history for Josephus and the circles to which he belonged. They had been woven together with the biblical story and shared equally the character of historical truth. We have express witnesses that this also happened with the *Haggadah*. In the 12th century a philosopher like Maimonides will be surprised at this and irritated. "Regarding the conception of the words of our Sages people may be divided into three groups. The one group—*and to this belong most people, whom I have learned to know, whose works I have seen, or who have been reported to me*— takes everything literally and does not suspect at all that much of it has a deeper, hidden meaning. Even the impossible they hold for reality. They do so because they have no understanding of wisdom and are far from all learning."[17] The caustic battle over his writings,

---

[17] Commentary on the Mishna, *Sanhedrin*, chap. 10, introduction.

which still raged during his lifetime and pitted his followers and his antagonists fiercely against each other, was in an important part precisely about that point: the literary conception of the *Haggadah*. The same is true in Islam. In the life of Muhammad or in the narratives about the prophets or in everything that the *Hadith* has preserved of history, the boundaries between truth and fiction, between history and legend, have gradually faded and disappeared. To the Muslim, both the one and the other have become reality.

We need to pause a moment to draw a few conclusions. First, a distinction needs indeed to be made between the original writer or composer of the story—we think of those cases where we have to do with free composition—and later people, who hear or read it. The former must have been conscious of the fact that he wrote poetry; for the latter it has become "tradition" and therefore an object of faith. Accordingly, the story is not told because it has happened, but the reverse, by its telling it becomes reality. The great authority attributed to oral tradition rests partly on that. Perhaps one may relate that to a general phenomenon that we notice with the ancients in general and that is particularly strong with the Oriental peoples: the intimate connection between representation and what is being represented; between image or drawing and the person or the object that is portrayed; between the name and its bearer. Why not also between the story and the event that is narrated? Be that as it may, the fact is certain. A similar sentiment we hear, too, from Herodotus: "Now I need to tell something, which does not strike me as trustworthy, but is, in fact, being told." That is to say, it is told, thus it is tradition; so there must be some truth in it.

Secondly, it is clear without further ado that the great freedom of treatment which we were able to indicate in Semitic narrative may easily lead to inconsistencies in representation—and will surely do so when recounted repeatedly. If the story does not aim at being a careful reproduction of historic events, there is no striving for strict coherence. A number which is only meant as type, a name which is exclusively given for a more concrete definition, and all sorts of other details that only aim at clarifying the situation, only serve to visualize the story and to make it tangible, as it were. However, another time these details could differ, and in the course of the tale the narrator may prove not to have bothered to keep all of those—incidental—details clearly in mind. When I say that in this world 20,000 is the same as 100,000 one will understand what I mean without further commentary. Such pictorial detail is intended for viewing at some distance.

Only later when, as we saw, pious faith had made those stories tradition and reality, the need arises to explain everything and to harmonize
the contradictions, a labor in which, e.g., Muslim theologians have
applied such unbelievable ingenuity regarding the *Hadith*. It is clear to us
that such attempts are not only hopeless, but they also lack any reason-
able basis and proceed from the wrong premises.

Summing up, we have found the following characteristics of
narrative in the Semitic literatures:

1. Narrative is a preferred means of framing thoughts.
2. It is characterized by an extraordinarily particularly strong inclination
   toward visualization and concrete representation.
3. It draws, if necessary, in a poetic manner on free fantasy and is not
   bound to reality, nor to older models, nor to historical tradition, nor
   even to a holy scripture. Mutually divergent representations exist side
   by side and initially do not give cause for critique.
4. In a longer or shorter period of time the narrative becomes tradition
   and tradition becomes reality.

Let us return for a moment to the Old Testament. Even as the later
development of a language may spread much light on the older periods,
it is likely to be the same with a literary genre. Yet, the material which I
have indicated rather than surveyed in this article has been put to little
use or not at all in the interpretation of Old Testament narrative.

To be sure, we meet here again various traits from those mentioned
above. A parable like Nathan's or the familiar fable of Jotham, in which
the trees choose a king, are of course, as everyone agrees, intended to
express a thought. The same is true of the conversations between God
and Satan in the introduction of the Book of Job. Liveliness of presentation and a need for visualization appear, e.g., in each and every speech of
the prophets, in the visions they describe and the curious acts accompa-
nying their words by way of "signs." Thus Jeremiah describes once[18]
how he takes "from the hand of God" a cup of wine symbolizing the
wrath of God and makes the leaders of Judah and many of the surrounding peoples drink from it. Elsewhere[19] a loincloth must be made unus-
able by letting it lie for a long time in the water of the Euphrates so that
he can tag it to the proclamation: "thus will I destroy the greatness of
Judah and Jerusalem." The thought must be demonstrated by something
concrete. Almost twenty centuries later the Muslim theologian Ibn

---

[18] Jer 25:17.
[19] Jer 13:1–11.

Taimiya illustrates a text from the Koran referring to the "descent of God" by descending a few steps from his lectern, saying: "just as I descend here."

Freedom toward older tradition? We can only be certain of that if we have in the Old Testament itself such an older tradition which the later writer must have known. Now, that is the case with the book of Chronicles. If we lay Chronicles beside the older historical books which narrate the same material, and if we compare here and there the numbers and names, the deviations prove to be quite numerous; but what is even more striking is that the narratives also differ remarkably in many essential points. Perhaps the most obvious fact is the description of the figure of King David.[20] The process that was just described for the *Haggadah* we see here, too, already in full swing.

In passing we may point out—even if it does not pertain to the narrative sections of the Old Testament—that, in cases where it happens that two recensions are preserved of a song or a psalm or even of a document as important as the decalogue, those two recensions are never identical. They always deviate from each other, whether with greater or lesser significance.

Finally we need to consider all those narratives and narrative cycles of which we do not have earlier editions. When we read them now according to our newly gained perspectives, we become certain that their character does not differ in any respect from that of later examples. Much presents itself to us in a different light from the one by which modern criticism has taught us to see. Our impression is confirmed that the story has unlimited flexibility and elasticity which resists not only a rigid belief in it, but also an unravelling and detailed analysis. Again, there is their predilection for concrete representation, for names and indications of places and for all sorts of details which give the impression of great accuracy, but which, on the other hand, won't accord either with regard to plausibility, or with other information about the same subject in a parallel text, or even within that passage. Renan[21] already remarked concerning the frequent localization in Genesis, *miqqedem*, "to the East": "I cannot believe, that its meaning is rigorously limited to the East...It seems to me, that in that fantastic geography, to orient places, they simply put them east of one another, without attaching a very precise conception to it."

---

[20] See Wellhausen, *Prolegomena*[3], 176–178.

[21] *Histoire générale et système comparé des langues sémitiques* (Paris: Imprimerie impériale, 1858) 466, n.2.

Everywhere incongruences and inconsistencies occur in the representation of, e.g., the dwelling place of the deity or concerning the course of
events in creation, in the flood, in the plagues which struck the
Egyptians, etc. We can now understand better how all of that has been
able to pass the critical eye of the final redaction. Moreover, we become
careful in assigning, without further ado, single components to different
written sources, even if the explanation surely rests in part on the
diversity within those sources. The question is whether we do not often
fall into the other extreme, of those Muslim theologians with their arts of
harmonization, with what is in essence and origin totally different.
Generally one does not sufficiently assimilate the ancients' ways of
thinking, illegitimately forcing our logic on them. Thus everything is
made much *too* logical and much *too* smooth and far more consistent in
representation than they had thought of themselves. They had their own
logic and never intended to build any *systems* at all.

Furthermore, we have so many detailed depictions, as, e.g., of the
capture of Jericho, which, upon closer examination, is hardly imaginable,
as with so many miraculous and fiction-like tales such as that of Jonah or
of Balaam; consequently, we may ask whether it is indeed necessary to
follow the writer exactly to reach the conclusion that everything is unhistorical. We have so many conversations, such as that between Amnon
and Tamar in 2 Samuel 13, of which it is impossible to see how a third
party might have such knowledge and when they might have been
written down; so many dialogues between God and man, between God
and, e.g., a servant who is charged by Him with a commission but who
excuses himself either because of his youth or his scant aptitude in
speaking. We believe we can recognize in all of these the same freedom
of form that we found in later periods. We have such stories as that of
Abraham who, upon learning of the judgment of Sodom, turns to God
and in a remarkable interview questions whether there are not 50 or 45 or
40 or 30 or 20 or 10 innocent people by whose merit the city might be
spared, a conversation which we cannot realistically imagine, nor can we
assume that it belonged to popular tradition in that form. It is apparently
a formulation of theme that is clearly indicated in Gen.18:25: "Is it possible that the Judge of the whole earth might do injustice," a theme that is
repeatedly treated later, too, as with Ezekiel. Remarkably, already in the
Middle Ages Jewish philosophers such as Maimonides and exegetes such
as David Kimhi thought they had to interpret this story and the ones
preceding it concerning the visit of the three angels to Abraham, as well
as similar ones, not as history but as visions. Their motive lay in their

rationalist conception or in that they deemed such stories unworthy of God. Via a different route, the way of literary-historical criticism, we do not reach the same but very similar results.

We could survey all of the literature of the Old Testament, but here, too, I have had to limit myself to a single illustration. Our conclusion must be in the first place that even the most ancient writers of the Old Testament—I speak purposely of writers and not of schools—must have taken a far more independent attitude toward the material and the tradition and must have composed much more themselves than one commonly assumes. The piety and conservatism toward an older tradition, to which one appeals to defend the opposite view, we do not find in later periods. Yet, even after the definite fixing of the text and its canonization, such piety cannot have decreased. The writers did not limit themselves to the reproduction of the sagas and histories that they found in oral and written tradition. The variety of their sources cannot <u>by</u> <u>itself</u> explain unevenness and inconsistencies in their representations. Neither can we agree with Gunkel when he says relative to the stories by these writers: myths, sagas, novelas, and legends: "Whoever tells and hears them, holds them naively for 'true' stories." To the contrary, in respect to this point we found a great difference between narrator and hearer. Only in the faith of later generations does the story become tradition and history. One "hears" a mood of faith in relating to tradition in the words of the psalmist: "O God, with our ears we have heard, our fathers have told us...,"[22] in which "with our ears we have heard it" (which has for us the emotional value of: "we have seen it with our own eyes").

By careful comparison and further classification one will have to determine what is history, what saga, and what is only a literary device in Old Testament narrative. We shall never reach complete unanimity, not even those among us who are prepared to let their investigations be guided by reason alone. Often enough empathy, our intuition, will have to decide. But, as a certain and significant result of this method, we may expect to be using criticism in a far less schematic way than has been done until now, in the way that Gunkel has overdone it. Moreover, we shall not be depending *exclusively* on an unraveling of the tapestry in order to weave the threads together again separately. Our view of the Hebrew narrative is incompatible with such an extreme dissection of the text as is exemplified, for example, by Haupt's so-called Rainbow Bible, which still finds much support among Old Testament scholars. Let us

---

[22] Ps 44:2.

remember that philology has not had the honor of being included among the exact sciences. Philology must turn this "deficiency" into a virtue in so far as it must not aim at too much exactitude. It is told of Rembrandt that he put off visitors to his atelier who wished to see his work from close up with the words: "The smell of the paint would annoy you." There is a lesson in this for us with respect to the paintings preserved for us in the Old Testament narratives. Certainly it is our scholarly duty to dissect the flowers that are offered here in the manner of a botanist. However, we also need to have a sense of and an eye for the flowers as a whole. Beside our critical sense, we ought to attempt to develop a delicate feel for this literature. That requires a certain congeniality to the spirit of the Old Testament and to the Semitic spirit in general, as well as a requisite adeptness for and literacy in the Semitic literatures in their entirety.

—⊸ 2 ⊱—

Saturation Points and Unfinished Lines in the Study of Old Testament Literature*

M. A. Beek

ABSTRACT

Jean Astruc's questions about the Pentateuch (how Moses could know the things written in these books and why two divine names were used) eventually produced literary historical criticism, classically formulated in the Graf-Kuenen-Wellhausen hypothesis.

Eerdmans' critique (1908–1910) was largely ignored, as were the questions of Volz and Rudolph later. Recently, critics of the documentary hypothesis have been heard more carefully, as was de Vaux, who pleaded for "a more flexible, less 'bookish' theory."

Form criticism, as first applied by Gunkel, occupied itself with the literature in its present form, but appears subjective and intuitive. Alt, in his distinction between apodeictic and casuistic law, proposed text corrections which are sometimes questionable from strictly literary considerations. The role of oral tradition, strongly emphasized by the Scandinavian school, is also to be seriously questioned.

---

* Translation of: "Verzadigingspunten en onvoltooide lijnen in het onderzoek van de oudtestamentische literatuur," *Vox Theologica* 39 (1968) 2–14. This essay was reprinted in: *Verkenningen in een stroomgebied. Proeven van oudtestamentisch onderzoek* (Beek Festschrift), ed. M. Boertien et al. (Amsterdam: University of Amsterdam, 1974) 8–19.

Our study of the Old Testament limits itself to large and small units of the MT according to their structure and function within the whole of the *Tanakh*. The text must be attended to carefully to discern its accents and motifs. Its purpose is not recreational but kerygmatic.

We might also pursue how literary science may impact on biblical studies. Alonso Schökel and Meir Weiss have used the insights of Staiger and Kayser, representatatives of *Werkinterpretation*. This method is concerned with the work itself and not with the historical circumstances surrounding its origin.

Historical literary criticism as well as form criticism have often produced atomizing analyses of the text. The type of study here proposed seeks to verify the integrity of texts, e.g., the psalm of Jonah 2, which has often been viewed as an intrusive addition. Actually, the song anticipates the rescue of the prophet.

Before the era of *Werkinterpretation*, Buber and Rosenzweig made contributions in biblical studies as in their concordant translation of the Hebrew Bible. They paid particular attention to motif words, as was done before them by midrashic exegesis. They also took great strides in their analysis of word usage, style, and structure. Yet, though they viewed the Bible as a literary work of art, it was created for proclamation: its aim is to change the hearer. The names of Benno Jacob and Cassuto may also be mentioned here; both authored significant commentaries on Genesis.

The literature of the *Tanakh* contains a number of leading thoughts which go well beyond the claims of Old Testament "Introduction" scholarship. Our ultimate goal, therefore, is the formulation of a biblical theology.

When Jean Astruc published his *Conjectures* in 1753, he could not have imagined that he would determine the course of Old Testament studies up to the present. As he read the Bible, this brilliant physician had asked two questions to which he thought he could give a single answer. He had wondered how Moses could have had any knowledge of events that had occurred since creation and long before his time. In addition Astruc was struck by the vexing problem of the seemingly disorderly use of two different divine names. He found the solution in postulating different sources, set down in writing, which had been available to Moses, the most important ones of which were later called the Yahwist and the Elohist. The problem he posed had originated in a reading of the Bible that had liberated itself from ecclesiastical and liturgical usage as well as dogmatic presuppositions. He did not doubt Moses' authorship of the entire Pentateuch, but he nevertheless thought it safer to publish his insights anonymously. He thereby became the father of literary historical criticism, which subsequently extended to the books of the prophets and the writings.

Since historical criticism achieved its classic form in the works of Graf-Kuenen-Wellhausen, in the circle which had accepted scientific biblical criticism in principle, the juggernaut of *Wissenschaft* has proceeded in between the demarcated roads, destroying whatever came in its path. *Alttestamentliche Studien* by Eerdmans, which appeared between 1908 and 1912, was not adopted.[1] It was ignored though it showed in a very penetrating way that the formation of the Pentateuch could also be envisaged in a different manner from what the source hypothesis claimed. Eerdmans opposed a hypothesis that had become a dogma of scholarship, and he did so on critical-scientific grounds and not from ecclesiastical-dogmatic considerations, as he told Abraham Kuiper in the Dutch Parliament.

The way of the literary historical school continues. Those who, like Volz and Rudolph, dared to speak of an *Irrweg* are hardly taken seriously by Koch in his *Was ist Formgeschichte?*[2] Yet, few new results were registered in the last decades, and if the study of the provenance and development of ancient Israelite literature kept apace nevertheless, this was due to the pursuit of new tracks. In the conclusion of his memorial speech in Copenhagen, which was dedicated to the second centennial of Astruc's hypothesis, de Vaux avers: "but one certainly tends toward a more flexible, less 'bookish' theory than the classic documentary theory, to a theory which is also less simple."[3] He reminded his audience among other things of the function of the question of the redactor, who reputedly joined the sources together, slavishly dependent on the material that he had received, and working so clumsily that he ignored the coarse seams of his compilation. He then wondered whether, for exam-

---

[1]   B. D. Eerdmans, *Alttestamentliche Studien* (Giessen: Töpelmann, 1908–1912). The first sentence of his preface: "In this treatise concerning the composition of Genesis I distance myself from the critical school of Graf-Kuenen-Wellhausen and attack the so-called documentary hypothesis in general" should be compared to the lapidary pronouncement of A. van Selms, *Genesis* (Prediking van het Oude Testament; Nijkerk: Callenbach, 1967) 1:21: "We find it impossible to make the different divine names the starting point of a literary operation such as the source division." Eerdmans had freed himself in his *Alttestamentliche Studien* of the fixed source hypothesis but not necessarily of a similar hypothesis in general. Only his later work gives evidence of a complete break.

[2]   Klaus Koch, *Was ist Formgeschichte? Neue Wege der Bibelexegese* (Neukirchen/Vluyn: Neukirchener Verlag, 1964) 77. English translation (from the second German edition): *The Growth of the Biblical Tradition* (New York: Scribner's, 1969).

[3]   R. de Vaux, "À propos du second centenaire d'Astruc—réflexions sur l'état actuel de la critique du Pentateuque," *VTSup* 1 (Congress Volume; Leiden: Brill, 1953) 198.

ple, in Genesis one might detect a conscious goal and intention, which could better be explained by the intervention of a personality who did not only collect information but also made it serve his purpose. His composition was that of an author, whatever he might be: writer or narrator.[4] With this we have landed on a different track, however: a method which does not intend to replace respectable source criticism, but which rather attempts to supplement it, partly because it seemed that a saturation point had been reached.[5]

This new method was first applied in the Old Testament by Gunkel who called it *Formgeschichte*[6] ("form criticism" in English). The study of literary units in the Bible is concerned with form and content together. The attempt is made to come to a division into basic units according to generally recognized stylistic norms in the history of literature. That is difficult enough since norms which are borrowed from European literary criticism are not directly applicable to Semitic literature, which is of a very different nature. The division into *Gattungen*, as we know them from Gunkel's commentary on the Psalms, therefore appears subjective. Such a division is more determined by intuition than by objective criteria, and one might therefore often question the *Sitz im Leben* which was to be derived with such certainty from the *Gattung*. The advantage of form criticism was that the exegete was not concerned with the *Vorquellen* but with the pericope or with the book of the Bible, with the song or the story at hand, in its fixed form.[7] Yet, form criticism remains an attempt to see the text as the result of a development and not as something in itself.

An objection against form criticism is, in particular, the reconstruction of so-called original forms on the basis of a model. Alt has impres-

---

4 Ibid., 194.

5 H. F. Hahn, *The Old Testament in Modern Research* (Philadelphia: Muhlenberg, 1954) 43 avers: "...criticism contributed to the increase of knowledge; it did not deepen understanding." But what does the increase of knowledge mean without the deepening of insight?

6 H. Gunkel gave the most thoughtful exposition of form criticism as "Form und Inhalt zugleich untersuchendes Verfahren" in his introduction to the Psalms: *Einleitung in die Psalmen. Die Gattungen der religiösen Lyrik Israels* (Gottingen: Vandenhoeck & Ruprecht, 1933).

7 J. Muilenburg, "The Gains of Form Criticism in O. T. Studies," *ExpTim* 71 (1960) 229–233. An example of balanced application is G. Gerleman, "The Song of Deborah in the Light of Stylistics," *VT* 1 (1951) 168–80.

sively applied the form critical method to the origins of Israelite law.[8] He clearly distinguished apodeictic from casuistic law according to an unquestionably literary norm. He also (correctly) discovered certain series which were recognizable by a refrain as, e.g., the *môt yûmāt* series, represented by Exod 20:15–17 and 22:18. Fascinated as he was with this series, he proposed to correct Exod 22:19 and to read a Hebrew text which might be translated as: "Whoever sacrifices to foreign gods shall be put to death." This is indeed a suggestive addition to the series, the first part of which is supported by the Samaritan Pentateuch and two manuscripts of the LXX. However, one might just as plausibly read the small series of apodeictic law of Exod 22:17–19 in its dissimilating force: a sorceress must not live, one who lies with an animal must be put to death, he who sacrifices to another god beside YHWH must be placed under ban. Three different transgressions of a divine command are punished by death, which is expressed in three different ways.[9] In the interpretation of the text, we are dealing with its given form and not with a supposed older form. Likewise, a supposed older formulation of the decalogue in a consistently negative series, no matter how suggestive by itself, lacks the objective character of the two nuanced decalogues preserved in Exodus 20 and Deuteronomy 5. Corrections *formae causa* may distract us from an intention determined by content and form.

Form critical investigation involves the question of oral tradition. What role did this tradition play before it was fixed in written form?[10] Is oral tradition more reliable in its verbal stability than written tradition? The Old Testament offers little material for a definite answer. Tall stories circulate concerning the mnemonic techniques of those who hand down religious texts, also and particularly when these texts are hardly understood. The memory of Baruch was not on this level, however. Jeremiah dictated to him a text which cannot have been long.[11] When this text was burned shortly afterward, the text had to be dictated anew. Neither do we know how widely the art of writing was mastered before the exile.

---

[8] A. Alt, "Die Ursprünge des israelitischen Rechts," *Kleine Schriften zur Geschichte des Volkes Israel* (Munich: Beck, 1953) 1:278–332. The cited example appears on 311, n. 2.

[9] Note the six different indicators of Ishmael in Gen 21:9–14, each of which derives its meaning from context. Similarly the alternating use by J and E of the divine names may have a significance which escapes the source hypothesis.

[10] The Scandinavian school particularly has occupied itself with this question. See the summary in E. Nielsen, *Oral Tradition* (SBT 11; Chicago: Regnery, 1954).

[11] C. Rietzschel, *Das Problem der Urrolle. Ein Beitrag zur Redaktionsgeschichte des Jeremiabuches* (Gutersloh: Mohn, 1966).

That a few boys could write the names of the elders of Sukkot is no proof for we are dealing with a story of uncertain date.[12] The Scandinavian school in particular has entered the debate on oral tradition. A provisional and cautious conclusion is that the relevant Old Testament material has been exhausted without finding a satisfactory answer. The supposition that the creators of ancient Israelite literature knew a large number of texts by heart and assimilated them, is acceptable. That the prophets drew on liturgical texts has been convincingly shown by Henning Graf Reventlow with regard to Jeremiah.[13] To what extent this adaptation occurred consciously escapes our judgment.

While the origin of the biblical text confronts us with so many unanswerable questions, we are strongly inclined to limit ourselves to the study of the available MT and to investigate large and small units according to their structure and function in the whole of the *Tanakh*. It is certain that the text has not been handed down intact, but corrections should not be based on hypothetical assumptions. Thus it is, e.g., a precarious matter to make a correction *metri causa* when we are uncertain of the Hebrew meter. What is certain is that we are confronted with texts from a time in which the written word was scarce. We meet daily with thousands of printed words of which some stick in our memory while most are wasted because they are cheap. The biblical text, by contrast, presupposes readers and hearers who taste the word slowly without hurry. Moreover, this word has a proclaiming function; its most gripping tale is not a *divertimento*. It is therefore important to hear the text with its accents, motif words, and serious, sometimes ironic, wordplay as the ancients heard it. One might therefore ask how we ought to treat deviant readings of authoritative manuscripts and ancient versions. The simple answer is:

---

[12] Judg 8:14. It remains an open question whether Jer 26:18 (Mic 3:12), Ezek 1:3, and Jer 1:1–3 testify to oral tradition.

[13] H. G. Reventlow, *Liturgie und prophetisches Ich bei Jeremia* (Gutersloh: Mohn, 1963). It is to be applauded that the objective character of Jeremiah's words presently receives more attention. The discernment of stereotyped language frees us from psychological analysis of the person of Jeremiah, which in some commentaries has descended to the sentimental. Moreover, it has become much clearer to what extent the prophet allowed himself to be led by theological motifs rather than by political events. With this a number of old questions (e.g., who are the enemies from the North?) have rightly been moved to a different plane.

they demand their own unique interpretation, which then forms a contribution to the history of exegesis.[14]

There has always been a process of osmosis between the developments in literary science and the methods of biblical study. Cassuto showed in his *The Documentary Hypothesis and the Composition of the Pentateuch*,[15] which appeared in 1953, that publications on the Bible and Homer in the same period not only used the same methods but even had the same titles. One may notice presently that the impact of methods which are called in English "New Criticism" and in German *Werkinterpretation* or *Werkschule* has made itself felt in publications on the Old Testament. The insights of Staiger and Kayser have found a response in, e.g., the work of Alonso Schökel, Meir Weiss, and Strauss.[16] Within the compass of this article only a few aspects will be mentioned, and that only insofar as they are relevant to the interpretation of Old Testament texts. It must be borne in mind that we are concerned with literature that counts as a work of art by virtue of its structure.

The interpreter of a poem according to the method of *Werkschule* does not look left or right, and above all does not endeavor to look behind the poem. The biography of the poet is unimportant for there is no identity between the poet as personality and the "poetic personality." A successful work of art shows no traces of its history of origin. The creator of the work proves for the most part unable to interpret it. Similarly, knowledge of temporal circumstances and milieu is no pre-condition for entry into the work of art because art expresses itself and not the time in which the artist lives. The work should not be read as a mirror of its time but as a product of the spirit that has begun to lead its own life, for after publication the umbilical cord is cut. The encounter with the reader or hearer results in a new creative process which is related to that of the artist.

---

[14] D. W. Thomas, "The Textual Criticism of the Old Testament," *The Old Testament and Modern Study*, ed. H. H. Rowley (Oxford: Oxford University Press, 1951) 238–40 avers that the corrected text lacks objectivity.

[15] Jerusalem, 1961 (English translation of: *Torat hatteᶜudot wesidduram šel sifre hattorah*, 1941).

[16] E. Staiger, *Die Kunst der Interpretation* (2nd ed.; Zurich: Atlantis, 1964); W. Kayser, *Das Sprachliche Kunstwerk* (10th ed.; Bern/Munich: Francke, 1964). [...] L. Alonso Schökel, "Erzählungskunst im Buche der Richter," *Bib* 42 (1961) 143–72. M. Weiss, "Einiges über die Bauformen des Erzählens," *VT* 13 (1963) 456–75; idem, "Weiteres über die Bauformen des Erzählens," *Bib* 46 (1965) 181–206; idem, *Hammiqra Qidmuto* (Jerusalem: Bialik Institute, 1962) (*The Bible from Within*; Jerusalem: Magnes, 1984). A. L. Strauss, *Bedarke hassifrut* (Jerusalem: Bialik Institute, 1959) points to the change of word meanings and its consequences for interpretation (p. 29).

Good reading, whereby the work of art masters us, is also a creative act, achieved by means of voice and soul.

In light of the foregoing it is clear that we are concerned with literary theory, a discipline that by definition will always be controversial from the point of view of method. This is the background of the well-known quip that in this field one concerns oneself either with literature or with science but never at the same time with both. It is also clear that the insights of the *Werkschule* can only be relevant to biblical literature if we are dealing with the structure of a work of art. The discovery of breaks, tears, and seams implies a value judgment. If one cannot speak of a closed composition, a solid reconstruction, extreme caution is in order.

Surely Old Testament study is influenced by what was happening in literary scholarship. In contrast to the atomizing analysis of historical literary criticism and form criticism came the attempt to understand large segments of narrative and poetic ancient Israelite literature as a whole. To illustrate what this means in the practice of interpretation: Jonah is a book that because of its tight structure satisfies the norms of a work of art. It is interrupted by a song as happens frequently in ancient and modern Oriental literature where narrative is interrupted by poetry. The psalm of Jonah 2 consists of citations which for the most part are paralleled in the Psalter. This does not necessarily imply that Jonah 2 is not a new creation. It is a song in which each word has its place. The Psalms of Thanksgiving, which were found near the Dead Sea, may likewise be analyzed with respect to their citations; yet they impress the reader as acceptable and carefully constructed compositions. Neither should the text of Jonah 2 be viewed as an intrusive addition. The song has its own function, anticipating the rescue of the prophet. To mention another example: when a commentator attempts to persuade us that Josh 5:4–8 is a compilation of five different sources and that only v. 8 may claim to be "genuine," I wonder how one pictures the final redaction and what objective character a supposedly "well-ordered" text might have.[17]

It is not surprising that the insights of the *Werkschule* have especially been taken into account in publications by scholars of the Hebrew University. Here the soil was prepared by the work of Buber and Rosen-

---

[17] H. Holzinger, *Das Buch Josua* (KHAT; Tübingen: Mohr, 1901). The commentary by M. Noth (*Das Buch Josua*; HAT; 2nd ed. Tübingen: Mohr, 1953) does not go this far, but it does put vv. 4–7 in parentheses and repeats not only here but also elsewhere the expressions so characteristic for these commentaries: "*nachträglich gestrichen*," "*ist wohl zu streichen*," "*der syntaktisch in der Luft schwebende ausmalende Satz*," "*deuteronomistische Bemerkung*," etc. etc.

zweig. Their valuable contributions to form criticism are completely ignored in the summary by Koch, proving how limited the horizon of *Wissenschaft* really is. Though the publications of Buber-Rosenzweig preceded by a few decades style- and structure analysis according to the methods of Kayser and Staiger, they are not superseded as far as Old Testament literature is concerned. One might only object that they did not get beyond a first start. Rosenzweig died young, and Buber had other concerns once he had to continue the task of translation alone; the more urgent is the duty to continue what they began and to test their insights by further and sound investigation.

Here, two principles come into play: the discovery of the motif words and of the structure of comprehensive literary units.[18] Whoever has "heard"—for hearing is particularly important—how a Hebrew root now modulates in conjugations and constructions and then returns with suggestive monotony, recoils at the atomization recommended on the basis of other norms. For Buber and Rosenzweig, hearing was a self-evident matter, as it was for my predecessor in Amsterdam, the Jewish scholar Palache, who knew the entire *Biblia Hebraica* by heart. Those who have not grown up with the text from their youth, can turn to the concordance.

The attention paid to motif words is characteristic of the halakhic and haggadic parts of the Talmud and of the Midrash, but there it is too often guided by assonance without taking context into account in interpretation. Midrashic exegesis therefore bears a fragmentary character; yet for scholarly exegesis there is a treasure of data concerning peculiar word usage, cruces, and implausible connections.[19] One does not need to accept their solutions to be impressed by remarkable examples of "close reading," which are neglected in contemporary commentaries. This occupation with the text, however unscholarly from an academic viewpoint, provides the background for the surprising and philologically acceptable interpretations by Buber-Rosenzweig, Jacob, Cassuto, and other Jewish scholars.

The extent to which the study of motif words may also be important in disparate texts I experienced recently in the exegesis of Isa 40:6–8,

---

[18] M. Buber, "Leitwortstil in der Erzählung des Pentateuchs," *Die Schrift und ihre Verdeutschung* (Berlin: Schocken, 1936) 211–38.

[19] L. Fuks: "The importance of the Midrash for modern scientific biblical exegesis lies more in its calling attention to *cruces interpretationis* than in the solution of the problems connected with them." (Thesis VIII of his dissertation, *Die Hebräischen und Aramäischen Quellen...*; Assen: Van Gorcum, 1964).

where the *ḥesed* of the flesh, transient as grass over which the *ḥamsīn* wind blows, is opposed to the eternity of the word, i.e., the promise, of God. In Ps 103:17 the mortality of humans is contrasted to the *ḥesed* of God. Hos 6:4 compares the *ḥesed* of Judah with a morning cloud and the dew that evaporates in the morning. The inner connection of these texts is indicated with the motif word, but how can a Bible reader perceive this when *ḥesed* is successively translated with the words "beauty," "mercy," and "love?" The first originated under the influence of the LXX because the Greek translator in Alexandria was at a loss with the Semitic idiom in which both "prolepsis" and "flashback" play their curious roles.[20] A concordant translation would have pointed the right way for exegesis. It is Breukelman's merit that he has tirelessly struggled for a more concordant translation in Dutch along the lines of Buber.[21] While Buber called attention to what he called *Leitwortstil*, Rosenzweig stressed the *Formgeheimnis* of the biblical narratives.[22] Actually the word *Geheimnis*, "secret," is incorrect in the context of his argument. We are dealing not with a secret in the sense that it might only be intelligible to the initiated, for what Rosenzweig reveals may be heard by anyone who wishes to listen. His stylistic analysis of the story of Jacob shows irrefutably that this is stretched in a "framework of a whole series of the same words, or words that are formally related, or formulaic sentences, which hang together with those preceding them as the turns of a quick-witted dialogue."

The aged Isaac says to the complaining Esau: "With deception your brother came and has taken away your blessing." After two chapters deception returns in Jacob's word to Laban: "Why have you deceived me?" Thus the deceived gave the motif word at the beginning. This word echoes in the name of Jacob, and his deceiver took it up in turn when he himself was deceived. It may also be noted that a popular etymological motif plays along in the Jacob-stories, as in many other short and long stories that play a serious game with a key word. An etymological game indeed—though not of "the people," but of the author or the circle of

---

[20] See: E. Fox, "A Buber-Rosenzweig Bible in English," *Amsterdamse Cahiers* 2 (1981) 9–22 and *In the Beginning: A New English Rendition of the Book of Genesis* (New York: Schocken, 1983); *Now These Are the Names: A New English Rendition of the Book of Exodus* (New York: Schocken, 1986).

[21] Good examples of a "flashback" are Jonah 4:5 and Gen 37:24 in comparison with 42:21.

[22] F. Rosenzweig, "Das Formgeheimnis der biblischen Erzählungen," *Die Schrift und ihre Verdeutschung*, 239–61.

authors who composed the stories and have made them function within the firm context of proclamation to Israel.

In the case of lengthy passages of a narrative and poetic character, it seems safer for the time being to abandon the idea of a compiling redactor and to attend to the work of creative writers. Perhaps it is still better to think of a circle of writers. In her dissertation on the *Iliad*, S. J. Suys-Reitsma mounts a solid argument that the work attributed to Homer may have originated in the milieu of a hetaery of poets who worked on the poem over a long period.[23] But such a hetaery does not come to the fore in the Old Testament. The "men of Hezekiah" who collected Proverbs (Prov 25:1) do not offer a connecting point for such a picture. We are better informed concerning the circles that already around the beginning of our era applied themselves to the written word and created a new literature in an orally memorized discussion. Is it a fruitful hypothesis to assume similar circles in the Babylonian exile, the exiled spiritual elite of Jerusalem, and to imagine that here a definite form was given, looking back at the past and looking ahead to the future? What, then, is genuine and what is not? Is the doom prophecy genuine and the prophecy of redemption spurious?[24] Is a midrash already growing in the canon not genuine? These are questions which drove Napier to despair at the Old Testament Congress in Geneva.[25]

Precisely because the discipline of the Old Testament introduction has run aground here, in a number of disputable hypotheses, it may be useful to return to the starting points of Buber-Rosenzweig, which are shared by Cassuto in his commentary on Genesis. In interpretation this amounts to an attempt to see the large units and to utilize some achievements of the *Werkschule*. The advantage of the Buber-Rosenzweig

---

[23] S. J. Suys-Reitsma, *Het Homerisch Epos als orale schepping van een dichter-hetairie* (The Homeric Epic as Oral Creation of a Poets' Hetaery; dissertation, University of Amsterdam, 1955). In my opinion the origin of the book of Job, e.g., may be explained in the same way as the work of a circle of sages, who had struggled with a typical "wisdom" problem for years and perhaps for several generations.

[24] H. A. Brongers in his address: *De structuur van de heilsverwachting bij de oudtestamentische profeten* (The Structure of the Expectation of Salvation according to the Old Testament Prophets; Nijkerk: Callenbach, 1967), reacting to S. Herrmann, *Die prophetische Heilserwartungen im A.T.* (*BWANT* 5; Stuttgart: Kohlhammer, 1965) showed himself inclined to reduce the number of authentic prophecies of šālôm. But what are "authentic" prophecies in the framework of the *Biblia Hebraica*? Is not šālôm prophecy given with "election," which is never disputed?

[25] B. D. Napier, "Isaiah and the Isaian," *VTSup* 15 (Congress Volume; Leiden: Brill, 1966) 240–51.

method is an analysis of word usage, style, and structure, that takes into account the innate character of the object. Ancient Israelite literature differs from a "work of art" in that it was not created for beauty but for proclamation. Therefore, analysis cannot stop at structure but must pay attention to content, which may amuse—ironically or as entertainment— but even then it aims at "changing" the hearer.

It will be clear from the foregoing that not all parts of the Old Testament lend themselves to such analysis. The narrative sections of the Pentateuch provide better results than the legal writings. In this connection we may take to heart what Palache remarked concerning the character of the ancient Oriental, Semitic story.[26] He concluded that the writers of the Old Testament took an independent stance toward tradition, were less inhibited by traditional material than is assumed by traditio-historical studies, and composed much more themselves than has been assumed by those who unravel the intertwined traditions.[...]

Besides the analysis of style and structure enough remains to be done in Old Testament scholarship. Whoever searches a well-balanced text for ancient religio-historical layers and contours behind the text, may count on our assent; but we tend not to view the reputed animistic, polytheistic, pre-Mosaic layers as essential. Old Testament literature, joined together by canonization, is borne by a number of leading thoughts, and these are recognizable in structures that are larger in extent and more massive in form than Old Testament introduction scholarship tries to tell

---

[26] J. L. Palache, "Het karakter van het Oud-Testamentisch verhaal,": *Sinai en Paran* (Leiden: Brill, 1959) 15–36, translated in this volume and discussed in Aleida G. van Daalen, *Simson* (Dissertation, University of Amsterdam; Assen: Van Gorcum, 1966) 43. See also: K. A. Deurloo, *Kain en Abel* (Dissertation, University of Amsterdam; Amsterdam: Ten Have, 1967; chapter I is translated in this volume) and K. A. D. Smelik's published address "Narrative in the Hebrew Bible" (translated in this volume). E. Auerbach, *Mimesis* (Garden City: Doubleday, 1957) 19 mentions as characteristics of biblical language: "certain parts brought into high relief, others left obscure, abruptness, suggestive influence of the unexpressed, a predilection for keeeping things in the background multiplicity of meanings and the need for interpretation, universal-historical claims, development of the concept of the historically becoming, and preoccupation with the problematic." That is quite a list! We need to pay particular attention to multiplicity of meanings (*Vieldeutigkeit*). Examples: Jonah announced that Nineveh would be turned upside down within forty days. The verb *hpk* used here of the "overturning" of Sodom and Gomorrah, also denotes a spiritual "turnaround" (Exod 14:5; Isa 63:10). The author is saying: Jonah announced something that he misunderstood. Nineveh was indeed "turned upside down" but by conversion and not destruction.

us, from the standpoints of literary historical, form critical, or traditional-historical methods.

Laying this bare is the undertaking I support, even if there is enough to do in other areas. The conviction that such inquiry will result in firming up the outlines of biblical theology and will inspire kerygmatic proclamation may not be advanced as a scholarly argument. Yet it may well be relevant in theological faculties and ecclesiastical training.

—◦ **3** ◦—

THE SCOPE OF A SMALL LITERARY UNIT IN THE OLD TESTAMENT

INTRODUCTION TO THE INTERPRETATION OF GENESIS 4*

K. A. Deurloo

ABSTRACT

Koch called the *Endredaktion* the unknown; von Rad, "the ways representing the small units." These two extremes touch one another. With both there is namely a certain form of *Dichtung* to be presupposed, resembling those of the nearest and most familiar traditional milieu: the oldest midrash genre. Usually, one can only reconstruct hypothetical contours behind the text. Methodologically this signifies preference of synchronics to diachronics. The historical disciplines are auxiliary to (synchronic) exegesis. Small literary units must be understood in their function within the cycle, i.e., the book whereby the entire ancient Jewish Bible, the *Tanakh*, forms the first hermeneutical horizon. According to the rule *verba valent usu*, (probable) borrowings from elsewhere and *cruces interpretationis* in the first and last place according to their *usus* ought to be interpreted in connection with their

---

* Translation of: "Inleiding. De vraag naar de scopus van een kleine literaire eenheid" = chap. 1 of *Kain en Abel. Onderzoek naar exegetische methode inzake een 'kleine literaire eenheid' in de Tenak* [Cain and Abel. A study of exegetical method concerning a "small, literary unit" in the *Tanakh]* (Dissertation, University of Amsterdam. Amsterdam: Ten Have, 1967) 9–23.

relevant unity. In this manner, the rule *scriptura scripturae interpres* remains valid. Decisive for the whole of the *Tanakh* is Beek's statement that the divine name is the center by which "everything that is within the circle is colored and determined by a totally unique character."

Israel *tells* history—she needs to, on account of the deeds of YHWH, and this telling becomes an integrating, participatory factor in this history.[1] One may not expect any custodians of a great or not so great past among those who tell the biblical stories but people who speak of the actuality of their history, which is implicit teaching: *torah*.[2]

Their story is no flowing, continuous argument, but rather develops by jumps from one discrete, well-rounded event to the other, which always seems to have its own typical theme. Thus a book like Genesis is a remarkable conglomerate of different stories, of literary units of greater or smaller magnitude. It is precisely in this diversity that historical critical science has found its inspiration (no source of joy for church and synagogue) and set in motion a thoroughgoing process of demolition that one would hardly want to undo if it were possible. The picture that the biblical writers in "their stories" have created of the history of Israel is split and atomized, the parts have been weighed historically and literary-critically and have become the building blocks of a new scientific image of history.

Critical exegetes also have problems, literally and figuratively, with "fragments." What are they to exegete? Small literary units, in the context of their *Erzählungsfaden* JEDP? Or are they to dig in the *tell* that every small unit appears to be in itself, and search for authentic origins? Von Rad had pleaded strongly that the *Jetztgestalt* and the *Letztgestalt* of the text be taken seriously, for "historical scholarship searches for a critically assured minimum—the kerygmatic picture tends toward a theological maximum."[3] The task is "to interrogate each document, much more closely than has been done hitherto, as to its specific kerygmatic intention."[4] He makes the interesting comment that "the particular way in which Israel's faith presented history is still far from being adequately elucidated. Admittedly, we are acquainted with the various basic historical and theological ideas of the Yahwist, or of the Deuteronomist's history, or the Chronicler's. But we are much less clear about the mode of

---

[1] Ps 118:17.

[2] See K. H. Miskotte, *When the Gods are Silent* (New York/Evanston: Harper & Row, 1966) 192.

[3] G. von Rad,, *Old Testament Theology* (New York: Harper & Row, 1962) 1:108.

[4] Ibid., 105, 106.

presentation of the smaller narrative units, although it is in fact the mass of these which now gives characteristic stamp to those great compilations."[5] He hopes that in such investigation certain patterns will be discovered that might offer greater insight into the manner in which Israel has absorbed historical data in its kerygmatic historiography. He adds the consideration that Israel's historical traditions must be regarded largely as *Dichtung*.

How must such investigations be conducted? Answers given to this question generally go in the direction pointed out by Gunkel: to ask for the particular *Gattung* of a literary unit; without this formal effort, exegesis would not be possible. In turn, a *Gattung* must not be characterized without first taking account of its *Sitz im Leben*, and thus inquiring into the situation, the speaker, the hearers, the atmosphere of the speaking, and the goal that the speaker or author has in mind. In addition, it should be considered that a literary unit, as *Gattung*, has its own history. *Gattungen* appear, flourish, and disappear in history just as a particular *Sitz im Leben* changes. These are general principles which the investigator must be alert to when one turns to a special literary unit, a tradition, which may be supposed to already have a long history behind it. One must then begin with the end product and make a retrograde movement, working traditio-historically. Such a small unit must have had an original *Sitz im Leben* that it has outgrown, once we find it in a framework; the narrative has been so powerful that it has not been ruined with the disappearance of the *Sitz im Leben*. It has found new situations in which it could function and it is obvious that this has affected the piece in form and content. If two versions of a tradition are known, the investigator has synoptic opportunities to penetrate to the tradition's unknown past. But it must generally rely on instances of unevenness in the document because there is only one version of the text. History, archeology, biblical and extra-biblical comparative materials are at one's service. Apart from the fruit that might be produced by such traditio-historical study for the discipline of the history of Israel,[6] the real goal is to get the final stage in sharper focus.

---

5 Ibid., 108.
6 "I am well aware that the writing of a history of Israel should be preceded by a thorough study of the nature of the sources. That is the sense of "traditio-historical" studies, engaged in so impressively by the school of Alt and Noth. At the same time, the danger threatens that the student becomes the captive of a too schematic representation of the origin of the traditions. Such a representation answers to the logic of the Western scholar, but fails to do justice to life itself. The oral and written tradition

The history of tradition...begins from the final stage of a single piece and illuminates its path through time (according to the laws of *Gattung* and *Sitz im Leben*) in order to determine the oldest *Vorstufe* possible. But it is up to the exegete from that point to return to the text as we have it presently. The exegete sees the final form of the text in a new light, however. Enriched by the knowledge of the traditio-historical dimension, he or she can comprehend and explain more clearly the meaning of the *Literaturwerdung*, of the inscripturation of that tradition. This (final) form-critical labor is called redaction-history. To proceed redaction-historically means interpreting a written text against the background of *Gattung, Sitz im Leben* and *Überliefer-ungsgeschichte*.7

In this it is presupposed that the "redactors," in the first place JEDP and possibly L, have occupied themselves not with creating, but collecting, ordering, shifting, while they also have introduced certain trends in their material and added explanatory or connecting remarks. That means, among other things, that certain small literary units in the context in which they have been placed, have a different meaning from when one views them in isolation, which suggests the question of at which stage the exegete must begin. Von Rad is inclined to say that in view of the fact that the earlier context in which the stories stood has been lost, the larger composition in which they have been absorbed must be the true scope of the exegete. One thinks, e.g., in the case of Genesis, first of all about the Yahwist; but because of the dynamic character of the traditio-historical method, one may not rest with that, for tradition continued after that stage. Von Rad asks whether we do not land in the camp of Franz Rosenzweig, who interprets the siglum R not as "redactor" but as *Rabbenu*: the one who has given us the Old Testament as a whole. This consequence, says von Rad, is valid only for Judaism. For Christianity, tradition has gone a step further: "We receive the Old Testament from the hands of Jesus Christ."8 The same inclination is noticeable in part 3 of his *Old Testament Theology* (volume 2), which deals with the relationship of the Old and New Testaments. Old Testament traditions appear to

---

of nomads and semi-nomads who have experienced the transition to settled agriculture, is too complex to discover laws in this. As a working hypothesis it is useless"; M. A. Beek, *Geschiedenis van Israel van Abraham tot Bar Kochba* (3rd ed.; Zeist: De Haan, 1964) 11.

7 K. Koch, *Was ist Formgeschichte? Neue Wege der Bibelexegese* (Neukirchen/Vluyn: Neukirchener Verlag, 1964) 62. The English translation was made from the second German edition: *The Growth of the Biblical Tradition* (New York: Scribner's, 1969).

8 G. von Rad, "Das hermeneutische Problem im Buche Genesis. Verkundigung und Forschung," *Theologischer Jahrbericht*, (1942/46) 50.

possess in their development a remarkable "openness to the future," which invites continual "new interpretations" in subsequent stages of tradition. But isn't the interpretation of the Old Testament in the New exactly the same process as may be discovered in earlier stages?[9]

Thus we land on the typical Christian problems of Old Testament hermeneutics,[10] in which reading Old Testament texts within the context of the New Testament is pleaded in various ways. For example, Frör says: "By drawing the Old Testament into the canon, the church announces how she wants to read and understand this book.... The material context for the interpretation of the Old Testament is therefore the witness to Christ in the New Testament."[11] That is essentially an invitation to a (possibly modern) way of typologizing.[12] The certain data then is the New Testament, with the Old Testament the problematic, instead of the reverse—as if, according to the New Testament, the *Tanakh* ("the law of Moses and the prophets and the psalms," Luke 24:44) did not first witness the Messiah and thus also needed to legitimize the witness concerning Jesus as Messiah in the New Testament.

The manner in which Barth has approached the relationship of the "testaments" is therefore not only dogmatically but also hermeneutically a propos and opens for the exegete perspectives for tackling one's work without having to force matters. "The history of Israel says 'before' (*vorher*), what the history of Jesus Christ says 'after' (*nachher*)."[13] In the words of Miskotte: "The testimony of the Old Testament goes out into the time of expectation, that of the New Testament into the time of recollection. What they have in common is their relationship to, their orientation toward, one and the same object, one and the same Name, one and the same Event, one and the same Salvation."[14]

That is to say, the term "witness to Christ" as applied to the *Tanakh*, may not be understood in a manner referring to the *witness* relating to

---

9 G. von Rad, *Theologie des Alten Testaments*, (4th ed.; Munich: Kaiser, 1965) 2:385. (The English translation is from the 1960 German edition).

10 See C. Westermann, *Probleme alttestamentlicher Hermeneutik. Aufsätze zum Verstehen des Alten Testaments (TBu*; Neudrücke aus dem 20. Jahrhundert; Munich: Kaiser, 1963) 2:363–72 has an extensive bibliography.

11 K. Fror, *Biblische Hermeneutik* (2d ed.; Munich: Kaiser, 1964) 131.

12 As, e.g., H. W. Wolff defends in his essay "Zur Hermeneutik des Alten Testaments." See Westermann, *Probleme alttestamentlicher Hermeneutik* 2:163, 164.

13 K. Barth, *Kirchliche Dogmatik* (Zurich: Zollikon, 1959) 4/3:71.

14 Miskotte, *When the Gods are Silent*, 113.

him *of the New Testament*,[15] as the latest authoritative traditional stage, which as such would determine the exegesis of the *Tanakh*. With that the conversation with the synagogue would essentially be cut off *a limine*. No special hermeneutical tricks are required for interpretation, not even those which present themselves under the appearance of traditio-historical methodology. For the rest, von Rad observes greatest caution particularly on this point; he speaks of a "double movement of reciprocal understanding"[16] of both the Old and New Testament traditions. In this way he keeps two paths open: on the one hand, the more dogmatic or practical discipline of theology—with all the dangers of irrelevant piety which this might produce—on the other hand, typical Old Testament scholarship, by which the various stages of tradition could speak for themselves. It is an equivocality writ large which we, as regards the Old Testament traditions, find in small compass with Koch. In vain does one look to him for an answer to the question, to which stage of a particular tradition must the researcher direct oneself. Both *Urgestalt* and *Endgestalt* may produce difficulties. The decision *"lies in the freedom* of the individual; the choice is not only directed to the mass of exegetical clarity, but also to what makes the congregation pious."[17] Accordingly, Koch introduces as a desideratum a synthetic history of literature in Gunkel's sense—to be built on the basis of *Gattungs-* and *Überlieferungsgeschichte*,[18] in the supposition that with this a practical need of the congregation has been served. We believe that the congregation is only served by an interpretation of the *Tanakh* in the unity of its traditional form, an interpretation which works realistically with this *certain* information.[19] The exegete

---

15 Often in the discussion concerning the "testaments" the mistake is made to treat "the time of revelation" and "the time of remembrance" as the same. This danger threatens when one identifies "it was said to the elders...but I say to you" (Matt 5:21, 22) with the New Testament. See G. C. van Niftrik, "Kroniek. Joodse en christelijke ogen" [Chronicles. Jewish and Christian Eyes], *Kerk en Theologie* 13 (1962) 51.

16 Von Rad, *Theologie*, 2:398.

17 Koch, *Formgeschichte*, 111. This quote is followed by the curious remark: "Presupposed is certainly the agreement that not only the biblical text at hand, but also its traditio-historical prior stages are guided by the Spirit of God, therefore are canonical."

18 Koch, *Formgeschichte*, 112–18.

19 "In the exposition of the Old Testament as well as the New it is an unpromising undertaking to try to discover or reconstruct a true text, a conception of what probably happened, the 'true' history behind the text. The traditional form of the text (in the broadest sense) is from first to last the material of exegesis. This is also of importance for a right insight into the unity of the Scriptures, for it is not in the continuity of the history but rather in the spiritual continuity of the words that this unity is

is thereby protected by the arbitrariness which Koch grants him, but his task also becomes more modest in the ambiguous sense of the word: *certus et modestus*.[20] However, according to Koch we know very little of the *Endgestalt*.[21] This comment is only possible when we reason from a particular traditio-historical view, in the supposition that traditions in the context in which we find them, still show all traces of the life they have led, even after they have been incorporated into the compositions of JED and P. The final redaction can only sporadically be observed. Might we not have here the threatening "danger become acute that the investigator becomes the prisoner of a too schematic representation of the originating of the traditions?"[22] Koch calls the *Endredaktion*, the unknown; von Rad the "ways of representing the small narrative units."[23] Might not these two seemingly divergent comments have everything to do with each other? That suspicion rises particularly when von Rad emphasizes that a large part of the historical traditions, too, are to be regarded as "products of a pronounced artistic drive."[24] Might not such supposed creativity be ascribed precisely to the unknown *Endredaktion*? "The piety and conservativism toward an older tradition, to which one appeals to defend the opposite view, we do not find in later periods," writes Palache after discussing the unlimited "flexibility and elasticity" of narrative among the Semites. "Yet, even after the definite fixing of the text and its canonization, such piety cannot have decreased."[25]

Inspired by this good Amsterdam "tradition," one could become convinced that much of the traditio-historical method is negotiable. When the "poetry" supposedly found in biblical texts is of the same character as the *Haggadah*—as Palache claims—that can mean nothing else but that in many cases we can hardly retrieve an earlier stage of a

---

located and becomes apparent." (Miskotte, *When the Gods are Silent*, 145; see n. 2, supra).

[20] See E. Rosenstock-Huessy, *Der Atem des Geistes* (Frankfurt: Frankfurter Hefte, 1951) 53.

[21] Koch, *Formgeschichte*, 111.

[22] See n. 1.

[23] Von Rad, *Old Testament Theology* 1:108.

[24] Ibid., 109: "...poetry was, as a rule, the one possible form for expressing special basic insights." Von Rad speaks in this connection also of "artistic narratives (*Kunsterzählungen*)—they reach from the Hexateuch to 2 Kings" (122).

[25] J. L. Palache, "Het karakter van het oud-testamentische verhaal" [The Nature of Old Testament Narrative] (inaugural address at his professorship at the University of Amsterdam, January 26, 1925; *Opera Minora. Sinai en Paran*; Leiden: Brill, 1959) 35. (English translation, chap. 1 above.)

narrative. And to what may we compare the *Tanakh* more appropriately than the oldest midrash? One is apt to arrive at even more drastic suspicions, such as the idea that there is no such thing as a tradition in the usual sense of the word. We may cautiously speak of "contours behind the text," but these cannot determine exegesis any more than the possible continuity of the different stages of traditions can. That may be done only through the coherence of words.

"Investigation of the exegetical method relating to a small literary unit" is the original Dutch subtitle of this study. That is to say, we are concerned with the story in the compositional unit of the book as a segment of the Torah, as one of the three main parts of the *Tanakh*.

Many reasons have led us not to speak about method. The thorough hermeneutical reflections that have been going on in theology and philosophy among Barth, Bultmann, Heidegger, and others,[26] compels anyone who only wishes to make a few marginal methodological comments to be modest; yet it also makes it impossible to limit oneself exclusively to a few technical exegetical labels. "For exegesis is only scientifically responsible, if one lets oneself be led by a thoughtful hermeneutic."[27] If correctly understood, the entire theological enterprise comes into view, which is in turn rooted in exegesis as "the concentration on the historical task of interpretation."[28] In this framework, the present study is concerned with the latter, the art of interpretation in the narrow sense. Its object must suggest its own method. However, the colorful phenomenon to which it directs itself, language in so many striking forms, makes it difficult to give an abstract, systematic theory of its procedure as *the* exegetical method. It is not characteristic of this discipline to describe its methods without applying it at the same time, and to verify it in its application.

Yet, exegesis has its own method and may and must be carried out independently. Methodologically considered, it finds itself in a precarious situation because its object is ever new and particular. Strictly speaking, to do exegesis means continually to begin from the beginning, to explore anew the means to understand a text. Even if there are ways to come closer to the text, as by asking questions about the authorship, time, and milieu of a particular work's origin, they do not belong to

---

[26] J. M. Robinson and J. B. Cobb Jr., eds., *New Frontiers in Theology II. The New Hermeneutic* (New York/Evanston: Harper & Row, 1968). Old Testament insights: Westermann, *Probleme alttestamentlicher Hermeneutik*. See the bibliography, 363–72.

[27] K. H. Miskotte, *Zur biblischen Hermeneutik (ThStud* 55 [1959]) 4.

[28] G. Ebeling, *Wort Gottes und Hermeneutik*, 145.

essential exegesis. The exegete needs to be careful with general insights gained in the practice of traditio-historical studies or the study of *Gattungen*. One runs the risk of tackling the text schematically while neglecting its unique character. Those who take too seriously what is commonly known, are inclined to level the particularity of the text being studied. *"Latet periculum in generalibus."*[29] This comment by Barth in connection with theology may also pertain to the work of exegesis.

The exegesis of Genesis 4 in the present study presumes to do more than establish a method, as if the method followed would only be applicable to this narrative and as if one by different paths might arrive at the same results. Exegetes introduce themselves in the process of exegesis and will therefore offer their own interpretations. However, if one asks realistically what is meant by the text, two interpretations may not exclude but supplement one another.

The method of this study presumes in its particularity, suggested by its stated objective, to give general rules which may be followed elsewhere by analogy. They may only be useful if they are focused anew on another text, since there is only one way in which the text may be approached, i.e., by being ready to listen according to elementary rules that should be valid in any human encounter.[30] That means that in principle the text has the first word, whatever information the exegete may have gained concerning it. It is therefore not entirely correct to speak about the object of the exegete. It is to the text that the exegete must above all be subject, and he or she will have to bow to it. As philologist, "lover of the word," and as servant of the word, the exegete may let the text be heard; he or she is comparable to a musician who performs a musical piece, "interprets" it. The word must be sounded and heard: the *Tanakh* is more *miqrāʾ* [what is read aloud] than Scripture. The words must be recited and heard. Even if one did not know that, the text makes it clear through repetition. "Brother" and "land" are themes that are discerned even upon hearing Genesis 4 for the first time.

Thus the exegete receives his or her first global impression of the story; possibly some salient details may have come to one's attention, but

---

[29] K. Barth, *Kirchliche Dogmatik* (Zurich: Zollikon, 1946) 2/2:51.

[30] "It is an inhuman way of treating a man's word to direct one's attention to the word itself and as such, or to direct it to the character of the speaker or his past or his authorities and then make this a matter of great importance. What does he want to say, to what matter which deserves all our attention does his word refer? Only when I see this matter do I really get back to the speaker himself and what he is saying." (Miskotte, *When the Gods are Silent*, 146.)

much remains unclear. Then the next step is taken and questions are asked. The exegete has entered the hermeneutical circle where, on a small scale, the rule of *scriptura scripturae interpres* is in force. The whole is understood from the parts, and the parts from the whole. If one is on the right road, answers are received to questions, and one confirms the other. "Every observation nods to the other. Each trait which becomes visible, confirms what is already recognized. The interpretation is evident. On such evidence rests the truth of our science," says Staiger, a scholar of stylistics.[31]

Not always does the interpreter get an answer, especially if the literary datum, such as biblical literature, stems from a totally different world from his own. Then it is necessary to step outside the hermeneutical circle and interrupt the conversation with the text to get information elsewhere. First, one may turn to the context that is closest to the text: the totality of biblical literature; next, the world of the ancient Near East. There auxiliary historical disciplines such as form criticism, archaeology, and ancient Near Eastern literature, are available. We may need them all, but we are not forced to consult any. With the necessary alterations or changes, we may adopt what Spoerri emphasizes concerning the science of literature, philosophy, the "love of words": "...all of history, philosophy and psychology may despite their best efforts, be only auxiliary sciences. The soul and end of all philological effort is the text, and everything that leads away from the written text and does not have as its goal the clarification of poetic form, is a sin against the creative spirit of language."[32] That seems to be the same as the answer that Bernhardt gives to "the question concerning the right method in Old Testament exegesis...No way may remain untrod which may somehow lead to the text,"[33] but in the title of his paper "The form critical study of the Old Testament as exegetical method," auxiliary science and exegesis are generalized. Exegesis itself does not merit attention in his treatment of the subject. Indispensable knowledge of the fact, information gained from outside the text, do not belong to exegesis itself but are preparation. This saying is of particular relevance: "*Latet periculum in generalibus!*" "Chasing after 'sources,' influences and parallel passages in itself can be a disadvantage to interpretation." They may tempt the interpreter not to

[31] E. Staiger, *Die Kunst der Interpretation* (Zurich: Zollikon, 1955) 20.

[32] Th. Spoerri, "Uber Literaturwissenschaft und Stilkritik," *Trivium* 1 (1942) 2–3.

[33] K. H. Bernhardt, *Die gattungsgeschichtliche Forschung am Alten Testament als exegetische Methode. Ergebnisse und Grenzen* (Berlin: Evangelische Verlagsanstalt, 1959) 18–19.

pay primary attention to "…the new, the uniqueness of the work at hand."[34]

Neither origins nor comparision is decisive for exegesis, but how, e.g., a certain motif or a direct borrowing is used within a text in question, according to the rule *verba valent usu*. If the *terminus technicus* "fatty part" used in Abel's sacrifice is understood by paying attention to the terminology of Leviticus, there is a danger that one might conclude that Abel's offering is cultically flawless unless one keeps in mind the function of the word in its context.

Thus, v. 4a must be read as a parallel to 3b:

> Cain brought an offering to YHWH from the fruit of the soil, and Abel brought one as well, from the firstlings of his sheep, from their fatty parts.

Thus, "firstlings" and "fatty parts" underscore that Abel's offering is also an offering to YHWH. (See, for example, Lev 3:16: "…all fat is YHWH's"). Abel is thus *implicitly* put on the same level as Cain, the central figure of the story.

The individuality and autonomy of this text, i.e., the *usus*, is therefore decisive. This is even more relevant if one moves even further outside of the direct framework of the data, as with the concept *qnh*.[35] With the search for parallels and analogies, on the other hand, a different usage may alert us to the unique character of the subject of study.

One certainly must take into account that the biblical authors did not create their material themselves, but that they borrowed from their own tradition and from elsewhere, or that they worked with fixed motifs or stereotypes, as perhaps in Genesis 4 with the "hostile brother" or "shepherd and farmer." "The ways of working presuppose certain knowledge, namely knowledge of elementary circumstances, which are given with the workings of a literary piece."[36] Among the "workings"

---

34 M. Weiss, "Wege der neuen Dichtungswissenschaft in ihrer Anwendung auf die Psalmenforschung. Methodologische Bemerkungen, dargelegt am Beispiel von Psalm XLVI," *Bib* 42 (1961) 268. See idem, "Einiges über die Bauformen des Erzählens in der Bibel," *VT* 13 (1963) 456–75; and "Weiteres über die Bauformen des Erzählens in der Bibel," *Bib* 46 (1965) 181–206.

35 On the basis of Ugaritic and Canaanite texts *qnh* must be rendered "create, bring forth." Thus: "I have *brought forth* a man, with YHWH" (Gen 4:1), contra, e.g., E. Fox, *In the Beginning* (New York: Schocken, 1983) 18: "*qānîtî*: I-have-gotten a man, as has YHWH!" Eve is, unlike Aṯarat: *qnytilm*: "the *bringer forth* of a creature" (Ps 104:24) *with* (by the intervention of, cf. the matriarchs) YHWH.

36 W. Kayser, *Das sprachliche Kunstwerk. Eine Einführung in die Literaturwissenschaft* (15th ed.; Bern/Munich: Francke, 1971) 54; cf. 55–186.

are also stylistic means, for style is not a surface phenomenon but the *opus ad extra* of the inner self (*innerlijkheid*).[37] For example, Buber had pointed out that the *Leitwortstil* in the *Tanakh* assumes an important role.[38] Again and again the exegete will need to ask oneself whether such elements of style as repetition, alliteration, chiastic construction, etc., have relevance in the text, whether they lead to a better understanding or even to the essence of the whole. "After much touching, pondering, attempting, stylistic analysis will interpret the object, the linguistic work of art. A general convergence will justify result and method; to show here means to prove."[39]

Discussions of words and segments of the text should dialogue with stylistic phenomena as they relate to the text in its wholeness.[40] Only if the given form produces true inconsistencies, is one forced to search for reasons, e.g., traditio-historical ones. But here also great care must be urged. It may relate to the character of the "Semitic tale" that everywhere "incongruences and inconsistencies are found in the representation."[41] Moreover, it may be that supposed cases of unevenness that have given occasion to source division may be well founded from an artistic point of view and easy to explain.[42] When one goes to work methodically, primarily hearing and questioning within the hermeneutical circle, where the whole is more than the sum of the parts, there may still be a dark segment such as Gen 4:7 which is to be interpreted in the context of "the man and his brother":

---

[37] "...and finally, style is not a formality, but an expression of human subjectivity, a necessary outcome of the power of the spirit, of human impetus toward the shaping of language and toward the communication by means of linguistic forms"; L. Alonso Schökel, "Die stilistische Analyse bei den Propheten," *VTSup* 7 (Congress Volume; Oxford 1959; Leiden: Brill, 1960) 164.

[38] M. Buber, "Leitwortstil in der Erzählung des Pentateuchs" in: *Die Schrift und ihre Verdeutschung* (Berlin: Schocken, 1936) 211–38; idem, "Das Leitwort und der Formtypus der Rede," *Werke II. Schriften zur Bibel* (Munich: Kösel, Schneider,1964) 1150–58. See F. M. Th. de Liagre Böhl, "Wortspiele im Alten Testament," *Opera Minora* (Groningen: Wolters, 1953) 11–25.

[39] L. Alonso Schökel, "Erzählkunst im Buche der Richter," *Bib* 42 (1961) 171.

[40] "Whoever interprets always runs the danger of producing only a collection of butterflies of purely independent observations" (E. Staiger, *Die Kunst der Interpretation*, 24).

[41] Palache, "Oudtestamentische verhaal," 33, 34.

[42] Alonso Schökel, "Erzählkunst" 168. Note his opposition to Eissfeldt, on pp. 169, 170.

Is it not thus:
If you do well, raise it (*scil.* face)!
But if you do not do well
you lie at the door of sin.

Doing well affects face to face communication with the brother. If that
does not take place the next step will be *sin*. Moreover, the younger
brother is dependent on the older (*těšûqāh* = orientation):

To you (Cain) he (Abel) is oriented
and you may rule over him.

This relationship is parallel to that of "the man and his wife" (Gen 3:16b):

To your husband you are oriented
and he may rule over you.

Many hold that one can understand a literary unit by comparison of
its intention and function within a certain "context," by which one then
understands the *Sitz im Leben*, which also determines the genre. A *Sitz im
Leben*, however, must generally be reconstructed from the exegesis, so
that one does not sufficiently reckon with the fact that the literary *datum*
in any case has received a *Sitz in der Literatur*[43] and lies therewith on a
different niveau from that of, e.g., an isolated aetiological saga. As to
genre, [E.] Jacob hesitates to apply the terms saga and *Legende* to biblical
narrative;[44] he deems the general indication "poetic narrative" more a
propos. That is not far from von Rad's description: "the product of
explicit artistic intentions."[45]

For the *Sitz in der Literatur* one must first take into account the
Tanakh, which is, in spite of its variety, an ordered collection of literature
with the name of YHWH in the center.

When Auerbach in his book *Mimesis. The Representation of Reality in
Western Literature* begins with a comparison of the biblical and Homeric
narrative method, he emphasizes that the former does not intend to
entertain but wants to bring the reader under the power of, and draw
him into, the narrated event. Saga, historical report, and history-theology
have melted together inseparably in the stories which are intentionally
told in such a way that they demand interpretation. Even when the
material seems to have the character of a saga, actual history appears to

---

43 Alonso Schökel, " Stilistische Analyse," 162.
44 E. Jacob, "Sage," *RGG3* 5:1302. "The *Sage* is a 'word' [*dāvār*]" (1307).
45 Von Rad, *Old Testament Theology* 1:109.

get the upperhand as the story progresses.[46] Even the Samson story has kerygmatic intentions.[47] Buber expresses this even more sharply when he says: "No matter what happened with the parts of the Bible before they were included in the Bible: in every part of its body the Bible is message (*Botschaft*)."[48] Not surprisingly, this has shaped the language of the *Tanakh*; the stories are not told to fascinate the hearer and to lead one along to another world, but the narrated history is presented as the story of the hearer oneself. To open the hearer's eyes the narrative must therefore take on a confrontational character, work with sharp light and dark contrasts to direct attention to the exclusively important, or draw the hearer with theme words at decisive and surprising moments, to instruct one implicitly in the narrative.[49] One may therefore expect certain similar stylistic means in different parts of the *Tanakh*, and one need not be surprised at the fact that the same narrative style is found in the gospels[50] —consciously imitating, one suspects.

By keyword (*Stichwort*) connections different stories appear to be connected in series, not only formally by way of narrative shaping, but also thematically, while the placing of literary units is most meaningful. The context in which a small unit occurs must therefore be drawn into exegesis and may even be the key to understanding the story. The exegete, moreover, must be alert to the fact that story complexes also are

---

[46] "The narratives of Holy Scripture do not, like Homer, solicit our favor, they do not smile at us to please and to enchant us—they want to subject us; when we refuse, we are rebels. It may not be objected that they go too far, that they do not expound history, but the religious teaching of a claim to dominion, for the narratives are not, like those of Homer, simply narrated 'reality'. Incarnated in them are teaching and promise which are inseparably melted together" (Auerbach, *Mimesis* 17).

[47] "As a gift of YHWH to Israel—thus Samson is preached"; A. G. van Daalen, *Simson. Een onderzoek naar de plaats, de opbouw en de functie van het Simsonverhaal in het kader van de oudtestamentische geschiedsschrijving* [A Study of the Place, the Structure and the Function of the Samson Story in the Context of Old Testament Historiography] (Dissertation, University of Amsterdam; Assen: Van Gorcum, 1966) 119.

[48] Buber, "Die Sprache der Botschaft." *Werke* 2:1095.

[49] See F. Rosenzweig, "Das Formgeheimnis der biblischen Erzählungen," in M. Buber & F. Rosenzweig, *Die Schrift und ihre Verdeutschung.* In a penetrating way he set forth that biblical narrative wants to be "public message, authoritative teaching" (248) and how this is expressed in form. He adds: "We would not claim at all that the form that is disclosed and illuminated in the previous material only occurs in the Bible; at least I would consider that very unlikely. I believe that there is hardly an element of the Bible that could not be attested elsewhere" (257).

[50] See F. H. Breukelman, *En het geschiedde...Concentratie op een pars pro toto. Lucas 2:1–20.* "Eltheto" brochure reeks 5 (1961).

positioned functionally in the larger composition.[51] But in the final analysis the entire *Tanakh* must be heard in the exegesis as *scriptura scripturae interpres*.

The theologian as exegete comes to the exegetical task with the presupposition that one knows what the text introduces, knowing, or thinking one knows, that in the final analysis the witness concerns YHWH the God of Israel and his people, and that the kerygma will be heard in this literature. To exegete means simply to ask for the marked path. No special theological hermeneutic is offered us, and we have no tricks at our disposal to facilitate our task, any more than what is available to an ordinary interpreter.[52] The exegete needs to set prior knowledge in the balance and accept the adventure that might lead to the discovery that the way was not so familiar after all—in spite of the fact that the *Tanakh* has a center by which "everything that is within the circle is colored and determined by a totally unique character."[53] The ways and footprints that must be followed are full of surprises!

---

[51] See van Daalen, 80, 81.
[52] Miskotte, *Zur biblischen Hermeneutik*, 14, 25.
[53] M. A. Beek, *Aan Babylons Stromen* [On Babylon's Rivers; 3d ed.] (Amsterdam: Kosmos, 1955) 236.

—◦⊃ 4 ⊂◦—

Narrative in the Hebrew Bible

The Approach to Biblical Narrative by Palache, Beek, and Others*

K. A. D. Smelik

ABSTRACT

This address memorializes Prof. Dr. M. A. Beek, late Professor of Old Testament at the University of Amsterdam.

The story of how the Amsterdam tradition deals with biblical narrative begins with Palache. Palache claimed that Israel's narrators felt quite free adapting traditional materials to their purposes. His independent approach also questioned the regnant documentary hypothesis on many points. He stressed that later writers (such as the Chronicler) were not slavishly bound to earlier sources but proceeded quite freely, depending on their particular emphasis. Contrary to common opinion, the history of David's succession was not an eyewitness report but a literary product (possibly from the exile)—a claim which Beek also made. Likewise, Van Daalen, a student and colleague of Beek, in her dissertation on Samson also warns against drawing historical conclusions from biblical literature.

Deurloo in his dissertation on Cain and Abel, stands in the same tradition, but also discusses hermeneutical and dogmatic interests, as well

---

* English translation of: K. A. D. Smelik, "Vertellingen in de Hebreeuwse Bijbel; De benadering van het bijbelse verhaal door Palache, Beek en diens leerlingen," *Amsterdamse Cahiers* 9 (1988) 8–21.

as the scholarship of Luis Alonso Schökel, Meir Weiss, and above all Martin Buber and Franz Rosenzweig. Deurloo also comments on the role of the Midrash. Instead of searching for a *Sitz im Leben*, he proposes that the reader look for a *Sitz in der Literatur*, thus giving a new significance to the Reformation dictum *scriptura scripturae interpres*. This means that a small unit must be interpreted from the context of the entire *Tanakh*: the Old Testament.

Gabriël Cohn's dissertation deals with Jonah. Since historical critical scholarship cannot solve historical questions, Cohn turns to New Criticism and *Werkinterpretation* for his method. He analyzes the rhythm, language, and content, concluding with a sketch of the book of Jonah as an organized unit.

The opinion that the Amsterdam school is not interested in historical questions must be opposed. Smelik's dissertation discusses the historicity of Saul and concludes that the Saul tradition represents prophetic reflection on the past, or narrating *paranaesis*, probably stemming from the exilic period. Beek's article "Saturation Points..." was a kind of programmatic introduction to the Amsterdam school. The Bible should not be seen exclusively as a literary work, for "this word has a proclaiming function."

Ladies and gentlemen:

Tonight is St. Martin's, November 11, 1987, a fitting opportunity to remember another Martinus, who unfortunately passed away last summer. Martinus Adrianus Beek occupied a special place as an Old Testament scholar and his influence will be noticeable for a long time through his writings and his students.

We are concerned with the nature of biblical narrative art, as seen by Beek and his students, a vision which was very controversial for a long time. Dr. Beek, as Professor of Hebrew language and literature, was always proud to be the successor of Juda Palache.[1]

Actually, that is not entirely correct. Between the forced dismissal of Palache as a result of anti-Jewish regulations by the German occupation and Beek's appointment in 1946 lies an interregnum in which the Rev. A. W. Groenman did not hesitate to occupy the chair of Palache on January 5, 1942. Palache and his wife were deported to Theresienstadt in 1944. Together they were murdered in a camp by the Germans on October 17, 1944.

---

[1] See, e.g., M. A. Beek, "Verzadigingspunten..." [Saturation Points, translated in this work as chap. 2 above]. In one of his publications, Beek referred to Palache as: "my predecessor in Amsterdam, the Jewish scholar Palache who had memorized the entire *Biblia Hebraica*."

But Beek was the true, spiritual successor of Palache, whose vision of Hebrew narrative became characteristic of the so-called Amsterdam school.

The Approach by Palache

Palache gave his inaugural lecture entitled "The Character of Old Testament Narrative"[2] on January 26, 1925. He had been named professor the year before, not without some controversy because as a Jew he would not only teach in the Faculty of Letters but also in the Faculty of Divinity. In his address Palache showed how his intense familiarity with tradition and Semitic literature (particularly Arabic) led him to take a standpoint on Old Testament narrative unique for that time.

During the twenties the historical critical approach to the Old Testament was current among non-orthodox Christian Bible scholars.[3] Palache warned against the one-sidedness of this method: beside the history of the *origin* of the biblical text there is also a history of *existence*.[4] He proceeded in his critique to call into question one of the most important presuppositions of the historical-critical method: the thesis that the biblical writers would have copied their sources virtually word for word. Indeed, a source analysis would only make sense if the original texts and traditions would be only slightly edited by the final editors. In this connection Palache cited Gunkel, who states that faithfulness vis-à-vis their sources would have been "*ihre erste Eigenschaft.*"[5]

To a certain extent Palache was willing to accept the existence of such piety toward tradition, but he pointed to "the pragmatic character of Israel's historiography...History is always seen from the viewpoint of a

---

[2] Reprinted in: *Sinai en Paran* 15–36 (and translated in this volume). Further citations will be made from this edition. There is a brief biography on Palache in Beek's introduction to J. L. Palache, *Inleiding in de talmoed* [Introduction to the Talmud] (3rd ed.; Amstelveen: Amphore, 1980) IX–XIV, and in the introduction of M. Reiser to J. L. Palache, *Sinai en Paran. Opera Minora* (Leiden: Brill, 1959) 9–12.

[3] Jewish exegetes assumed more independence toward the historical-critical school and pointed out the weaknesses of this approach. See the works of U. Cassuto, *The Documentary Hypothesis and the Composition of the Pentateuch* (Jerusalem: Magnes, 1961); *A Commentary on the Book of Genesis* (2 vols.; Jerusalem: Magnes, 1964); Benno Jacob, *Das erste Buch der Tora Genesis* (Berlin: Schocken, 1934; reprinted: New York: Ktav, n.d.), Buber's writings on the Bible are collected in his *Werke II. Schriften zur Bibel* (Munich: Kösel, Schneider, 1964); Franz Rosenzweig has several essays in *Die Schrift und ihre Verdeutschung* (Berlin: Schocken, 1936).

[4] Palache, *Sinai en Paran*, 18.

[5] Ibid., 21.

certain idea."[6] Such an approach "precisely presupposes a freer and more independent treatment of the data at hand."[7]

Palache elaborated this by briefly discussing genres from later Semitic literature that shows a kinship with Old Testament narrative: the Jewish *haggadah*, the Arabic *ḥadīth*, and the Syriac *tešʿītā*. His theses are as follows:

1. Narrative is a preferred means for the presentation of thoughts.
2. It is strongly inclined to visualization and concrete imagination.
3. It therefore, draws, if necessary, in a poetic manner from the imagination and is bound neither to reality, nor to older examples, nor to historical tradition, nor even to a holy scripture. Mutually diverging presentations exist side by side and initially do not give cause for criticism.
4. In the course of time the narratives become tradition, and tradition reality.[8]

These conclusions have major consequences. Palache is somewhat reticent and cautious, but if his four theses also apply to Old Testament narrative, the applicability of the historical critical method (both source analysis and later approaches such as form criticism and tradition history) has become problematic. Also, the use of the Hebrew Bible as a historical source began to appear in a very different light. The Old Testament narratives are paranaesis and not historiography. Only at a later stage, when the text had become tradition, was it assumed that the stories had really happened, and many worked diligently to harmonize contradictions. In this connection it is lamentable that Palache did not have the opportunity to elaborate his ideas and that he did not include Akkadian literature in his overview. The numerous studies of the Gilgamesh epic would have offered him interesting comparative material.

Palache demonstrated in the remainder of his address that his four theses also apply to stories in the Hebrew Bible. The "great preference for concrete representation" prompted their authors to tell in great detail, whereby the reader (very wrongly) receives an impression of "high accuracy."[9]

Palache also saw in the Hebrew Bible everywhere "incongruencies and *non sequiturs*." He did not exclude the possibility that some of these

---

6   Ibid.
7   Ibid., 22.
8   Ibid., 31, 32.
9   Ibid., 33.

contradictions might go back to different sources, but he warned against forcing modern logic on the biblical writers. What appears illogical to us may not have been so to the original author.[10] Unlike later exegetes, neither the biblical writers nor the final editors were greatly disturbed by these contradictions.[11]

Supposed piety toward the *Vorlage* is hardly noticeable when one sees how the Chronicler has utilized the books of Samuel and Kings for his own composition.[12] According to Palache the oldest writers of the Old Testament also took a "much more independent attitude toward the material and the tradition and must have composed much more themselves than is generally assumed."[13]

With this Palache laid the foundation of the fundamental critique of the historical critical method by the Amsterdam School. The Amsterdam method cannot be applied beside the historical method (as opposed to most of the other synchronic methods). Amsterdam exegetes are indeed interested in the history of the text, but they view it quite differently from the historical critical school, as will be explained below.

The History of the Succession

Palache gave an application in a story which could not go back to historical information: the dialogue between Amnon and Tamar in 2 Samuel 13.[14] An interesting example, for in his time the Succession Narrative of David, of which this story is a part, was considered the high point of ancient Israelite historiography, objective and historically very reliable.[15] The narrative character of this part of the book of Samuel was hardly recognized.[16]

Beek in this respect stood completely with Palache according to a lecture on the occasion of the 340th anniversary of the University of Amsterdam on January 10, 1972, entitled: "David and Absalom: A

---

[10] Ibid., 34.

[11] Ibid.

[12] Ibid., 33.

[13] Ibid., 35.

[14] Ibid., 34.

[15] See, e.g., the positive judgment of the work in Th. C. Vriezen & A. S. van der Woude, *Literatuur van Oud-Israel* (5th ed.; Wassenaar: Servire, 1976) 209.

[16] See also K. A. D. Smelik, "De Hebreeuwse Bijbel als historische bron," *Amsterdamse Cahiers* 8 (1987) 9–22, esp. 14, 15.

Hebrew Tragedy in Prose?"[17] While most Old Testament scholars at that time assumed that the Succession History was the report of an eyewitness from the opening years of King Solomon, Beek began by saying: "I emphasize at the outset that we are dealing with narrative and not the report of an eyewitness, as has been suggested."[18] And further: "It is clear that we are dealing with literature here. The narrator was not an eyewitness to David's flight and the emotions which this called forth among his supporters, any more than Aeschylus witnessed the uproar at the court of Xerxes when he returned in defeat from Greece; he did not hear the speech of Hushai any more than Shakespeare heard the speech of Mark Antony at the forum of Rome after the murder of Julius Caesar. Historical motifs are perceptible in the background, but above all else we hear what narrators and tragic poets essentially are telling us."[19]

In note 2 of Beek's published lecture he tells us that he gave up his former opinions concerning the Succession History. He says: "Influenced by an article by Th. C. Vriezen...the present author thought for a long time that we are dealing with a report from someone very close to the events, if not the report of an eye witness...Observing the literary shape made me conclude otherwise and provided me at the same time with more insight into the function and the message of the story. I cannot give an opinion on the date of the author, but I do not necessarily exclude an exilic date."[20] It is interesting to compare this statement with the close of Beek's lecture in which he says: "The historiographer who questioned what might be the cause of this humiliation [the Babylonian exile], had already been answered by the prophet Jeremiah."[21] Here Beek assumed that the writer must be dated later than Jeremiah and the destruction of Jerusalem in 586 BC. It is typical of his approach that he always expressed himself very carefully. He asked questions and suggested possibilities rather than establishing theses. In this there may be a clear difference between Beek and his students.

[17] M. A. Beek, *David en Absalom; Een Hebreeuwse tragedie in proza?* (Lecture on the occasion of the 340th anniversary of the University of Amsterdam, January 10, 1972; English translation, chap. 11).
[18] Ibid.,5.
[19] Ibid., 11.
[20] Ibid., 17.
[21] Ibid., 16.

The Influence of van Daalen

The late dating of the story of Absalom was then still quite remarkable; in the meantime other proposals have dated these chapters later still,[22] but in 1972 no one doubted their dating in the time of Solomon. The influence of Aleida G. van Daalen on Beek may be considerable. She had been Beek's closest colleague since 1948; in 1966 she received her doctorate from him for a dissertation entitled *Simson*.[23] Beek also remarked in his "extravert biography"[24] *Wegwijzers en wegbereiders* (Signposts and Preparers of the Way), how much he was influenced by his students: "Thus I have learned from all my students, and if I ask myself seriously to whom I owe the most, to my teachers or to my students, I do not know which way the scale tilts."[25]

Van Daalen's dissertation is subtitled: "An investigation of the place, structure, and function of the Samson story in the context of Old Testament historiography." "Place," "structure," and "function" have become characteristic words in the Amsterdam manner of exegesis. Remarkably van Daalen also speaks of *historiography*, a term which might easily create confusion. But van Daalen is not referring to historiography in the modern sense; the second thesis of her dissertation is: "One must be extremely chary of drawing of historical conclusions based on biblical stories." She is referring to the salvation history embedded in Genesis–2 Kings and assumes that these biblical books were written by a group of authors in the period of the Babylonian exile to proclaim God's salvation in history in that time of misery for his people.[26] Beek may have taken over this dating from van Daalen.

Upon perusing the Samson dissertation again recently, I was struck by how definitely van Daalen settled scores with the traditio-historical method by name and how stubbornly the misunderstanding persists that the Amsterdam school is not interested in the origin of the text. Van Daalen offered a reconstruction of how the whole of Judges 13–16 came

---

[22] See J. Van Seters, *In Search of History. Historiography in the Ancient World and the Origins of Biblical History* (New Haven/London: Yale University Press, 1983) 290: "We may conclude from these observations that the Court History is a post-Dtr addition to the history of David from the postexilic period."

[23] A. G. van Daalen, *Simson; Een onderzoek naar de plaats, de opbouw en de funktie van het Simsonverhaal in het kader van de oudtestamentische geschiedschrijving* (Assen: Van Gorcum, 1966).

[24] The expression is Beek's; see *Wegwijzers en wegbereiders; Een halve eeuw oudtestamentische wetenschap* (Baarn: Bosch & Keuning, 1975) 5.

[25] Ibid., 12.

[26] See Van Daalen, *Simson*, 117, 118.

into being: when a group of authors wrote the Books of Samuel, the Book of Judges, which in that phase ended with 13:1, was supplemented by chapters 17–21. Subsequently, one of the writers composed the story of Samson as a counterweight, to show readers that YHWH redeems his people in hopeless situations, too, by the hand of not entirely blameless figures such as Samson and David.[27]

Diversity within the Book of Judges does not therefore go back to different old traditions, which were joined by a redactor, but is the trace of various groups of authors, who wrote a number of narratives from which they selected some to create the final text of the biblical book. To quote van Daalen: "It is clear that the history could not be written as a whole immediately. The manner of writing suggests that several motifs have been utilized and various designs and proofs of stories have been made, used, and smoothed, before they were made into a whole. Ancient stories and traditions were possibly utilized, but in that case the motifs and data have been worked over by the 'scribes' and rewritten in light of their view of history."[28] On this van Daalen and Palache agree completely.

Important also is her subsequent remark: "As they wrote, they [the Bible writers] have had to review and rework their material where the treatment of their subject demanded it; it might even happen that certain fragments demanded emphases that contradicted statements made elsewhere."[29] In this van Daalen has given a very acceptable explanation of the incongruences and inconsistencies that tempted earlier generations of Old Testament scholars to use scissors on the text.[30]

The Dissertation of Deurloo

A year after van Daalen, in 1967, Karel Deurloo, who was to be Beek's successor, received his doctorate. His dissertation is entitled *Kain en Abel. Onderzoek naar exegetische methode inzake een "kleine literaire eenheid" in de Tenakh* (Cain and Abel. A Study of Exegetical Method Con-

---

[27] Ibid., 79–84, 117–19.
[28] Van Daalen, 47.
[29] Ibid.; see also 43.
[30] In my article "De dynastieën van Omri en Jehu; De compositie van het boek Koningen I" [The Dynasties of Omri and Jehu; The Composition of the Book of Kings], *Amsterdamse Cahiers* 6 (1985) 43–69, esp. 55. I venture the thesis that the book of Kings was never completed. The missing final redactor's hand might explain a number of inconsistences in this book, particularly in 2 Kings 13 and 14.

cerning a "Small Literary Unit" in the *Tanakh*).[31] Deurloo quotes Van Daalen with approval but stresses other emphases as well. This appears already in his introduction, where he quotes Miskotte and von Rad in his plea to take the *Jetztgestalt* and *Letztgestalt* as the starting points of exegesis and of biblical proclamation.[32] He also refers with approval to Frans Breukelman's vision of Genesis.[33] Deurloo's hermeneutic and dogmatic interest is rarely found in Beek's other students.

In addition, he links up with developments in modern literary theory as applied to Old Testament literature, as found in the work of L. Alonso Schökel and M. Weiss.[34] In this connection the names of Buber and Rosenzweig must also be mentioned: all members of the so-called Amsterdam School have accepted their discovery that motif words play an important role in the structuring of Old Testament narrative; their stress on idiolect translation has likewise found a hearing in Amsterdam.[35]

In his dissertation Deurloo pays much attention to the later reworking of the story of Cain and Abel in the Midrash.[36] He shows that this genre may already be illustrated in the Hebrew Bible.[37] As the writers of the Midrash treated the traditional text with remarkable freedom, so have the biblical writers not felt themselves bound by the tradition which they received. Behind the text one cannot discover more than "contours."[38] These contours may be important for interpretation, but only because of their function in the text. "Those who search for a romantic Never-Neverland in order to discover the original text may become so mesmerized that they forget the real object of their study."[39]

Instead of his search for the *Sitz im Leben* of the original traditions, Deurloo places all emphasis on the *Sitz in der Literatur*.[40] With this he

---

[31] K. A. Deurloo, *Kain en Abel; Onderzoek naar exegetische methode inzake een 'kleine literaire eenheid' in de Tenakh* (Amsterdam: Ten Have, 1967). (The introduction to this work has been translated as chap. 3 above.)

[32] See, e.g., 9.

[33] See 7 (Preface).

[34] See 19–21.

[35] The standard work is M. Buber and F. Rosenzweig, *Die Schrift und ihre Verdeutschung*. Concerning the idiolect translations of the *Societas Hebraica Amstelodamensis*, see F. J. Hoogewoud, "Stap voor stap. Een kroniek bij 'Een vertaling om voor te lezen' (NBG/KBS)" [Step by Step. A Chronicle of "A Translation to be Read Aloud"], *Amsterdamse Cahiers* 1 (1980) 102–15.

[36] Deurloo, *Kain* 49–73.

[37] Ibid., 70–73.

[38] Ibid., 73.

[39] Ibid., 84.

[40] Ibid., 21.

gives the Reformation dictum *scriptura scripturae interpres* a new significance. The text must be understood in its totality. That is in the first place
the small literary unit (in this case Gen 4:1–16), but: "The context in
which a small literary unit occurs, must... be drawn into the exegesis and
may be the key to understanding the story. Moreover, the exegete should
be sensitive to the fact that complexes of stories function in the larger
composition. Ultimately the entire *Tanakh* as Scripture must find
expression in the exegesis."[41]

It should be noted that Deurloo limits "Scripture" in both cases to the
Old Testament. For him the New Testament is also Holy Scripture, but
he does not wish to go along with the familiar habit of Christian Old
Testament scholars who refer in the last paragraph of a book to New
Testament texts and use Jesus almost as a *deus ex machina.* "The *Tanakh*
may and must speak for itself in its given unity."[42] Though Deurloo
refers here to Barth and Miskotte, the influence of Beek may be
discerned. From him he learned respect for the Hebrew Bible as a separate writing and reverence for Judaism as a distinct way to God. Beek
once said that when a Jew informed him that he wanted to become a
Christian, he seriously advised him against it.

Cohn's Vision of Jonah

For this reason it is not surprising that Beek as a liberal Dutch
Reformed theologian had a number of Jewish students. Surely, his
double appointment both in the faculty of Divinity and in Literature was
not the only reason for that. Beek felt himself closely related to Jewry,
and he demonstrated that kinship.

One of his Jewish doctors is Gabriël H. Cohn, presently at Bar Ilan
University, Tel Aviv. He received his doctorate on July 11, 1969 with a
dissertation entitled: *Das Buch Jona im Lichte der biblischen Erzählkunst.*[43]

Following an overview of the present state of investigation Cohn
arrived at the conclusion: "Since beside the named problem, the problem
of a possible historical background cannot be solved along the lines of
accepted historical critical scholarship, a new style of critical method is
desired to approach the literature."[44] Cohn wanted to join the currents
within literary scholarship that are known as New Criticism and *Werkin-*

[41] Ibid., 22.
[42] Ibid., 13.
[43] G. H. Cohn, *Das Buch Jona im Lichte der biblischen Erzählkunst* (Assen: Van
Gorcum, 1969).
[44] Ibid., 113.

terpretation, the same direction in which Deurloo pointed.[45] In this approach the investigator's interest concerns itself with the "being" and not the "becoming" of the text.

Cohn's literary analysis is threefold: rhythmic, linguistic, and thematic. Among the rhythmic aspects he counts structure, the parallelism between chapters and motif words, besides sound effects and the dimensions of time and space. Finally in chapter 7 he gives a sketch of the book of Jonah as an organic unit. This is probably the strongest part of his dissertation, and one of the best analyses of this biblical book.

Typical for this literary-analytical approach is the treatment of the psalm in Jonah 2, which most exegetes see as a later addition. Cohn simply includes it in his analysis,[46] so that it has a clear position in the book. He concludes: "The following overall analysis of the psalm demonstrates that it seems to be, linguistically and thematically considered, an integral part of the book of Jonah."[47] Beek put it as follows: "The text of Jonah 2 does not need to be regarded as an addition out of context. The song has its own function, looking forward to the saving of the prophet."[48]

Historical Interest

We have previously referred to the stubborn misunderstanding, holding that exegetes of the Amsterdam School proceed ahistorically. This is plainly incorrect, as already indicated in van Daalen's dissertation. Beek's historical interest, whose *Geschiedenis van Israel* [History of Israel] is one of his best known publications, continues in the work of his students as well. This is particularly notable in my dissertation, *Saul. De voorstelling van Israel's eerste koning in de Masoretische tekst van het Oude Testament* [Saul. The Representation of Israel's First King in the MT of the OT].[49] In this study an attempt is made to trace the historicity of the Saul stories in the Book of Samuel according to criteria which, on the one hand, are borrowed from the modern study of Graeco-Roman antiquity, on the other hand, originate from the Amsterdam method of exegesis.

---

45 Ibid., 32–42.
46 See 43, 44.
47 Cohn, 93 n. 1.
48 Beek, "Verzadigingspunten," 12, 13. (Translated in this volume).
49 K. A. D. Smelik, *Saul; De voorstelling van Israels eerste koning in de Masoretische tekst van het Oude Testament* [Saul; The Representation of Israel's First King in the Masoretic Text of the Old Testament] (Amsterdam: P.E.T., 1977).

Much attention is given to an accurate determination of the genre of Old Testament narratives. Van Daalen still spoke of "Old Testament historiography," but on comparing ancient Near Eastern historiography it becomes clear that the Former Prophets may not be labeled historiography. Instead, I introduce the term: "prophetic reflection on the past," i.e., "a consideration of the past from a world view based on what the great Israelite prophets proclaimed and the attempt to arrive at a narrating paranaesis... addressed to contemporaries."[50]

The expression "narrating paranaesis" betrays the influence of Palache,[51] but in addition I chose ancient Near Eastern texts particularly in comparison with those of the Old Testament. As to dating of the Former Prophets in *Saul*, I agree with van Daalen.[52]

The second part of the dissertation deals with unity and historicity of 1 Samuel 9–31. The result of the investigation of literary unity is summarized in the first thesis: "The Book of Samuel must be regarded as an original literary composition, which probably stems from the period of the Babylonian exile." In this composition the authors have made use, on a limited scale, of older historiographical sources which they have freely utilized and completely subordinated to their literary and ideological purposes. By means of a very critical historical source investigation of the biblical text it was possible to recover some historical data concerning King Saul and to arrive at a historical reconstruction of his career.[53] In this the genre of the text plays a significant role.

Saturation Points and Unfinished Lines

After discussing four dissertations published under Beek's direction, a possible misunderstanding should be cleared up. It is certainly not true that there is no difference between Beek's vision of Old Testament narrative art and that of his students. While Beek expressed himself more cautiously and reticently than his students, he was open to their ideas and stimulated them to proceed in new ways. He created a climate for them which made them feel free to explore in new directions.

In 1968 Beek wrote an important article on method. It has become a kind of confessional writing for the Amsterdam School, and it has the eloquent title: "Verzadigingspunten en onvoltooide lijnen in het onder-

---

50   Ibid., 18.
51   Palache, "Karakter" 22.
52   A more nuanced view is developed in my article "The dynastieën van Omri," cited in n. 31.
53   Smelik, *Saul* 207–13.

zoek van de oudtestamentische literatuur" [Saturation Points and Unfinished Lines in the Study of Old Testament Literature].[54] Beek wished to sketch the background of the work in which some of his students were engaged, and he remarked: "I am responsible for this work because I have made them aware of a number of unintegrated and yet valuable contributions by Eerdmans and Palache, by Buber-Rosenzweig and a few scholars in Jerusalem writing in Hebrew."[55] Thus Beek clearly described how he, on the one hand, felt himself responsible for the work of his students, while on the other hand acknowledging that they went their own way.

In his article Beek declared "that the juggernaut of *Wissenschaft* has proceeded between the demarcated road signs and destroyed whatever came in its path."[56] He then pointed to the work of his teacher Eerdmans, who in the beginning of this century criticized the source hypothesis (though not from ecclesiastical-dogmatic considerations). However, the source hypothesis reached its saturation point, and form criticism did not offer any essential relief. What then?

"While the origin of the biblical text confronts us with so many unanswerable questions, we are strongly inclined to limit ourselves to the study of the available Masoretic Text and to investigate large and small units according to their structure and function in the whole of the *Tanakh*."[57] Here we are reminded of the dissertations of van Daalen and Deurloo. Beek continued by pointing to the fact that the reader is confronted by texts from a time in which the written word was rare. Daily we meet with thousands of printed words of which some are caught in our memory but most, because they are cheap, are wasted. "The biblical text presupposes readers and hearers who taste the word slowly without excessive hurry."[58]

Yet another point must be cited from this important article. Beek saw possibilities that the *Werkschule* method might be profitably applied to certain biblical texts, but he warned against seeing the Old Testament exclusively as a literary work of art. "This word has a proclaiming func-

---

[54] See n. 1.
[55] Beek, "Verzadigingspunten" 13 (see n. 1). (This citation does not appear in the translation of the article in this volume.)
[56] "Saturation points..." (in this volume).
[57] Ibid.
[58] Ibid.

tion, it is not a *divertimento*—even in its most gripping narrative form it was not intended as such."[59]

Times have changed since 1968—in Old Testament scholarship, too. The historical-critical school, which Beek questioned and which his students criticized, has been through a crisis and is busy surveying new ways whereby the final shape of the text receives more and more attention. Abroad also, particularly in the United States and France, one notes various forms of synchronic and structuralist study. "Rhetorical criticism" is a trend that is closely related to the so-called Amsterdam School. One of their representatives, Martin Kessler, cited Beek in an article about 1 Samuel 16 in 1970.[60] In The Netherlands, the Amsterdam School has many supporters and sympathizers. In addition, many exegetes are similarly engaged with structuralist methods, even if they would not count themselves among the adherents of the Amsterdam School. Precisely because of these new developments, both within and outside the historical-critical school, a new reflection on the bases of the Amsterdam method is a pressing desideratum.[61] With such reflections the work of Beek will again prove to be a source of inspiration, and his students will always remember him in gratitude for what they received.

---

[59] See also 15.
[60] M. Kessler, "Narrative Technique in 1 Sam 16,1–13," *CBQ* 32 (1970) 543–54, esp. 544, 545.
[61] A first attempt may be found in R. Oost, *Omstreden bijbeluitleg* [Controversial Biblical Interpretation] (Dissertation, University of Groningen; Kampen: Kok, 1986).

— ∾ 5 ℮ —

A CRITICAL HERMENEUTIC*

Rochus Zuurmond

ABSTRACT

The definition of the word "hermeneutics" is largely dependent on the school of thought within which it functions. The last half century has seen a certain dominance of German *Hermeneutik*, in which the interest was on the understanding subject rather than on the texts. When applied to biblical exegesis, it tended to impose ideological preconditions on a text in order to be understood. This danger, however, is not confined to this particular type of hermeneutic; it occurs wherever texts are interpreted without a general theory of understanding.

We reject the thesis that a text, in the last analysis, is nothing but the interpretation of that text. A text has an authority of its own, which in principle is capable of asserting itself even if it moves beyond our immediate cultural horizon. The emphasis, therefore, is more on breaking down the barriers in our approach of the text than on bringing the text under our intellectual control. A hermeneutical theory may well be helpful in that respect, though it will not be in an unassailable position.

Many biblical texts expressly try to convey a message, in the sense that they try to involve us in a particular praxis. Whether the message is accepted or not is a different matter, but serious exegesis cannot overlook something that is an intrinsic element of these texts. A purely historical

---

* This is a translation of "Een kritische hermeutiek," in *De Bijbel maakt school. Een Amsterdamse weg in de exegese* (Baarn: Ten Have, 1983) 15–29.

approach not only surrenders—often unconsciously—to a concept of "history" which is by no means neutral, but also distances itself from this practical aspect.

Both in Old and New Testament studies many exegetes tend to be more interested in the (hypothetical) "sources" than in the actual texts, a position which in the case of Pentateuchal criticism is definitely connected with a low estimate of post-exilic "Judaism" among German scholars in the late nineteenth century. In Amsterdam we began to counterbalance historical methods by a more structural approach and "close reading" of texts in their literary context in the 1950s, long before these methods became fashionable.

In order to come to grips with our own presuppositions, it is often helpful to study the history of exegesis. Even textual criticism, by explicitly confronting us with what the text does *not* say, can help the text open itself up to us, its readers.

1. *The concept of hermeneutics*

Hermeneutics is a relatively young branch of theology. The first book dealing with biblical interpretation with the word "hermeneutics" in its title was published in 1654.[1] However, hermeneutics began to assume a prominent role only in the nineteenth and twentieth centuries. First, at that time it was definitively emancipated from theology and was therefore no longer exclusively concerned with the interpretation of Holy Scripture but with the interpretation of historical documents in general. Second, Schleiermacher gave a new content to the concept of hermeneutics.[2]

This article deals with the biblical hermeneutics that was called *hermeneutica sacra* in the seventeenth century. It should be said at the outset, however, that what is valid for the interpretation of the Bible must *mutatis mutandis* also be valid for the interpretation of other texts and vice versa. There is no fundamental difference between *hermeneutica sacra* and *hermeneutica profana*.[3]

---

[1] J. C. Dannhauer, *Hermeneutica sacra, sive Methodus exponendarum Sacrarum literarum* (Argentoratum; Strasbourg: J. Staedelius, 1654).

[2] The first reference to *hermeneutica profana* was by the theologian J. M. Chladenius in his *Einleitung zur richtigen Auslegung vernunfftiger Reden und Schriften* (Leipzig, 1742). See Peter Szondi, *Einführung in die literarische Hermeneutik* (Frankfurt: Suhrkamp, 1975) 27–29. The standard work on the development of hermeneutics remains: Joachim Wach, *Das Verstehen, Grundzüge einer Geschichte der hermeneutischen Theorie im 19. Jahrhundert* (3 vols.; Tübingen: Mohr, 1926–33; reprinted 1966).

[3] See Karl Barth, *Kirchliche Dogmatik* (Zurich: Zollikon, 1938) 1/2: 515. The terms "general hermeneutics" and "special hermeneutics" are sometimes also used, for

Though biblical hermeneutics is a rather recent phenomenon under that name, the problems relating to this science are as old as the Bible itself. Hermeneutics is, according to its current definition, a theory of interpretation. Wherever biblical texts were or are interpreted and applied, hermeneutical questions come into play whether one is conscious of this or not. Thus, there is a hermeneutic of the Old Testament in pre-Christian Judaism, as for example in the pĕšārîm (actualizing biblical interpretations) in Qumran. Hellenistic-Jewish allegorizing such as we meet in Philo of Alexandria rests on hermeneutic assumptions. Rabbinic Judaism deals with hermeneutical viewpoints when it interprets Scripture within the framework of the hălākā (Jewish rules of life). Ancient Christian concepts concerning the Old Testament may also be called "hermeneutic," particularly the assumption that this book is only significant because, and insofar as, it points to Jesus and the church.

With most of the examples cited here the interpreter is not, or hardly, aware of one's hermeneutic presuppositions. However, as soon as explicit theories concerning biblical interpretation appear—the first is Origen's in the first half of the third century, the most important is Augustine's in the beginning of the fifth century[4] —it may be said that hermeneutics has in fact gained a place within theology.

For the sake of clarity it is important in this connection to define the concept of hermeneutics more accurately because there is not the least unanimity on this.[5] One's definition is related to the school to which one belongs. A German means by "Hermeneutik" mostly something different than a Frenchman with "herméneutique" or an American with

respectively, for the theory of the interpretation of the Bible generally and the theory of the interpretation of biblical genres such as parables, typology, and prophecy.

4 Origen, Peri Archoon IV (see, e.g., the bilingual edition of Gorgemans and Karpp for the Wissenschaftliche Buchgesellschaft, Darmstadt, 1976). For Origen the starting point and guide for exegesis is the unity of Spirit and Reason (logos). Scripture cannot therefore be opposed to the logos, which means in practice for Origen that Scripture (particularly the Old Testament) is made to agree with the Logos with the help of Platonic schemes. Hence the doctrine of the "threefold sense of Scripture." Augustine, De Doctrina Christiana (many editions and translations; see H.-I. Marrou, Saint Augustin et la Fin de la Culture Antique [4th ed.; Paris: Boccard, 1958] 331–33) posits love (agape, caritas) as a hermeneutical principle. All texts must be interpreted in such a manner that they serve love (see Matt 22:37–40; Rom 13:10). The rabbis developed their hermeneutical rules probably as early as the second century.

5 Richard E. Palmer gives in his Hermeneutics. Interpretation Theory in Schleiermacher, Dilthey, Heidegger and Gadamer (Evanston: Northwestern University, 1969) 33–35 no less than six modern definitions of hermeneutics, each one of which indicates a stage in the historic development which he has sketched.

"hermeneutics," which may lead to some confusion at international meetings.[6] Our definition of hermeneutics is very broad: *all theoretical reflection on exegesis and its functioning in the present and the past.*

That means that for us hermeneutics also includes studies which many classify under literary scholarship. The use and tenor of both terms is a matter of convention. Till the nineteenth century hermeneutics included all aspects of interpretation, as we may notice, for example, with Chladenius (n. 2). After Schleiermacher there is a change. His hermeneutic, under the influence of Kant, concentrates increasingly on "understanding" (*Verstehen*), i.e., on the question of how it is possible that a text which in the first instance is strange to us may be understood, and what the conditions and presuppositions are for understanding.[7] The study of texts themselves, their literary forms, their origin and tradition, were gradually removed from hermeneutics and became the domain of literary criticism, which arose at the end of the eighteenth century as an independent (historical) discipline.

The type of hermeneutics introduced by Schleiermacher, which was targeted more on questions dealing with understanding than texts themselves, was developed in Germany by Dilthey, Heidegger, and Bult-

---

[6] For example, the Portuguese Fernando Belo writing in French at the end of the 1970s, used to object strongly when someone dared to speak about his *herméneutique.* He wanted no part of hermeneutics! What he, influenced by structuralism, rejected, was in fact the modern German philosophical *Hermeneutik.*

[7] Schleiermacher's hermeneutic between his *Erste Entwurf* of 1809/10 and his last *Randbemerkungen* of 1832/33 characterized itself with increasing emphasis as a philosophically responsible doctrine of interpretation. The accent came increasingly to lie on the activity of the understanding (*verstehende*) consciousness of the interpreter. Of course texts, too, interest Schleiermacher; how could that be otherwise with someone who translated all of Plato into German! An interpreter who "wanted to bungle beyond the linguistic" becomes a "nebulist" (*Akademiereden* of 1829, 15). But the concrete texts interested Schleiermacher less and less. His need to develop a generally valid (as opposed to a specifically biblical) hermeneutic drove him ever farther from the texts in the direction of pure *Verstehen.* In the last phase of his hermeneutic this *Verstehen* hardly refers to text but rather to the process in which the author externalizes his inward thinking in language. Language becomes a code of pure thought that is particularly conceived as a movement of the mind. Hermeneutics is the *Kunstlehre* (art) that breaks this code by, as it were, crawling into the skin of the author. (This is a key to the emphasis on biography in the nineteenth century). With Schleiermacher the interpreter may be compared to a musician who interprets a piece; "interpreting" in this sense is indeed one of the meanings of Greek *hermeneuein.* The performing artist executes the entire composition (a beloved word with Schleiermacher) afresh, as it were. See Fr. D. E. Schleiermacher, *Hermeneutik, Nach den Handschriften neu herausgegeben und eingeleitet von Heinz Kimmerle* (Heidelberg: Carl Winter, 1974).

mann.[8] We call this "philosophical hermeneutics." In the 1950s and 1960s this movement was so dominant that the word "hermeneutics" practically came to mean philosophical hermeneutics. This also influenced literary criticism. The hermeneutical method that included all of literary criticism came into being.[9] Hermeneutics and literary criticism were united once more, under the banner of philosophical hermeneutics.

This was not an altogether favorable development for theology, as will be shown below. But value-free literary criticism is also problematic. Therefore, for a definition we return to the classical position, whereby "hermeneutics" includes the entire field of interpretation, so that the entire tradition of interpretation of synagogue and church may remain within our horizon.

2. Hermeneutics and history.

It is no accident that the emergence of modern hermeneutics and historical scholarship coincide. Questions concerning the interpretation of documents written long ago became acute when one, with Lessing,[10] became conscious of the "ugly broad ditch" that separates historical truth from truths that may be recognized by any rational, thinking human being. Hermeneutics presupposes a way of thinking in which history becomes a category of its own. Modern hermeneutics rises on the foundation of modern historical consciousness.

Meanwhile the nature of that historical consciousness colors not only hermeneutics but also exegesis. If one thinks (with Lessing) that we can understand literature of a totally different culture because, and insofar as, the writer expressed generally valid truths, then one in fact brings the texts before the bar of reason, which is, however, strongly determined historically. This is the position of the hermeneutic of the Enlightenment

---

[8] See esp. W. Dilthey, "Die Entstehung der Hermeneutik," *Gesammelte Schriften* (7th ed.; Göttingen: Vandenhoeck & Ruprecht, 1964) 5:317–38. The article was written in 1900. A summary of Bultmann's concepts on the subject are found in his article "Das Problem der Hermeneutik," *ZTK* 47 (1950) 47–69, reprinted in *Glauben und Verstehen, II*, (Tübingen: Mohr, 1952) 211–35. Bultmann's students, particularly E. Fuchs and G. Ebeling, have developed the so-called *Neue Hermeneutik* of the sixties (based on this work). See, e.g., J. M. Robinson & J. B. Cobb (eds.), *New Frontiers in Theology, II: The New Hermeneutic* (New York/Evanston: Harper & Row, 1968).

[9] The fundamental work for this school is H.-G. Gadamer, *Wahrheit und Methode* (4th ed.; Tübingen: Mohr, 1975). (English trans.: *Truth and Method* [New York: Crossroad, 1982].)

[10] See G. E. Lessing, *Uber den Beweis des Geistes und der Kraft* (cited according to *Lessings Werke* [Stuttgart: Deutsche Verlags-Anstalt, 1901] 789–91).

and of liberal theology. On the other hand, if one thinks, with Schleier-macher, that understanding rests on the possibility of "entering into the life" of an ancient author because he or she also participates in general human nature, then the texts quickly become ciphers of human experi-ences while the attention of the interpreter moves from the text to the personality of the writer. That is the position of Romanticism and the biographical movement of the nineteenth century. Along the lines of Lessing, theologians wrote books on Jesus' teaching,[11] and along the lines of Schleiermacher they wrote a "Life of Jesus."[12] It should be possible to describe the hermeneutical development in the nineteenth century as modifications and/or combinations of these two viewpoints.[13]

What these two have in common, and what characterizes all of mod-ern hermeneutics, is the experience of historical distance that dominates the entire hermeneutical problem. The feeling of estrangement, experi-enced by interpreters when they attempt to look beyond the boundaries of their own culture, notably irritated people of the late eighteenth and nineteenth centuries, much more than it did their predecessors. They wanted to know precisely how it was. They undertook journeys of discovery to the interior of distant continents; if possible, they would do the same to the remote corners of history. In that context hermeneutics is ontologically either structural (with Lessing) or anthropological (with Schleiermacher). Historians—and exegetes of the nineteenth century saw themselves mainly as historians—obsessed by the problem of history,

---

[11] A good Dutch example is J. H. Scholten in *De Leer van de Hervormde Kerk* [The Teaching of the Reformed Church] (4th ed.; Leiden: Academische Boekhandel, 1861): "The basis on which the Reformed Church recognizes the Word of God in Scripture lies in the agreement of what God has revealed in Jesus Christ according to the Scrip-tures with what he still reveals through his Spirit to human reason and conscience." (Part 1, chap. 3, introductory thesis).

[12] The climax of romanticizing Jesus-biographies is, of course, Ernest Renan, *Vie de Jesus* (rev.13th ed.; Paris: Michel Levy Frères, 1867): and D. F. Strauss, *Das Leben Jesu* (rev. ed.; Tübingen: Osiander, 1838)—the first book in which scholarship consciously searched for the "historical Jesus"—may be much more sober. Strauss' Jesus looks suspiciously like Strauss himself! (Cf. the judgment of Karl Barth, *Die Protestantische Theologie im 19. Jahrhundert* [Zurich: Zollikon, 1947] 490ff.)

[13] Such a modification, which strongly determines the later development, is found, e.g., with Martin Kahler in his *Der sogenannte historische Jesus und der geschichtliche, biblische Christus* (3rd rev. ed.; Munich: Kaiser, 1961). Kahler drops the historical Jesus for we know next to nothing about him. He starts from "the Christ" witnessed to in Scripture. But we do not know him on account of his having spoken generally valid truths but because of the faith of his disciples, which created a tradition.

wished to regain the lost past to make it participate in their own existence.

Already in the nineteenth century Nietzsche protested this "historical fever."[14] He saw an excess of historical consciousness as a culturally paralytic phenomenon and a harbinger of the end. His pupil Overbeck, positing that modern Christendom had been totally estranged from its historic roots, finally sounded the death knell on all attempts to draw the past to the present on a massive scale. The task that hermeneutics set for itself, namely to give true, free access to the past, became an impossibility.

But perhaps this task had been stated altogether wrongly. Perhaps it reached too high, so that it instantly fell too low. Perhaps it is, after all, not much more than a form of spiritual imperialism which, as a shadow of political imperialism, is doomed to ruin by its own over-confident self-consciousness.

A much more modest and practical approach is possible. Instead of trying to break into the past, wouldn't it be better to let the past present itself to us? Instead of taking a problem as one's starting point, wouldn't it be better to begin hermeneutics with the fact that voices may be heard across the centuries, enabling us to enter into conversation with them?

In reference to Scripture, this is what happens in Barth's theology. If the biblical texts on the basis of their inherent power (which might be called "inspiration" or "theopneusty") could not on their own gain access to our heads and hearts, and thus in a sense by their own force become contemporary with us, we might well write off exegesis. In that case our hermeneutics might not be much more than a camouflage of failure. If God's history is not present in one way or another, all our attempts to actualize that history will be in vain.

This Copernican turn in hermeneutics should not be misunderstood. It surely does not mean that there are no problems with interpretation, or that there are no conditions that we must satisfy to understand these texts. But such concerns are secondary. Ontology and anthropology lose their dominance and must return their central position in hermeneutics to the text itself. The reality of the text that addresses us precedes the possibility of its interpretation.

---

[14] Friedrich Nietzsche, "Vom Nutzen und Nachteil der Historie für das Leben" in *Friedrich Nietzsche Werke* (ed. K. Schlechta; 3rd ed.; Munich: Carl Hanser, 1962) 1:209–85. The article was written in 1874.

3. *The poverty of hermeneutics*[15]

Hermeneutics as it functions in Amsterdam, particularly as influenced by Breukelman, distinguishes itself from common (philosophical) hermeneutics in that it cannot be an autonomous discipline preceding exegesis, but is gradually developed and adjusted by the texts that are read. Exegesis must be kept free from every hermeneutical a priori.

That agrees with the theology of Karl Barth, his views on history, and his "hermeneutics." We put the word in quotes, for Barth is not by profession a hermeneut. Hermeneutical problems were largely forced on him, particularly by Bultmann and his school. He did not spend any more time on the subject than was strictly necessary to keep his attackers at bay. Meanwhile he went his own way, not so much answering the questions of his opponents as showing the objectionable and theologically irrelevant character of such questions. In that sense there emerged with Barth, a sort of hermeneutic, but not a traditional one.[16] Barth's implicitly proposed hermeneutic in his *Kirchliche Dogmatik* turns current hermeneutics upside down: the secret "Hermeneutics as Dogmatics" becomes openly "Dogmatics as Hermeneutics":[17] philosophical hermeneutics becomes theological hermeneutics.

The reason for Barth's reticence concerning hermeneutical questions is clear. Hermeneutics, as we have seen above, has in the course of the eighteenth and nineteenth centuries ever more clearly become an autonomous discipline. What might be called "exegetical physics" was gradually replaced by a *metaphysics of interpretation*, which reaches a provisional high point with Heidegger: with him hermeneutics becomes ontology; his philosophy might, in a way, be typified as *hermeneuo ergo sum*. It is this phase of hermeneutics which confronts Barth via Bultmann

---

[15] This was the title of my contribution to the *Festschrift* for Frans H. Breukelman, *Verwekkingen* (Amsterdam: Universiteit van Amsterdam, 1976) 82–89. I cite (adapted) parts of this article in this paragraph. The title was a conscious reference to Marx's *Misère de la Philosophie* (Brussels: Vogler Paris: Frank, 1847); authorized German translation in *Marx Engels Werke* (Berlin: Dietz, 1972), vol. 4, which in turn was an answer to Proudhon's *Système des contradictions économiques* (Paris, 1846). There is a structural parallel between Marx's concepts of the relationship between philosophy and economics, on the one hand, and Barth's concepts on the relationship between hermeneutics and the biblical text, on the other.

[16] For Barth's hermeneutics, see G. Eichholz, "Der Ansatz Karl Barths in der Hermeneutik," in *Antwort. Festschrift für Karl Barth zum siebzigsten Geburtstag* (Zurich: Evangelischer Verlag, 1956) 52–68.

[17] "Karl Barth's *Kirchliche Dogmatik* as hermeneutics" is one of the mottos of F. H. Breukelman's work.

and against which he polemicizes, for this type of hermeneutics projects itself as the totally dominating prelude to revelation. In this hermeneutic a framework is set up, willy nilly, within which theology might still be done sensibly. Always begun as servant, hermeneutics ends here as absolute master. Natural theology here receives the form of natural hermeneutics. Natural theology eventually ousted revelation; natural hermeneutics will eventually oust Scripture.

The discussion between Barth and Bultmann is in many respects exemplary of every discussion on the place of hermeneutics in theology. What is notable is the non-theoretical, completely non-speculative way in which Barth combats Bultmann. The dominant question is: what does this hermeneutic produce?[18] Barth is not opposed to philosophy as such; he is absolutely not anti-philosophical (nor pro-philosophical for that matter). He is not even opposed to philosophical hermeneutics in principle. He is willing to admit that his "eclectic procedure is somewhat gypsy-like,"[19] and definitely does not recommend it for imitation. It is quite possible that a well-thought-out hermeneutics might be of great service to exegesis. The rejection of Bultmann's hermeneutics has an *inductive* proof for its foundation: in practice it appears that Scripture resists such a hermeneutical framework.

It is no different with Breukelman. For example, the battle for the translation—and if any theologian is a *hermeneut* it is the translator!—does not take place in the first instance in the valley of translation theories but on the plain of exegesis. Here applies the saying, "A tree is known by its fruit." The criterion for each hermeneutics is and remains: whether or not it can maintain itself in the face of the texts themselves. Along the lines of Miskotte[20] and Breukelman we seek in Amsterdam a "critical hermeneutic," being quite aware that the *krites* can be none other

---

[18] In addition to a number of passages in *Kirchliche Dogmatik* and the little book *Rudolf Bultmann, ein Versuch ihn zu verstehen (ThStud* 34; Zurich: Zollikon, 1953)—a revealing title!—see esp. Karl Barth-Rudolf Bultmann, *Briefwechsel 1922–1966* = Barth, *Gesamtausgabe* (Zurich: Theologischer Verlag, 1971), vol. 5/1. See especially letters 48 and 95.

[19] "Briefwechsel," letter 48 (p. 85).

[20] For Miskotte's hermeneutics see: *Om het levende Woord* [Concerning the Living Word] (The Hague: Daamen, 1948; reprinted: Kampen: Kok, 1973); *Als de goden zwijgen* (Amsterdam: Holland, 1956; English trans.: *When the Gods are Silent* [New York/Evanston: Harper & Row, 1967]); "Zur biblischen Hermeneutik," in: *Geloof en Kennis* [Faith and Knowledge] (Haarlem: Holland, 1966). See also G. H. ter Schegget, "Adhaesie aan de Naam," in K. H. Miskotte et al., *De Weg der Verwachting* [The Way of Expectation] (Baarn: Ten Have, 1975) 82–90.

than the text itself. What is unique with this hermeneutic? What makes it a specifically theological, rather than philosophical, discipline? We have indicated it formally in the previous paragraph: it is a consistent application of the thesis that the reality of the Word of God in all its forms precedes its possibility. This hermeneutic proceeds from the fact that God speaks intelligibly in and through the biblical text, and it investigates the postulates of that text, all for the sake of leaving room for the freedom of the acting speaking and speaking acting (the *dābār*) of God and the implied critique therein of our acting and speaking. This God must be able to be GOD, and the theologian may think twice before one tries to put him under the yoke of our view of the world, of humanity, or of life.

However, we may not remain with these formal definitions. A purely formal acknowledgement that "the finite cannot contain the infinite" is a paradox. The religious person has no trouble with that. On the contrary, religious consciousness is nourished by such inward contradictions. A "wholly other" of God's Word may very well be built into a philosophical hermeneutic, as, for example, with Bultmann. When we say that God's Word is a *free word*, such a formula carries within it, its own denial, unless we allow this Word to testify concretely, in preaching and scriptural interpretation.

Such a hermeneutic is naturally a *biblical hermeneutic*, one that lets its categories continually be interrogated and corrected by Scripture itself, that cannot be applied to Scripture without at the same time having Scripture applied to that hermeneutic and therefore ever anew beginning with the basics, because they are the ABC of the witness of the history of God-with-us, the basic movement by which we are related by hearing. "Wir sein pettler, *hoc est verum*." This saying of Luther, Miskotte rightly made the *Leitmotiv* of his hermeneutic.[21]

Thus, there is no *hermeneia perennis*. We know only a continuous dialectic between Scripture and interpretation. We reject every hermeneutic which judges this dialectic unnecessary, undesirable, or impossible, and every hermeneutic which, appealing to whatever presuppositions, refuses to be, and to remain, accountable to Scripture itself.

A fundamental decision is to be made here. One possibility is the thesis that "Scripture itself" (or: "the text") is really nothing but our own interpretation of Scripture. The dialectic here proposed, then, cannot be anything but a *petitio principii*, a meaningless tautology. This is a common view that to many in our culture appears to be a logical necessity. It

---

[21] Miskotte, *Geloof en Kennis* 202 and passim.

might be roughly characterized as vulgar neo-Kantian ideology. Everything is made subservient to the categories of my thinking, the *Ding an sich* finally disappears behind the horizon, everything that is different from myself can only exist in the interpretation which I suggest. That is how imperialism thinks.

The other possibility is—acknowledging the tautological element that is present and of which one should be conscious lest one become a victim of it—not to exclude in advance that the Logos (*dābār*) that is witnessed to in Scripture, in these texts, itself provides access to the heads, hearts, and hands of the hearers. In the first place, nothing else is asked of the hermeneut, the exegete who reflects on his or her work, than to remain faithful to the texts as a hearer and continually critical vis-à-vis oneself and one's implicit or explicit hermeneutic. The text is the *krites*, the critical authority. We can only interpret Scripture if at the same time we let Scripture interpret us.

This forms the connection with preaching in the church. Scripture wishes to be explained because the Word to which it witnesses wishes to be preached. That is not something additional, but is fundamental to the texts from the outset. Whoever thinks one is able to explain texts *without* honoring this connection to preaching, whoever wishes to exegete without bearing in mind that these are texts that have something to announce, estranges an essential element of Scripture. Of course, it sometimes makes sense to defer this viewpoint. Grammatical problems are not solved by an appeal to the proclaiming function of the text; neither may historical details be derived from the kerygmatic thrust. But in a considered exegesis of a text the kerygmatic tendency will not be lacking. A *distinction* between preaching and teaching may occasionally make sense, but a *separation* of the two is an impossibility. The thesis heard here and there—"if you have done the exegesis of a text, you cannot preach on it anymore"—is *unscientific*, the result of an academic self-understanding that has moved beyond its perimeters. Ultimately neither the academy nor the pastor's study is the place where these texts are at home. The exegete *borrows* the text—from the synagogue and the church. As Barth's dogmatics seeks to be church dogmatics, so our hermeneutics wishes to be in the final instance *church* hermeneutics—not in the last place by dint of our scientific conscience.

It should be clear from what has been said here that this does not mean in the least that Scripture should be surrendered to confessional prejudices. On the contrary, the only way to discover and eliminate (not only confessional!) prejudices is to participate in the movement (Spirit) of this Word, and with that, one takes one's place in the Church. Outside of this Church (which is not the same as the institutional church!) there is a poor future for exegesis.

4. *Hermeneutics of the praxis, praxis of hermeneutics*

But how does all of this work in practice? In principle we do not reject any hermeneutical theories except those that do not take the text seriously. We are philosophically eclectic: nothing is to be rejected a priori, everything is welcome if it serves the explication of Scripture. We are not opposed to the *historical* approaches to Scripture that are presently dominant. But if an uncritical concept of "history" sometimes leads exegetes to pile hypothesis upon hypothesis, then to publish the results as "science," we become suspicious. Nor are we opposed to the developing *structural-analytical* methods. But we are aware of the danger that threatens here to view the hearer of the texts as a noble computer; in that case this method, too, would overstep the mark. Hermeneutical reflection will critically view everything that pertains to scriptural inter-pretation, search out its (hidden) presuppositions, and test the results, with the texts themselves in context as the final critical authority. Naturally, a good biblical theology is indispensable to this.

If in Amsterdam circles there is sometimes a slight preference for structural-analytical methods of exegesis, that is only because such methods pay more attention to the text in the form they have been deliv-ered to us than is the case with historical methods, which sometimes seem more interested in the (hypothetical) earlier stages of the text than in the text itself. Nevertheless, a historical approach that tries to analyze the process by which the texts have originated, can furnish the text with a profile that is helpful for the interpretation of that text. That is particu-larly the case when something is known of those earlier stages, such as with the book of Chronicles (based on Kings) or the evangelists Matthew and Luke (on the basis of Mark). The heuristic function of textual history must also be mentioned in this connection, including the versions (older translations) by which exegetes do not only perceive what is there but also what is *not* there.

Hermeneutics also includes a critical analysis of its own explicit or implicit presuppositions. The function of the text itself in this connection has already been pointed out. Disciplines such as sociology and psychol-ogy may be helpful. Everyone knows people's inclination to appropriate Bible texts for themselves, then to justify this by means of a theory. If we are aware of this, and if we are alert to the ideological field of gravity within which we do our exegesis, individually and as a community, we may be able to remove barriers which hinder a correct understanding of these texts. Listening as closely as possible is fundamental. It could hardly do any harm to check whether we might have ideological cotton in our ears, as long as it is in the service of the interpretation of the texts and these aids do not begin to behave as masters.

In this connection "materialist exegesis" and "feminist exegesis" and similar approaches also have their place.[22] They are valid analytical methods vis-à-vis the texts as well as the hearer. When "materalist exegesis" (a most unfortunate term) tries to read the texts as elements of a resistance movement, that may be at least a useful supplement, and in certain instances also a necessary corrective, to existing methods. However, as soon as these new approaches degenerate into new philosophical prolegomena that seek to impose their will on the text, they overshoot their goal. No less than with other exegetes, "materialist" or "feminist" exegesis must remain aware of the tendency to self-justification that is present in every understanding of Scripture, namely, an inclined plane on which one easily lands but remains standing with difficulty.

The history of exegesis may furnish us with useful material for hermeneutical finger exercises. The totality of exegetical work that has been done may be compared to a tell. On the foundations of the old collapsed structures new buildings were erected, which in turn collapsed and became the foundations for the following phase. The history of exegesis tries to dig up that tell, as it were, layer by layer. The cross-section makes visible how old motifs sometimes remain active, much longer than the situations in which they originated, and how new conditions modify the old motifs and sometimes annihilate them. It may be shocking sometimes to see how in previous generations certain examples of exegesis were held as uncontroverted which today are confronted by exegetes with a shrug of the shoulder. Are we so sure that this may never happen with our own exegetical work?

In the cross-sections one might try to see the connections of a theology (and, within that, of exegetical work) and the society in which it operated. Exegesis undeniably has ideological components that are at

---

[22] This is not the place for a full discussion of these views. For my position concerning "materialist exegesis" (let the reader beware against premature conclusions!) I refer to the article cited in n. 15 in *Verwekkingen* and to my contribution in A. F. J. Klijn (ed.), *Inleiding tot the studie van het Nieuwe Testament* (Kampen: Kok, 1982) 153–64. In this context I might also mention fundamentalist exegesis.

times more easily visible from some historical distance than in one's own situation. Let us hope that the critical sense developed by historical examples can help us further in our exegetical endeavors.

The study of the history of exegesis does not reach beyond that. No one should think that we only need to blow the dust of the ages off the texts to see their pure truth before our eyes. It is not that simple. There is *always* a layer of dust on the texts; it remains impossible to gain direct access to them. Ultimately, only the words themselves can shake off the dust and reveal themselves.

There is no such thing as a single true exegesis of Scripture, valid everywhere and always. It could not possibly exist in view of the witnessing character of the bibilical writings. Every age will need to tackle the interpretative task of the Bible anew; in every situation the Bible speaks afresh. There is no problem with exegetes accenting certain things more one time and less another. The Bible does not reveal static or cosmic truths and will not let itself be caught in a timeless system of thinking. Correct exegesis is a perspective, though there is such a thing as *incorrect* exegesis, misled and misleading exegesis, distorted by interests of groups or classes. It is the task of biblical hermeneutics to help avoid such problems as much as possible.

B

Studies in Genesis

—⚬ 6 ⚬—

THE STORY OF THE SONS OF GOD WHO TOOK THE DAUGHTERS OF HUMANS AS WIVES*

F. H. Breukelman

ABSTRACT

The elaboration of the theme "the genesis of Israel amidst the nations" ties the book of Genesis together as a composition in which all elements have their function. First, in 1:1–2:3 the story of creation and in 2:4–4:26, the complex of stories about man on his land *coram Deo*, are told. Next, in 5:1–50:26 (with three main parts 5:1–11:26; 11:27–37:1; 37:2–50:26), the "Book of the *tôlĕdôt* of Adam, man" follows. Throughout the book the crucial issues are *fathers* and *sons*, who are each other's *brothers*. In the first main part attention is focused on the contrast between the lives of Israel's fathers *ante et post primogenitum natum* and the lives of all peoples *ante et post diluvium*, which contrast is maintained during the next main parts. Israel, being *firstborn* among the brothers, is the blessed, representative of man among mankind.

In the way that God is *vere Deus* among the gods, so Israel as the partner of God is *vere homo* among all men. In this connection Gen 6:1–4 functions as a "fragment" to express the way in which the Torah criticizes popular myth. It was inserted here to make clear, with reference to the giants and the

---

* This article is a translation of: "Het verhaal over de zonen Gods die zich de dochters des mensen tot vrouw namen," *Amsterdamse Cahiers* 1 (1980) 9–21.

heroes, who is *not* the real man. As a contrast to the hero in popular myth, the ṣaddîq of Israel's Torah appears.

I

Whoever tries to understand the book of Genesis needs to consider how the book came into being. This question must not, however, become the sum total of our studies. Neither must it as "tradition history" form the framework in which all the parts of the book are explained. What ought to engage us is not the becoming of the book but the result of that becoming, the book itself, given to us as a unified composition.

However, the components which we meet in the book of Genesis are so different in nature and origin that unity of composition is a very controversial question. Thus, Otto Eissfeldt says at the beginning of his book *Die Genesis der Genesis* : "In the form in which they lie before us, these 50 chapters offer a continuing narrative of events which stretch over more than 2400 years, from creation... to the death of Jacob and Joseph. However, the 50 chapters do not represent a closed totality, according to a unified plan."[1] Eissfeldt could not see that they who worked on the formation of the book of Genesis busied themselves with unfolding a theme and that they thereby created a grandiose unity of composition in the manner in which they arranged all the components, gathering them up in the book and attuning them to one another. Our thesis is that one needs to know the theme and composition of the book as a whole to be able to interpret each of its components. With the interpretation of many components the correctness of this thesis has been amply confirmed. This time we wish to see how far we can get with this thesis in the interpretation of Gen 6:1–4.

First, we need to describe briefly the theme and composition of the book of Genesis. After 1:1–2:3 (the creation story) and 2:4–4:26 (the complex of stories concerning *hāʾādām* on the *ʾadāmāh coram Deo)* there follows in 5:1–50:26 (the three major divisions being: 5:1–11:26, 11:27–37:1 and 37:2–50:26) the *sēper tôlĕdôt ʾādām*, "Book of the Generations of Adam, the human" (hereafter abbreviated BGA. This entire book deals with *fathers* and *sons* who are each other's *brothers*. In the first major part of this book of generations (5:1–11:26), in generation after generation (*dôr wādôr*) the generation of the firstborn son is always the decisive event in the life of each of the fathers, first during the ten generations before the

---

[1] O. Eissfeldt, *Die Genesis der Genesis. Vom Werdegang des ersten Buches der Bibel* (Tübingen: Mohr, 1958) 3.

flood of Adam to Noah (5:3–32; 9:28, 29) and thereafter during the ten generations after the flood from Noah to Terah (9:1; 11:10–26). In generation after generation, the concern is ever for that *one* among others, the one who will (in the second major part of the book) be called Abraham, then Isaac, and finally Jacob-Israel.

We meet with an enormous contrast in the first chapter of the book of generations, the contrast between the firstborn and the others (*ante et post primogenitum natum*) of the life of everyone of Israel's fathers, and those before and after the flood (*ante et post diluvium*) of humanity at large. We meet the same contrast in the story of the generations of Terah (11:27–25:11), in which Abraham is juxtaposed to Lot, who went with him. Like the lives of all his fathers, Abraham's life is again a life before and after the birth of the firstborn, and Lot's life is again a life before and after the catastrophe, like the life of all humanity out of whose midst they were drawn.[2]

The *dābār* (word), which each time in the first major part of the BGA (5:1–11:16) may be told in a bicolon or tricolon—the movement of the father to the son, whereby the father is each time represented to us as living before and after the birth of the firstborn, and the son as the first-born among many brothers—this *dābār* is now broadly unfolded in the second major part of the BGA (11:27–37:1); first the *father* is mentioned (in the story of the generations of Terah, 11:27–25:11), and then the *son* in relation to his brother (in the story of the generations of Isaac, 25:19–35:19). The story of the *tôlĕdôt* of Terah deals mainly with Abraham, whose life is again presented before and after the birth of the firstborn; and the story of the generations of Isaac thereafter deals with Jacob in his struggle with his brother for the right of the firstborn (*bĕkōrāh*) and the blessing (*bĕrākāh*). In this movement from generation to generation, from father to son, which reaches its goal in the appearance of Jacob-Israel, we are dealing with the theme of the book of generations: the becoming of Israel in *ʾereṣ kĕnaʿan* in the midst of "the-peoples-on-earth" (*haggōyîm bāʾāreṣ*), 10:32. In this becoming of Israel in the midst of the nations a *dābār* of God takes place that is just as miraculous as the creation in the beginning. Hermann Gunkel remarks about Gen 11:10–26: "Those named are always the firstborn, as in Genesis 5; Israel, who has descended from them, is the firstborn among the peoples."[3] From the outset all of our attention in the BGA is concentrated in that *one* among all others. If you

---

2   See Gen 19:29 *hhpkh*, LXX *katastrophe*, Buber: *Umsturz*.
3   H. Gunkel, *Genesis* (5th ed.; Göttingen: Vandenhoeck & Ruprecht, 1911) 155.

wish to know what is happening to the others, then pay attention to that one, for in that one the story concerns all. The entire problematic of *hāʾādām* in his existence on the *ʾădāmāh coram Deo* will be thematically treated toward a solution. As the firstborn among his many brothers, he is a uniquely representative person among humankind, the blessed one, in whom all are blessed with a salvific future. As his God is the true God (*vere Deus*) among the gods, as a partner of God he is the truly human (*vere homo*) among humankind.

Another comment: to unfold the theme of their story as thoroughly and precisely as possible we see the narrators constantly painting contrasts. The earth under the sky is placed in the light of day as opposed to *tōhû wābōhû*, which is negated by the *bārāʾ* of *ʾělōhîm* and is definitely excluded from any effective role. Those born before and after the birth of the firstborn (*ante et post primogenitum natum*) are juxtaposed to the scheme: before and after the catastrophic flood (*ante et post diluvium catastropham*). Nimrod appears in the "Table of Nations" juxtaposed to Abraham, who is called away from the peoples, and Abraham is juxtaposed to Lot, Sarah to Hagar, Isaac to Ishmael, Jacob to Esau (and within Israel, Joseph to Reuben). The No is in the service of the Yes. The one who is not (chosen) is mentioned to help us visualize as sharply as possible who the divinely chosen is.[4] In that *one* the others are all dealt with!

These remarks on the theme and composition of the book of Genesis will have to suffice. We are concerned with the small fragment Gen 6:1–4, which refers to the sons of God who saw the daughters of humans and took them as wives, had intercourse with them with the result: they *gave birth* to them…! What moved those who were engaged with the formation of the book, we ask, to include this small fragment in the proclaiming narrative of the BGA? How does this little fragment, which, follows immediately on 5:1–32, function within the book and how does what we hear in this fragment relate to the theme of the book as a whole?

II

Since our exegesis is based on the colometric representation of Martin Buber's translation,[5] the Hebrew text according to Buber's divi-

---

4 It should be noted here that the concepts "elect" and reject," the concern of the *bkwrh*, do not occur in the BGA.

5 M. Buber & F. Rosenzweig, *Die fünf Bücher der Weisung* (9th ed.; Heidelberg: Schneider, 1976).

sions is reproduced below to facilitate reference to each of the twelve cola in our exegesis.

ויהי כי החל האדם לרב על פני האדמה
ובנות ילדו להם
ויראו בני האלהים את בנות האדם כי טבת הנה
ויקחו להם נשים מכל אשר בחרו

ויאמר יהוה
לא ידון רוחי באדם לעלם בשגם הוא בשר
והיו ימיו מאה ועשרים שנה

הנפלים היו בארץ בימים ההם
וגם אחרי כן
אשר יבאו בני האלהים אל בנות האדם
וילדו להם
המה הגברים אשר מעולם אנשי השם

1a   It happened, however, when humankind began to become
 numerous on the face of the land
1b   and daughters were born to them,
2a   then saw the sons of God the daughters of humankind,
 how beautiful they were,
2b   and they took to them women from all they chose.
3a   And YHWH said:
3b   My spirit may not remain in humankind forever,
 since they too are flesh,
3c   their days will be a hundred and twenty years.
4a   The giants were on the earth in those days
4b   and also afterward,
4c   when the sons of God went into the daughters of humankind
4d   and who bore them—
4e   those are the heroes, from early times, the men of name.

In Gen 5:3–32, in each of the pieces (mostly tricola) we hear the following:

A lived _____ years and he generated B
and A lived, after he generated B, _____ years,
and he generated sons and daughters (bānîm ûbānôt)
Thus were the days of A _____ years and he died.

When the new pericope in 6:1 begins, with the words "It happened, however, when humankind began to become numerous on the face of the land / and daughters were born to them...," it is a meaningful con-

nection to the preceding material. Not only this opening, but other significant components of the pericope, too, demonstrate a clear connection to
what preceded in 5:1–32. In 5:3–32 we heard in each of the tricola the
hiphil hôlîd, "to generate," three times. The narrators reserved this *hiphil
hôlîd* for what happens in the main story line about the BGA. In the short
pericope 6:1–4, therefore, we do not hear this *hiphil hôlîd* again but in v.
4d we hear the *qal yālad*, "to bear": "the sons of God saw the daughters of
humankind and took those they chose and went into them and they *bore*
them...(*wĕyālĕdû lāhem*; the reading *wayyôlîdû* of the Samaritan Pentateuch is to be rejected as *lectio facilior*)." A fixed expression in the stories
of the *Tanakh* has: she (a named woman) bore him (a named man) a son
(e.g., Gen 16:1, 15; 17:19, 21; 21:3, 9; 22:20; 24:24, etc.). In the words "and
they bore them..." we hear this fixed expression here in 6:1–4—in v. 4d.
Although the narrator in v. 4 with great reticence fails to say directly and
openly to whom "they bore them" refers, he does not leave us in uncer-
tainty on the subject. Undoubtedly he meant the *nĕpîlîm* mentioned in the
first line of v. 4; they "were on the earth in those days / and also afterward" (LXX *hoi gigantes*). They are, as we hear in the last line of that verse,
the heroes, from early times, men of name (v. 4e).

As in the narrative complex in which 2:4–4:26 precedes 5:1–32, in the
pericope 6:1–4 *hā'ādām* on the face of the *'ădāmāh* is mentioned again (v.
1a). This time the reference is to the appearance of *hā'ādām*, which is in
glaring conflict with the essence of *h'dm*, namely in the form of the
nĕpîlîm, the notorious giants and titans from early times (*Urzeit*), the half-
divine heroes of the mythology of the *gôyîm*. Apparently the narrators
and tradents took over this fragment concerning the origin of half-divine
heroes in the story of the BGA after 5:1–32 in order to make visible by this
means a contrast within the whole of the BGA. Opposed to the truly representative human among humankind, indicated in the main story line of
the BGA, the absolute opposite of the true human is portrayed here. Here
in the BGA the human who is *not* the one, is set over against the one who
is the one. YHWH wants to deal with humanity, involving himself as
covenant partner in justice and mercy on behalf of humanity. He wants
to deal with people and associate with them. But what is he to do with
such superhuman giants? He wants to be a God of people, not a God of
giants. Whatever may happen dialogically between the true God and the
true human is a history of *dĕbārîm*—not the humanizing of God and the
deification of humanity. Such a blurring of the boundaries is out of the
question. By placing this fragment at this point of the story, the narrators
also share the Torah's critique of the myth of the *gôyîm*.

That we are dealing in this fragment with a critique of the myth of the *gôyîm* is also evident in the manner of expression. The narrator lets us know quite clearly that he speaks with aversion on the matter introduced here. We do not get to hear a real story. In the three parts of the pericope (vv. 1, 2 and 3) the narrator lets us hear successively three statements that relate to each other only insofar as all three refer to the same subject. We shall discuss each of them briefly.

1. *Vv. 1–2*

What is said in the four lines of the first part can only be heard as the normal opening of a story to be told. In Buber's *Verdeutschung* (German translation) the story opens as follows:

> Es geschah als der Mensch auf dem Antlitz des Ackers sich zu
>   mehren begann
> und Töchter wurden ihnen geboren,
> da sahen die Gottessöhne die Menschentöchter, wie schön sie waren,
> und nahmen sich Weiber, welche all sie wählten.[6]

To arouse our attention after what was said in 5:1–32 and to prepare us for something totally different that is suddenly about to happen, the story opens with the words: "It happened, however, when..." (LXX: *kai egeneto henika*; VT: *et factum est postquam*).[7] Most translators like Luther, Zürich, and the Dutch Bible (1951) follow Jerome, who deleted the words *"et factum est"* as a Hebraism so that with him the story begins with *"cumque coepissent homines multiplicari....."* Buber also still had in the first edition (1926), "Als nun der Mensch auf dem Erdacker sich to mehren begann...."[8] Already in the second edition (1930) he changed this to *"Es geschah* als der Mensch auf dem Antlitz des Ackers sich zu mehren begann...."[9]

We hear the word *hāʾādām* in vv. 1a and 3b. In the following pericope it is repeated thrice (vv. 5b, 6b and 7b). Because the narrator wants to say something new about *hāʾādām*, the word *hāʾādām* in v. 1a must not be translated as plural but singular (in spite of virtually all translations since the LXX):

---

6 *Die Schrift, zu verdeutschen unternommen von Martin Buber gemeinsam mit Franz Rosenzweig: Im Anfang* (first ed.; Berlin: Schneider, 1926).

7 For *wayĕhî kî* see also Gen 26:8; 27:1; 43:2; Exod 1:21, etc.

8 See note 6.

9 *Die fünf Bücher der Weisung*, verdeutscht von M. Buber gemeinsam mit Franz Rosenzweig (2d ed.; Berlin: Schneider, 1930).

> It happened, when *"the man"* began to become numerous
> on the face of the earth,
> and daughters were born to them.

After we hear the word *hāʾādām* in v. 1, and *běnôt* in v. 1b, we hear
these words combined twice: *běnôt hāʾādām*, first in v. 2a—the sons of
God saw *běnôt hāʾādām*—and then in v. 4c: the sons of God went in to
běnôt hāʾādām. When we realize how the words *běnê hāʾělōhîm—běnôt
hāʾādām* occur in these two places in the story, we understand that Buber
did not render v. 2a with: "Da sahen die Gottessöhne, dass die
Menschentöchter schön waren," but with: "Da sahen die Gottessöhne die
Menschentöchter, wie schön sie waren" (for the sentence construction,
see the following references: 1:4; 12:14; 13:10; Exod 2:2).

In 5:1–32 we hear, generation after generation, each time at the conclusion of the second line: *wayyôled bānîm ûbānôt*, "and he begot sons and
daughters." These sons are *běnê hāʾādām*, the sons of humans, and these
daughters are *běnôt hāʾādām*, the daughters of humans. Naturally, generation after generation, these were "the sons of *humans*," who saw "the
daughters of humans," taking them as wives. But in 6:1–4 we suddenly
hear something very different. We need to listen to 6:1–4 and 5:1–32 and
compare them, to realize fully what an appalling order-disturbing viola-
tion of boundaries is taking place when not "the sons of humankind" but
"the sons of gods"—note: *"die Gottessöhne"*—"took the *Menschentöchter* as
wives," that is, married them (see *lāqaḥ ʾiššāh*, e.g., Gen 24:3, 4, 7, 37, 38,
40, 48, 67 and 4:19; 11:29; 12:19; 34:9, 16, 21, etc.). They took women for
themselves *mikkōl ʾăšer bāḥārû*, which we might translate "from all that
they chose" or else "whoever they chose" *(quascunqe)*.[10] In any case, it
means that the sons of God were free and unrestrained in their transgression of boundaries.

2.   *V. 3*
Barely begun with his story, the narrator immediately stops. What
follows after what was starting to happen we do not find out. Suddenly
the narrator lets us know what the Lord said:

> Not...my spirit in man forever...flesh he is.
> His days will be a hundred and twenty years.

---

[10] See *GKC* §119w, A1.

Thus, for the sake of being truly human, of which Israel had never been ashamed (Psalm 8), all mixing of the divine with the human is declared invalid, and the clear distinction between YHWH and his *rûaḥ*, on the one hand, and humankind which is flesh, on the other, is maintained. The words of v. 3c, "his days will be 120 years," remind us of the third line of the tricolon in Genesis 5: "Thus all his days were .... years." The human will remain human and will not become a god or a half-god.

We left the words *yādôn* and *běšaggam* untranslated because they are difficult to explain. Dillman concludes concerning both words: *non liquet*.[11] The most obvious explanation from the textual context, and the most widely accepted as well by interpreters and translators, is found in, e.g., Cassuto, who explains *yādôn* as a form of *dnn* with the meaning "to abide permanently," and the word *běšaggam* as *bāʾăšer gam* , "inasmuch as he, too."[12]

3. V. 4.

After the first four lines (vv.1, 2) v. 3 is not a continuation of the story but a sudden interruption. After this interruption, however, v. 4 is not a true continuation either. What we do hear in the five lines of this verse is, namely,"a note on the *nepîlim* then and later."[13]

The *něpîlîm* were on earth in those days
and also afterward,

———————

———————

They are the heroes, those from early times, the men of name.

The identity of the *něpîlîm* of the first line is explained in the fifth line: they are the heroes from early times, the men of name. That these *něpîlîm*, notorious people from the *Urzeit*, are a gigantic type of human we learn from elsewhere in the *Tanakh* that the word occurs: Num 13:32b–33; and see Deut 2:10–12, 20–23). However, it was indeed the narrator's intention to inform us in this third part of the pericope of the continuation of what had begun to happen in the first part. To do this as reticently as possible, he tucks it away in a subordinate clause (introduced by *ʾăšer = kaʾăšer*): That the *něpîlîm* were on earth / and also thereafter, that was: when the sons of God went into the daughters of men—and they bore them—. By

---

11   A. Dillmann, *Genesis* (Edinburgh: Clark, 1897).
12   U. Cassuto, *A Commentary on the Book of Genesis. Part One: From Adam to Noah* (Jerusalem: Magnes, 1972).
13   Dillmann, *Genesis*.

speaking thus, the narrator could avoid saying openly that these *něpīlîm* from the *Urzeit* had been produced by the marriages of the sons of God to the daughters of men.

From this brief discussion of the three parts of the pericope we can now understand that Buber printed them not in the form of a continuous narrative but separately from each other.

Concluding our explanation of Gen 6:1–4 we must refer to a few passages from the exegetical argument of Hermann Gunkel: "Narratives dealing with gods or sons of gods are according to their type mythological, according to their origin probably non-Israelite...From Israel we have only this sample of such narratives."[14]

Regarding v. 4 he says: "The author, anxiously concerned to tone down what was objectionable tells only the synchronic ... but one must be very naive not to read between the lines that, according to the original tradition which the author seems to shy away from sharing, the giants were those children...The characteristic cumbersome sentence construction may be explained by the embarrassment of the writer who had to say things that he would prefer to suppress."[15] In a brief concluding remark he adds the following: "The present truncation may be explained from the highly mythological content of the tradition which offended the narrator. The heathen [!] tell dispassionately of the time 'when gods and goddesses loved'; but Israel [!] experiences revulsion toward the mixing of the divine and the human. Thus the narrator could share only little...and do it very carefully." See v. 4.[16]

Gunkel is certainly correct in what he says concerning the "offense" and about the "anxiety," the "aversion," and the "embarrassment" on the part of the narrator, whom we hear speak in Gen 6:1–4. However, we would ask the shapers of the book of Genesis why they did not resolutely leave this fragment out along with all the rest that they excluded. If they felt it necessary to speak with so much aversion and dislike, why did they not keep silent? Why are they saying things here that they would have preferred to keep silent about? It does not suffice to say that they wished to express a critique on the myths of the *gôyîm*. In its anti-pagan witness the entire *Tanakh* continually shares its critique of mythology directly and indirectly. Why did this have to be done so openly and

---

14 Gunkel, *Genesis*, 56.
15 Ibid., 58.
16 Ibid., 59.

emphatically in this place and in this form? It must be related to the theme that is unfolded in the whole of the BGA.

Therefore, the answer as to why this fragment was included in this form and in this place must be because they wished to point to the giants and heroes of pagan mythology and to declare as emphatically as possible who is *not* the true representative human among humankind.

The brief creation report at the beginning of the BGA (5:1, 2) ends with the words: "and he (God) called their name Adam, *human*, on the day they were created." The truly representative human among humans on earth is *coram Deo* the one who is indicated in the main line of the BGA: not the hero of pagan mythology, but the *ṣaddîq* of the Torah of Israel (see Luke 23:47).

III

In this section we should like to dialogue with other interpreters of Gen 6:1–4 from the voices we hear in some commentaries.

It may be profitable to begin with a brief note on the exegesis of Claus Westermann, who read this pericope very differently in his commentary on Genesis.[17] His commentary is not a new beginning but an end, the consummation of two centuries of biblical scholarship. He begins with an investigation of the origins of the text through a history of traditions approach (*Traditionsgeschichte*). The result (like Gerhard von Rad's in his commentary)[18] is that Gen 6:1–4 is explained not as a part of the book of Genesis but as a segment of the *Urgeschichte* of the Yahwist. However, contrary to von Rad, Westermann says that the real intention of the Yahwist in composing Genesis 2–11 is not "to represent the heightening, but the multiplicity of sin in its fundamental possibilities."[19]

We must not begin with the question (as has been done in all of the history of exegesis till the present): "*Who* are the 'sons of God' and the 'daughters of man'?" The question should rather be: "Which history is represented in this narrative?" The event with which Gen 6:1–4 deals becomes clear to us, says Westermann, when we compare this text with Gen 12:10–20 and 2 Samuel 11–12.[20] We are dealing with "the history of love."[21]

---

[17] C. Westermann, *Genesis Kapitel 1–11* (BKAT; 2nd ed.; Neukirchen/Vluyn: Neukirchener Verlag, 1976) 498.

[18] G. von Rad, *Genesis* (OTL; Philadelphia: Westminster, 1961) 109–12.

[19] Westermann, *Genesis*, 498.

[20] Ibid., 496.

[21] Ibid., 497.

In stories about love, passions can sometimes become too powerful and lead to dangerous transgressions of boundaries. "A specific scenario may occur when someone possessing superior power may violate boundaries upon observing a woman's beauty…This motif in Gen 6:1–4 is also found in Gen 12:10–20 and 2 Sam 11f.; the powerful may choose the beautiful among many that please him and he can do so because he has the power to violate boundaries … the narrator is referring to a human phenomenon which he represents in the manner of mythological speech."[22] V. 3 deals with "the repulsing of the transgression of the boundaries of humanity by the limiting of the span of life."[23]

Thus the text is dealing with "a human phenomenon." The mythical is only the clothing (*inkleding*). "The radical critique of myth in the Old Testament and the fact that Israel did not produce any myths does not change anything of the fact that for J, mythical events had an undeniable meaning for humanity before and outside of Israel's history[!]. Therefore it is possible for him to present *urzeitliche* events in mythical dress."[24]

After reading the 27 pages on Gen 6:1–4 in Westermann's commentary,[25] we have become even more convinced that there is much to be said for the attempt, at the outset, to interpret a text from its context, in which the narrators—who knew what they were doing—placed it and treated the subject in context.

---

[22] Ibid., 501.
[23] Ibid., 508.
[24] Ibid., 515.
[25] Ibid. 491–517.

—∾ 7 ∾—

THE WAY OF ABRAHAM

ROUTES AND LOCALITIES AS
NARRATIVE DATA IN GEN. 11:27–25:11*

Karel Deurloo

ABSTRACT

Within the thematic two-part Abraham-cycle ("land," chaps. 12–14 and "progeny," chaps. 15–22), after the haphazard migration (11:31) and the accomplished migration (12:5) "to go to the land of Canaan," all attention is directed to the marking of *the land* by the three altars in the North, center, and South, with the provisional conclusions of the blessing in the place which qualifies the land: "Salem" (Jerusalem). In this place, the second part of the cycle concerning the *son* will also conclude: the mountain of YHWH (Zion, 22:14). That this son, on the basis of God's "oath," receives his location in the land in Beersheba ("Well of the Oath," 22:16, 19) is prepared by the oath that gives its name to this place (21:31). In contrast to Isaac, the other son of Abraham may live in the deadly desert because God hears ("Ishmael," 21:17). Lot, as contrasting figure to Abraham, receives via the motif "Zoar" (13:10, 14:2, 19:17,18) in "Moab" (*mēʾāb*, "by the father," 19:36) his incestuous progeny.

In the two additional ancestral mothers' stories the first theme is sounded in relation to Sarah's grave, as a sign of the gift of the land, in

---

* This article was expressly written (in Dutch and translated) for this volume.

Genesis 23; while Rebekah in Genesis 24, repeats Abraham's migration for
the sake of progeny.
    Routes and locations in the Abraham cycle correspond completely with
the theme of the narrative.

"'Go, you (*lēk-lĕkā*)' is written twice (12:1, 22:2), and we do not know
which was the most precious [in the eyes of God], whether the first or the
second." This statement by Rabbi Levi in *Gen. Rab.* 39:9 indicates the
indissoluble connection of these two perspectives: the first concerns
Abram's journey on account of the *land*, the second—within a sentence
with the same rhythm and climax—his journey on account of the *son*.
The two texts form the framework for the series of the Abraham narratives and indicate the themes of the two parts of the cycle: 11:27–14:24,
which must be read under the heading of the phrase: *lāleket ᵓārṣāh
kĕnaᶜan*, "to go to the land of Canaan," and chaps. 15–22, which must be
read as an intensification of the first part: *lĕzarᶜ ăkā nātātî ᵓet hāᵓāreṣ hāzzôᵓt
*, "to *your seed* I give this land" (15:18). Thus, the Abraham cycle is a con-
cretizing of the previous stories concerning *humanity on earth* in the
particularizing of *the people in the land*. One might say that Abram leaves
for this "particularizing" the world of nations, the "families" (*mišpāḥôt*,
see, e.g., 10:2, etc.) on the "earth" (*ᵓădāmāh*), or: the "nations" (*gôyîm*) on
earth (*ᵓāreṣ*). The world of nations frames the real cycle with these two
terms: "with you will all *families of the earth* be blessed" (12:3) and, as a
parallel: "with your seed will all the *nations on the earth* bless one
another" (22:18). The stories concerning this land and this son have the
world of nations as their horizon. Two narratives concerning the matriarchs Sarah and Rebekah repeat the two themes as in an epilogue. The
grave of Sarah is mentioned with an eye on the land (chap. 23), the journey of Rebekah—parallel to that of Abram—is mentioned in connection
with the progress of the "seed" via the *son*.

Twice "to go to the land of Canaan"

When we follow the *tôlĕdôt*-division of Genesis, we note that the
Abraham cycle begins with: "These are the descendants of Terah"
(11:27).[1] After the genealogical notations which, particularly through the
names of Nahor and Milcah, form a framing with 22:20–23, mention is
made of a first move from Ur of the Chaldees at the instigation of Terah.
The remarkable manner in which this migration is narrated corresponds

---

[1]   See K. A. Deurloo, "Narrative Geography in the Abraham Cycle," *OTS* 26 (1990)
48–62.

with the summarizing address of YHWH to Abram in the opening chapter of the second part, entirely along the lines of the exodus formula: "I am YHWH who brought you out of Ur of the Chaldees to give you this land to inherit it" (15:7).[2] On the one hand, this is a prelude to the *vaticinium ex eventu* concerning Israel's stay in Egypt (15:13); on the other hand, the author indicates with this that the first exodus (*yṣ*ʾ) at the initiative of Terah was already the work of YHWH, though Abram's call took place at Haran (12:1–3). Though Terah acted at first, it was Abram who went out. That point becomes clear when one reads synoptically the two sentences concerning the theme *lāleket ʾārṣāh kĕnaᶜan*:

> Terah took Abram his son and Lot, the son of Haran,
> his son's son and Sarai his daughter-in-law, the wife of Abram his son.[3]
> They set out *with them* from Ur of the Chaldeans, to go to the land
> of Canaan.   They came
> as far as Haran, they settled there (11:31).
> He (Abram) took Sarai his wife and Lot his brother's son, all...and all...,
> and they set out to go to the land of Canaan
> and they came in the land of Canaan (12:5).

The difference between the coincidental initiative of Terah—if things would look favorable in Haran, they would stay there—and the intentional initiative of Abram—"they came in the land of Canaan"—catch the eye. In between stands Abram's call *lēk lĕkā*, "go, you." In the first case the narrator relates that Terah takes the clan of Abram, whereby he omits the other members of Terah's house (particularly Nahor and Milcah, see 22:20ff.). Thus he makes it possible to say in the following sentence: They (Abram and his people) went out (*yṣ*ʾ) *with them* (*ʾittām*),[4] i.e., with Terah and all of his house. Without knowing it, Abram has already gone out of Ur according to the exodus formula of 15:7. Just as Haran dies at Ur, "before the face,"[5] in the presence of, his father Terah (13:28), thus Abram will leave his father's house during Terah's life. Terah dies at 205 years old, Abraham takes the initiative for his exodus at the age of 75.

---

[2] The most striking parallel is found in Lev 25:18, but see also Exod 20:2.

[3] The repeated word "son" forms a thematic contrast with: "Now Sarai was barren, she had no child" (13:30).

[4] The special significance of *ʾittām* is generally not noted (see critical apparatus). Translations incorrectly choose "together," or the word is simply omitted (e.g., NEB). U. Cassuto interprets: "all the members of the family went forth *with them*—that is, with Abram, Sarai and Lot"; *A Commentary on the Book of Genesis* (Jerusalem: Magnes, 1964) 2:280, 281.

[5] See *Gen. Rab.* 38:13.

The theme "to go to the land of Canaan," the only land with boundaries that is already named in the list of nations (10:19), receives special emphasis by this repetition. That land, however, is already inhabited by the twelve "clans." When Abram arrives there he sounds alarmed: "The Canaanite lived in the land then" (12:6). Abram will be a *gēr*, a sojourner, there.

The marking of the land by three altars

The author has Abram, like Jacob in his return from Paddan Aram (33:18), arrive at the "cultic site" (*māqôm*) Shechem, the oak of Moreh. The land that YHWH will "show" him (12:1) is, first of all, the land where YHWH appears, "lets himself be seen," with the promise that this land will be given to his "offspring." The supreme moment of this series of narratives, the *seeing of the land*, is still postponed. In this northerly part of the land Abram erects an altar of the theophany (12:7).

In the following stage Abram, by the building of the altar, creates a place, namely between Bethel to the west and Ai to the east. It is not so much the exact geographical as the "historic" center of the land, the boundary between the southern and the northern kingdom.[6] In this new location Abram proclaims the name of YHWH.[7] When the journey moves further south, the reader naturally expects that there, too, an altar will be built, but the shameful descent to Egypt, because of famine in the land, thwarts that expectation. Partly for compositional reasons the author inserts the scene of the matriarch in a royal harem. It is one of the "doublets"[8] of which the Abram-cycle makes conscious use: Sarai at the court of the Pharaoh introduces, after the exodus from Egypt, the great moment of *seeing the land*, just as Sarah in the harem of the king of Gerar (chap. 20) introduces the *birth of the son*. Abram, who, just as his people later, goes out with much property, returns to the location in the "center," which now is called *māqôm* (place), and he again proclaims the name of YHWH. Before the provisional goal of the first series of narratives is reached, Lot has to separate from him, to direct all attention to the first patriarch and to him alone. Lot "who went with him" (12:4; 13:1, 5) can-

---

6   See Josh 18:13; 8:9.

7   With this the last sentence, which is full of perspective, is taken from the narrative anthropology of Genesis 2–4: "Then men began to call out the name of YHWH" (not "call on"!). See H. A. Brongers, "Die Wendung *bešem jhwh* im AT," *ZAW* 77 (1965) 12.

8   See J. Rosenberg, *King and Kin* (Bloomington/Indianapolis: Indiana University Press, 1986) 73–75.

not reside in the land with Abram because he represents the peoples of
Moab and Ammon. Similarly, Ishmael (the southern desert peoples) and
Esau (Edom) must separate from Jacob (*prd*, hiphil 10:32; 13:9, 11, 14;
25:22). These contrasting figures represent the nations surrounding Israel
in the Genesis story, which describes Israel's development among the
gôyîm. "They could not 'settle' (*yšb*) together...the land could not support
them" (13:6; 37:7). In Lot's selection the narrator draws a contrast to
Abram: "Lot lifted up his eyes and *saw* the plain of the Jordan, how well-
watered it all was, before YHWH brought ruin upon Sodom and Gomorrah, like YHWH's garden, like the land of Egypt (!), as far as you come
toward Zoar" (13:10).

After Lot's separation comes the moment promised to Abram: "the
land that I will *show* you" (12:1).[9] "Lift up your eyes and *see* from the
place where you are (i.e., the 'place between Bethel and Ai!', the middle,
on the boundary between the northern kingdom and Judah) northward,
southward, eastward, and westward, indeed, all the land that you *see*, I
give it to you..." (13:14). Abram's going (*hlk*) to the land now becomes
"walking" (*hlk*, hitpaʿel). Now he may take his own place in the South to
build his third altar. Everything is told very briefly, because the narrator
will return to this place in connection with the theophany concerning the
son (18:1).[10]

Abram has marked the land with three altars: the northern one at
Shechem/*oak* at Moreh; the southern one at Hebron/the *oaks* of Mamre.
In the "middle" he has created a "place" with his altar. Provisionally, the
narrative has concluded with seeing of the land from this place. But is it
indeed *the* place in the land? In any event, Abram will build yet another
altar in the story.

Lot as contrast figure of Abraham

Though Lot does not appear in the pericope of the sojourn in Egypt,
his choice of the "plain of the Jordan" reminds us of this history: "like the
land of Egypt." His choice also presages what will take place, not only by
the remark "now the men of Sodom were exceedingly wicked and sinful
before YHWH" (13:3) but also by the notice that Lot saw "as far as Zoar"
(13:10). In that direction will he proceed. The name of this place returns

---

9   Translation: "To the land that I will let you *see*." Thus after Buber: E. Fox, *In the
Beginning. A New English Rendition of the Book of Genesis* (New York: Schocken, 1983)
48. Citations are accommodated to this translation.

10   See T. L. Thompson, "The Origin Tradition of Ancient Israel," *JSOT* 55 (1978) 85,
91, 92.

in the story concerning "the war in the land"—the rescue of Lot, in "doublet" with chaps. 18/19—where the kings of four empires war with the five—and not, as one might expect, the four[11]—local kings. The author lets the fifth city, obviously added to the traditional names, stand out stylistically. The fifth king is nameless, and his city is glossed: "and the king of Bela, that is Zoar." This city "Bela" ("devoured") will be the only city that is not "devoured" in the catastrophe of chap. 19, because the city receives the name of Zoar.

Lot, who is removed from the catastrophe by the divine messengers by virtue of Abraham's intercession (19:29), is afraid to flee to the mountains and raises the question: "that town is near enough to, flee to and it is so tiny (*miṣ'ār*)." The amazing answer is: "Make haste, escape there, for I am not able to do anything until you arrive there." That is how great is the power of Abraham's intercession! Thus peoples are blessed in him: Moab and Ammon. Of that, the nearby city of Moab, near the Dead Sea (see, e.g., Isa 15:5), is the remaining sign: "therefore the name of the town was called Zoar/Tiny" (19:17–22).

Thus Lot finally approaches his own *land* (*'āreṣ*). But will he also have a *son*, will he have "seed"? From the names[12] Moab and Bene Ammon (thus is this people always indicated in the Old Testament) the author develops a story dialectically opposed to the miraculous birth of Isaac (21:1ff.), which truly evokes laughter (*ṣḥq*). A different kind of humor is found in 19:30–38. Lot's hesitating between Zoar and "mountains"—one almost might add: "of Moab"—is decided in favor of the latter. There he sits in a cave with his two daughters. The narrator has excluded his wife in an original manner (19:26); the sons-in-law have disappeared in the catastrophe (19:14). It seems as if Lot, like Abraham, will have "seed" through a miracle—but it becomes an all too natural miracle. The firstborn (!) daughter says: "our father is old" (we need to hurry) "and there is no man in the *land*." But it is a land of wine (see Isa 16:8; Jer 48:11ff., 32ff.) and with its help it is possible to revive "seed...from our father" (*mē'ābînû*); 19:32, 34). The daughters get pregnant by their father. The firstborn gives birth to Moab (*mô'āb*) by the father (*mē'āb*). The youngest bears a son, the father of Bene-Ammon, "Ben Ammi," "son of the blood

---

[11] See the four names at the boundaries of Canaan (10:19; Deut 29:23). On the basis of 14:2, Wis 10:6 speaks of "Pentapolis."

[12] See J. Van Seters, *Abraham in History and Tradition* (New Haven/London: Yale University Press, 1975) 219, 220. The motif the post-deluge situation at best filters through in this story; see C. Westermann, *Genesis* (BKAT I/2; Neukirchen/Vluyn: Neukirchener Verlag, 1981) 379, 380.

relation/father." The daughters' will to survive takes care of the natural miracle: Lot begets, without "knowing" (*yd^c*), his *land*, his *seed*, his descendants. Thanks to Abraham's effort on his behalf, Lot, too, has also "land and progeny." The sign of this is Zoar.

Royal-priestly blessing at Salem

Contra Emerton[13] and with Van Seters,[14] the chapter that has been typified as "independent and secondary in the development of Genesis"[15] may be seen as a late narrative in which psalmic motives have been incorporated. Nevertheless, the chapter is firmly anchored in context. Lot's sojourn in Sodom is presupposed, while the word *mgn*, the *delivering* of enemies in Abram's hand (14:20), occurs again in an ambiguous sense in 15:1.[16] The chapter plays with names. The king of Sodom is called "Bera," "in anger" (*bĕra^c*), the king of Gomorrah "Birsha," "in evil" (*bĕrāšā^c*) in line with 13:13. Reference has already been made to "the king of Bela, *that is* Zoar" (14:2, 8). The formula "that is (now)" is repeated a number of times: the valley of Siddim, *which is* (now) the Dead Sea (see chap. 19). The journey of the four great kings forms, in the first instance, the reverse of the people's route in the wilderness to the land, that is to say, to "En Mishpat, which is Kadesh" (cf. Num 13:36, 20:1). Abram as a "Hebrew"—the name of someone from Israel in international context, see Jon 1:9 et al.—is initially involved in battle when he is told that Lot has been taken captive. The rescue of Lot, which is a major motif in chaps. 18 and 19, appears to be an ancillary motif here. Kingship is central. The narrator makes this clear with the sentence: "The *king* of Sodom went out to meet him (Abram) upon his return from the strike against...the *kings*...to the valley of Shaveh, *that is* the *king's* valley (see 1 Sam 18:18). Now *Malki*-Tsedek, the *king* of Salem..." (14:17, 18). Salem does not need to, and cannot be, explained as: that is, Jerusalem,[17] for that name and *Zion* are avoided in the Torah. Who is Malki-Tsedek? This name and *Salem* occur in the Zion psalms

---

[13] J. A. Emerton, "Some False Clues in the Study of Genesis XIV," *VT* 21 (1971) 24–37, and "The Riddle of Genesis XIV," *VT* 21 (1971) 403–39.

[14] Van Seters, *Abraham*: "Its dating points at the close of the fourth century B.C. as the time when biblical tradition of Abraham received its final chapter" (308).

[15] Thompson, "Origin Tradition" 87.

[16] "Shield," but 15.2: "what will you *give* me." Martin Kessler suggests in "The 'Shield' of Abraham?" (*VT* 14 [1964] 494–97) that *mgn* be vocalized *mōgēn*, "to give," translating: "I am about to give you your very great reward."

[17] See 1QapGen 20:13.

with the defeat of the kings who threaten the divine city (Psalms 76 and 110). This king and priest represent the good among kings—one might be tempted to say, *that is,* Davidic kingship. The words he speaks cannot be: "ʏʜᴡʜ, the maker of heaven and earth, bless you from Zion," as in the Psalms. With a sense of the "historic" situation, the author lets him use his own language: "Blessed be Abram by God Elyon, Founder (*qôneh*) of heaven and earth," a saying that Abram can take over with the addition of the divine name (14:19, 22).

The blessing of the one who was blessed at the beginning of this series of narratives (chaps. 12–14) is a fitting conclusion. Moreover, what does the name Salem mean at the end of the treatment of the theme "going to the land of Canaan?" Is the land that is marked by three altars not particularly characterized by this place? Here Abram already brings his tithes, here he will bring the substitute sacrifice for his firstborn son, in chap. 22, as Israel will do later (e.g., Deut 12:6). Then Abram, who in chaps. 15, 18, and 20 has a prophetic function, will himself act as priest. The compendium character of the Abraham cycle—many central themes that typify the essence of Israel are present here—does not only concern, but in chaps. 12–14 the land especially and its central place. Here Abram will build the altar par excellence (22:9) in connection with the second main theme, the *son.*

The preparation of Isaac's location, Beersheba

In addition to the place of Abraham's sacrificial journey,[18] which is indirectly emphasized through the purposeful omission of a name, the location Beersheba plays a most important role in the chapters concerning the *son* (chaps. 12–22). The pericope 21:22–34 does not receive the attention it deserves exegetically and homiletically, however. Discussion deals mainly with source analysis[19] or the literary prehistory.[20] It is generally concluded that we have here a weaving together of two motifs: Abraham shrewdly makes use of a previously given etiological explanation of the name "Beersheba": "seven-well," to get this well into his possession by the gift of seven lambs. In this settling of a shepherds'

---

[18] See K. A. Deurloo, "Abraham, profeet (Gen 15 en 20)," *Amsterdamse Cahiers* 9 (1988) 35–46 and chap. 8 below.

[19] Westermann, *Genesis* 424–26.

[20] Van Seters, *Abraham* 183–91. Concerning the episode, vv. 25–26, 28–31a, he says that we are dealing with a folkloristic motif rather than a tradition. Etiologies like these concerning the place Beersheba "were very common as literary devices in the ancient world" (185).

argument one notes the local color of semi-nomadic life.[21] The other motif stems from the political sphere: the Philistine king recognizes (in Abraham) Israel as the superior power in the land. One does not need to deny the correctness of these observations to deem another, namely, the compositional question, of greater significance for exegesis.

The question arises, however, why it was not sufficient to raise this theme in the story of Isaac, where it is staged so much more clearly?[22] Why is the narrative (also) situated here, and why does it contain such an obvious double motif? The answer to the first question might be that an interlude between the birth of Isaac/the sending away of Ishmael and Abraham's sacrificial journey is in place from a literary point of view.[23] Van Seters has pointed out that with respect to content, Abraham's admonition concerning the stolen well connects better with Gen 20:17 or 18 "to counterbalance the previous charge that Abimelech made against Abraham."[24] That is an apt observation which, however, makes the question concerning the present composition the more pressing. In the first place, one might say that if the narrative concerning the well had been situated there, the direct connection of the sterility in Gerar with Sarah's infertility would be broken: the plague of Abimelech's impotence and the infertility of his wives are healed after the intercession of Abraham the prophet (20:18), as an introduction to Sarah's pregnancy (21:1, 2).[25] Moreover, it would not have been appropriate to burden the pericope, in which Abraham's low point is described, with a countermove by Abraham of a settlement: an admonition concerning the stealing of a well by Abimelech's servants. All emphasis must fall on Abraham's degenerate behavior in Genesis 20. Because the prophet did not *see* (20:10) that he was in Gerar in the midst of a godfearing people, he wanted to secure his own life through his "sister" excuse, and that while Sarah had just been promised fertility (18:10). The entire goal of his life placed Abraham in the balance, and, after God intervened by making Abimelech impotent,

---

[21]   V. H. Mattheus, "The Wells of Gerar," *BA* 49 (1986) 118–26.

[22]   Westermann, *Genesis* 425 strongly emphasizes the parallelism with Genesis 26. In spite of identical expressions, differences attract attention in this chapter, which is so full of the repetition of Abraham motifs. Abimelech, for example, looks up Isaac after he sent him away from his sphere of influence. Beersheba had already become the place of Isaac.

[23]   See T. L. Thompson, "Origin Tradition" 96, 97, and Fox, *In the Beginning*: "This interlude, which usefully separates the life threats to Abraham's two sons..." (79).

[24]   Van Seters, *Abraham* 185.

[25]   K. A. Deurloo, "Die Gefährdung der Ahnfrau (Gen 20)," *Dielheimer Blätter zum Alten Testament* 25 (1988) 17–27.

he fabricated a tale about his family relationships (20:12), using abject terminology about his call: "when gods made me wander...." Abimelech listened to him and made no comment, or is there an ironic note in his statement to Sarah: "I am giving a thousand pieces of silver to your *brother*...." Abraham's "counter-balance" needed to be postponed a while, as well as Abimelech's conscious reaction to Abraham's lie.

Just as the story of Sarai in Pharaoh's harem (12:10–20)[26] directly precedes, via an exodus from Egypt, the great moment of *seeing of the land*—connected with the separation of Lot (Moab and Ammon), Genesis 13—thus the story of Sarah in the harem of Abimelech directly precedes the decisive moment of the *birth of the son*, which is coupled to the separation of Ishmael (the southern desert peoples). To Abraham, the questionable prophet and intercessor from Abimelech's viewpoint, a son is born through Sarah. He has a future in the land that Abimelech hospitably offered him: "See, my land lies before you..." (20:16). Connected to the episode 20:1–21:21 is the temporal clause, "it happened at that time..." (21:22).[27] At the beginning of it Abraham placed himself in the direction of what would appear to be Isaac's own location. The description has intentionally been kept vague: the Negev between Kadesh and Shur, also with a view toward Ishmael (16:7, 14). The name of the location, "desert of Beersheba" (21:14), is named proleptically in a casual manner. That name will soon be accented emphatically, however, but not without connecting to it a second motif. The deceit of Abraham calls for redress. That redress leads to a pact and to a boundary settlement with the Philistines, one of the surrounding peoples beside the southern nomads (Ishmael) and the peoples of Moab and Ammon (Lot) and Edom (Esau)—and like the Chaldeans, an anachronism in these stories. Though the Philistines are not brothers, Abraham and Isaac (26:28) have a covenantal relationship with them.

At the conclusion of the first part of the cycle the reader has already met references to the north of the land (*Dan*, Damascus, 14:14ff.); here in the south, at the conclusion of the second part of the cycle, the names of *Beersheba* and the Philistines are heard. In this part of the land, too, which is not called the land of Canaan but still the land of the Philistines, Abraham is a guest and a stranger (*wayyāgor bigrār!*) 20:1; see also "the land in

---

[26] See K. A. D. Smelik, "Verhaal en context" [Story and Context] in: B. Becking & K. A. D. Smelik, (eds.), *Een patriarchale leugen. Het verhaal in Genesis 12 verschillend belicht* [A Patriarchal Lie. Different Approaches to the Story of Genesis 12] (Baarn: Ten Have, 1989) 54–57.

[27] For this redactional connection see 31:10; 38:1.

which you have sojourned [lived as guest and stranger]," 21:23. No matter how stringently it is indicated that the well was dug by Abraham and in spite of the fact that Abimelech and Phicol return to "the land of the Philistines" (21:34), the marking of Beersheba is still provisional for "Abraham sojourned in the land of the Philistines" (21:34). Nevertheless, now that his son is growing up, Abraham is presented as a powerful figure from the perspective of the future. This is made clear in the story by having Abimelech accompanied by his army commander when he "at that time" addressed himself to Abraham with words that, for the reader who knows what the patriarch had actually done (Genesis 20), have a somewhat ironic sound. It is indisputably true, however, that Abraham is blessed:

> God is with you in everything you do.
> Now then,
> swear to me by God:
> See, do not deceive me, nor my kith, nor my kin!
> According to the "loyalty" (*hesed*) which I have done to you,
> do thus to me also
> and to my land where you have sojourned (21:23).

The language Abimelech uses (*nînî-nekdî*, "progeny-posterity") is well chosen for Abraham, who had become the father of a son. *Deceit* reminds one of Abraham's deed, the *hesed* of Abimelech's straightforward conduct in Genesis 20, where he had to speak the words: "Deeds that one does not do, you have done to me" (20:9).

The Well of the Oath

After Abraham has thus sworn (*šbᶜ*) at Abimelech's request, the author connects to this moment the "counterbalance" to Abraham's reproach concerning the stolen well (*bĕʾēr*), so that the theme Beersheba (*bĕʾēršebaᶜ*) is sounded. In his answer Abimelech appears to be the same upright figure the reader met with in his defense before God (20:5, 6 *gam-gam!*):

> I do not know who has done this.
> Neither have you informed me,
> neither have I heard about it before today! (21:26).

Abimelech approached Abraham in his deceit with a present of small livestock and cattle (20:14). Abraham now does the same in this case of the theft of a well (21:27). The covenant may be concluded, but it needs to be underlined with the etymological motif of *seven* (*šebaᶜ*) lambs. In vv. 26–31 this results in the series: *beʾēr-šebaᶜ-šebaᶜ-šebaᶜ-beʾēr*, after which the name Beersheba appears in the etiological formula. This name, like *beʾēr* and *šebaᶜ*, is sounded three times in the story. The sworn covenant and marking the place in the south of the land stand in the sign of the *already* and the *not yet*. That is the case not only on account of the ambiguity of the two sentences: Abimelech and Phicol, "they returned to the land of the Philistines" (21:34), and "Abraham remained as sojourner in the land of the Philistines" (21:34) but also because of the fact that Abraham does not build an altar in Beersheba. That is left to Isaac to do (26:25).

Abraham had already built three altars that indicate the northern and southern divisions in the land of Canaan: Shechem as the central northern (cultic) place (12:7), Mamre/Hebron in the Judean south (13:18), and between Bethel and Ai (12:8; 13:4) in the middle, the point from which he can see the *land* in all directions (13:14). The only altar that he builds not in connection with the *land*, but with the *son* on the mountain of YHWH, has its central place in the following chapter. The fact that Abraham here in Beersheba, just as in the middle of the land, proclaims the name of YHWH[28] (13:14), calls the more attention to his failure to build an altar. And it is precisely here, in his special locale, that the name of his son is lacking. What the reader misses is compensated for in the story of Genesis 22, which forms the climax of the cycle. The pericope 21:22–34 is not only an interlude that makes a division between narratives concerning a threat to the life of the two sons Ishmael and Isaac, but also forms a preparation to the sacrificial journey of Abraham[29] and the only altar on the mountain of YHWH.

At the beginning of Genesis 22, the place of the night call—"Take your son…"—remains in the dark. Everything turns on the secret of that other place that God mentions to Abraham (22:2, 4, 9). When, however, the tension concerning that riddle is dissolved (22:14), the starting point of the sacrificial journey may be mentioned for the sake of the son, and repeated for emphasis: "They went together to *Beersheba*, and Abraham lived in *Beersheba*" (22:19). It is the Well of the Oath. Does it connect with the sworn covenant that Abraham concluded with Abimelech? Indeed, thus Isaac's own location, the extreme south of the land, opposite the

---

[28] Identification of YHWH with El Olam, which is unique in the Old Testament, as with El Elyon in 14:22.

[29] The inner necessity of Abraham's temptation relating to the son whose birth is also prepared by his lie to Abimelech (Genesis 20), and the explicit mention of that lie (21:23), as framing of Isaac's birth.

Philistines, is spelled out in plain sight, after his birth and after his separation from Ishmael. With this son Abraham's seed is called by name (21:12). But the fact that he can make his place there rests still more on that other *oath*: "By myself I swear, saying of YHWH…" (22:16–18). That oath YHWH will confirm (26:3f.!) when Isaac settles in the land of which YHWH would tell him (26:2; see 22:2ff.). Beersheba will be the place where Isaac builds an altar and where he, following Abraham, proclaims the name of YHWH.

Ishmael as contrasting figure to Isaac

The well Lahai Roi is the geographical point connecting Ishmael (16:14) and Isaac (24:62; 15:11), the two sons of Abraham. None of the figures who form a contrast to the patriarchs and those who represent the peoples among whom Israel is said to originate—Abraham versus Lot (Moab/Ammon), Isaac versus Ishmael (the southern desert peoples), and Jacob versus Esau (Edom)—is characterized so similarly to his brother as Ishmael. The stories concerning Hagar and Ishmael, as "doublet,"[30] form the framework of the announcement and birth of Isaac, and/or the command to give a name (17:19), and their execution (13:3); of the command to circumcise on the eighth day (17:12) and its execution (21:4): in chap. 16 Ishmael is born and in 21:9–13 Hagar is sent away with him.

The prophetically colored "call" chapter (chap. 15) introduces the second part of the Abraham cycle concerning the theme "son." The going-to-the-land of Canaan has not yet been developed after ten years (16:3) because of Sarai's infertility. Abram's answer to YHWH's call echoes his call *lēk-lĕkā*, "go, you!": *wĕ°ānōkî hôlēk ʿărîrî*, "I go childless" (15:2).[31] After the proposal that Abram's *major domo*[32] be his heir is rejected, a

---

[30] G. W. Coats, *Genesis with an Introduction to Narrative Literature* (FOTL 1; Grand Rapids: Eerdmans, 1983) 135, rightly remarks: "The crisis in the narrative, introduced in Genesis 16, is rejoined in 21:8–13, a continuation of the counterpart rather than a doublet."

[31] Participle with the connotation "to die," see Gen 25:32. In addition, ʿărîrî is a counterpart to ʿăqārāh that is only used of men (Lev 20:20, 21; see Jer 22:30).

[32] Eliezer, in *gematria* [numerology] 318, see 14:14, is mysteriously called *ben mešeq*, son of the house (see F. Pomponio, "*ben mešeq* di Gen 15,2 e un termine amministrativo di Ebla," *BibOr* 25/136 [1983] 107–9). A. van Selms, *Genesis* (Nijkerk: Callenbach, 1967) 1: 214 translates "son of the legal claim" and sees an allusion to the legal claims of Aram to Israelite territory; with reference to the name Hadad-ezer in connection with "Damascene Eliezer." The explanatory "gloss" *that is Damascus* recalls the formula in Genesis 14, however. One might think of the progress of the "blessing" in

new emergency solution comes into view: "Abram hearkened to the voice of Sarai" (16:23, see 21:12; 2:18; 3:17). Hagar must first furnish a mirror image of Israel's *slavery* in *Egypt* where the people are *oppressed* (15:16). Hagar must have herself *oppressed* as an *Egyptian slave* (16:9) by Israel's matriarch. But with this fate she also shares in blessing in the same manner as Abraham. Her seed, too, cannot be counted (16:10, see 15:5). Her son, too, will be a "great nation" (21:18), like Isaac (21:3, see 12:2; 17:20; 18:18). Though Abraham's "seed" will receive a name in Isaac (21:12), and though YHWH will make his covenant with Isaac (17:21), Ishmael is no less a son of Abraham,[33] and according to chap. 17 he is the prototype of the circumcised proselyte. When Hagar, the Egyptian mother of this son of Abraham, seeks an Egyptian wife for him (21:21), this is partially suggested by the fact that in Ishmael the people located between Israel's land and Egypt is defined. In this land the two Hagar stories take place. As to the latter, both the contrast and the parallel with chap. 22 have been pointed out correctly.[34] The son, threatened by death, is kept alive at the last moment by the call from heaven by the messenger of God (with Hagar), by the messenger of God (with Abraham). In addition to the parallel promises to Israel and to Abraham's "seed" already mentioned, there are corresponding motif words of which *see* is the most striking. As far as Abraham is concerned, the "seeing of the land" has its counterpart in the role the word *see* plays in Genesis 22. In the first Hagar story the reader is struck by the crucial words: "Have I even here seen after him who sees me?" (16:13 in reference to the name of the boundary between Ishmael and Isaac: Lahai Roi). In 21:19 her eyes are opened so that she sees the well, which means life in the desert for her son. Because "God hears" ("Ishmael"), Hagar *sees*. Abraham, who confesses that "God sees" (22:8, cf. the name "YHWH sees," 22:14), is the one who by his "going" *hears* God's voice (22:18).

How does Ishmael reach his location? His people's secret lies precisely in that and is explained by his name. His name explicitly resounds in connection with Hagar: "God-hears," for "YHWH has heeded your affliction" (16:11). But the name resounds more impressively in an implicit manner, with the child—his name is intentionally withheld in chap. 21—dying under a desert shrub. When Hagar then raises her voice

Damascus-Aram in place of Salem-Israel. The second solution of the progress of the "blessing" refers to "Ishmael"—the southern desert nomads.

33 Fox, *In the beginning* 79: "The same exalted status as his brother."

34 In a rather stubborn manner by, e.g., H. C. White, "The Initiation Legend of Isaac," *ZAW* 91 (1979) 1–30.

to weep, it is not said as in 16:11 that God hearkens to her voice, but: "God hears—*wayyišmaʿ ʾĕlōhîm* and (*k*)*yšmʿ ʾl*(*hym*): "Ishmael!"—the voice of the boy *where he is*" (21:17), namely, in the desert where one cannot live but dies of thirst. These "Ishmael-people" must have been observed with amazement: they live in a place where Israel could only live by God's providence, in the exodus from Egypt. How else could this people live except because "God hears"? No matter how dangerous these desert nomads (16:12) might be with a bow (21:16, 20), they are nevertheless, in the shadow of the wonder of Israel's origin and existence, a sign of life in the midst of a land of death: "Ishmael," "where he is," in the desert.

Machpelah, the grave of Sarah: Sign of the gift of the land

After the story in which the Abraham cycles reaches its climax, the sacrificial journey to "the place," the "body" of this series is closed by a genealogical notice: 22:20–24. Among the twelve(!) sons of Nahor, surprisingly, a daughter is featured: "And Bethuel begot Rebekah." The reader will learn later that he is also the father of Laban. The name Rebekah introduces two epilogical stories concerning the matriarchs, which once more raise the two great themes of the cycle: land and son. Meanwhile Rebekah is introduced as the new matriarch before Sarah dies. Clearly it is not her death and burial that is the central theme of chap. 23, but her grave, or more specifically: the *field* with the cave of Machpelah.[35] The inclusio puts the reader on the right track: "Arba, that is Hebron, *in the land of Canaan*" (23:2), "Mamre, that is Hebron, *in the land of Canaan*" (23:19). This statement the narrator lets the owner of the cave, Ephron, say accidentally, as it were. Ephron hopes to take clever advantage of the situation by also selling the adjoining field (*śādeh*, 23:9) at a high price. First, Ephron says, among the ʿ*am hāʾāreṣ*, the "people of the land," the legal dignitaries who were competent to act: "That field I *give* you, with the cave on it I *give* you, before the eyes of the sons of my people I *give* it to you; bury your dead!" (23:11). Upon naming the price he says, however: "*land* (ʾ*āreṣ*), of 400 shekels, what is that between you and me!" (23:15). The reader detects a double bottom (the buying of the field, but with the words: *giving* of the *land*), and he is reminded of the theme of Genesis 12–14. After the purchase Abraham, who no longer "faces" his wife Sarah—see the play on the word *pānîm*, 23:3, 4, 8—is now "facing" her burial plot from his place Mamre (23:17, 19) as the first

---

35 Translation by Th. Booij, "Hagar's Words in Genesis XVI 13b," *VT* 30 (1980) 1–7.

piece of land belonging to him. Abraham said:[36] "I wish to bury my dead *from before my face (millĕpānay)"*; the legal contract mentions the field that stands (*wayyāqom*) in name of Abraham *facing (ᶜal pĕnê)* Mamre, Abraham's place. "After that Abraham buried his wife Sarah in the cave of Machpelah, (situated) before the face (ᶜal pĕnê) of Mamre, that is Hebron, in the land of Canaan." The grave is a sign of the future fulfillment of the promise of YHWH: to your "seed" I will give this land.[37]

Rebekah's journey from Haran as sign of the future for the son

On the "seed" turns the last great narrative of the cycle. Therefore, Abraham has the servant whom he sends to fetch a wife for his son, swear an oath "on his testicles" (24:2). The big question is whether that woman from Haran might be willing to follow the servant *"to go to this land"* (24:5). This phrase calls to mind again *lāleket ᵓārṣāh kĕnaᶜan*, "to go to the land of Canaan," and thereby the great move of Abraham himself. This effect is strengthened, moreover, by the use of the characteristic terms of 12:1, namely *land, family (môledet)*, and *father's house* (see 24:28): *mother's house*.[38] Abraham's journey is irreversible. Thus, in his oath the servant must swear he will not let the son return to the land that Abraham had left. In the grave of Sarah the promise of the gift of the land lies, as it were, anchored sacramentally. With a new exodus from the mother's house the woman must go the way that Abraham went to guarantee the offspring of Isaac. It is up to her whether what began as so *exciting and marvelous* in chaps. 15–22 will have a future. The narrator arranges the story so that with every patriarchal negotiation the decision is made by the woman herself. Through the figures in the story the reader hears the fact of her willingness "from her own mouth:" "I will go" (24:57f.). The continuation of the double *lēk-lĕkā*, "you go," of Abraham is thereby guaranteed: the story will continue in the *tôlĕdôt* of Isaac.

---

[36] Therefore, Thompson says wrongly that Genesis 23 must be read as a "self-sufficient tale that has no integral connection with the preceding Abraham narratives" ("Origin Tradition" 99). For an opposing view see F. W. Golka, "Die theologischen Erzählungen im Abrahamskreis," *ZAW* 90 (1978) 193–95.

[37] Thus, the life of Abraham and Sarah was   one "from face to face."

[38] About the patriarchs and their burial site G. Von Rad strikingly remarks: "In death they were sojourners no longer"; *Old Testament Theology* (New York: Harper & Row, 1962) 1: 169.

The blessing Rebekah receives thus corresponds with the statement concerning Isaac: "your '*seed*' shall inherit the gate of their enemies" (22:17). To her is said:[39]

> Our sister, may you become thousandfold myriads!
> May your "*seed*" inherit the gate of those who hate him! (24:60).

In going to the land of Canaan Rebekah becomes the new matriarch. In the land that bears as a sign the grave of Sarah, Rebekah assumes her function: "Thus was Isaac comforted...after his mother" (24:67).

Epilogue

In the course of investigating routes and locations above, comments of a genetic and traditio-historical nature were made very sparsely; the given composition was our starting point. The question of the texts' origins[40] is (also in connection with new concepts concerning the history of Israel)[41] much discussed. Old Testament scholars of the Amsterdam School have, since the 'sixties, carefully worked with the hypothesis that the exile was the period when literary production flourished, and that it came to fruition especially after the exile. It is assumed that pre-exilic material was often worked with. However, the emphasis has always been on rhetoric and criticism. Yet, historical questions cannot be ignored. In the diversity of style and word usage, the texture of, e.g., the Abraham cycle is more and more evident. We must agree with Diebner when he speaks of Genesis as a book of the "ancient Jewish Bible" that speaks so fully about fundamental data concerning Israel that it might be characterized *cum grano salis* as a sort of "dogmatics."[42] The completely hypothetical, very old dating of J segments of Genesis is aptly called a scientific relic of historicism. Theologically speaking, dating in the ninth or eigth century, or even after the sixth century, cannot have any decisive significance. But the difficult question concerning the when and how of the liturgical use of this text is of theological interest. Must we not imag-

---

39 A. van Selms, *Genesis* (Nijkerk: Callenbach, 1967) 2: 45, correctly points to the (here democratized) royal blessing (see 22:18; Ps 72:17). For a Ugaritic parallel see *CTA* 10, II, 20–21.

40 See R. N. Whybray, "The Making of the Pentateuch. A Methodological Study." *JSOTSup* 53 (Sheffield: Academic Press,1987).

41 See N. P. Lemche, *Ancient Israel. A New History of Israelite Society* (Sheffield: JSOT Press, 1988).

42 B. J. Diebner, "Genesis als Buch der Antik-jüdischen Bibel." *Dielheimer Blätter zum Alten Testament* 17 (1983) 81–98.

ine this in connection with the origin of the synagogue? Is not everything that is brought up here focused on the identity of Israel and its God?

As long as external evidence is lacking, all attention will have to be directed to compositional data. In this the exegete needs to be conscious that "single authorship" is not a matter of course. The diversity of Genesis points to a process lasting generations. Narrators, accordingly, had to reckon with ancient traditional data such as the locations of Abraham at Mamre and Isaac at Beersheba. But such names could become the nuclei of new stories, as is the case in the Midrash. The true binding factor is concentration on the name of Israel's God and in connection with that: the existence of God's people in the midst of other peoples; this is the factor that must have guided the process of Genesis' origins. Therefore, in spite of the wide diversity of this book, a fundamental coherence—even in small details—may be discovered.

—∾ 8 ∾—

BECAUSE YOU HAVE HEARKENED TO MY VOICE (GENESIS 22)*

Karel A. Deurloo

ABSTRACT

Efforts to create a historical or traditio-historical setting for the chapter about the sacrifice of Abraham, in which the second main cycle of Genesis (11:27–25:19) reaches a climax, frequently result in embarrassment because of the intense theological content of the pericope. Also unsatisfactory is Westermann's dating of Genesis 22 based on the individual character of Abraham's God-fearing described in this chapter, which he claims is only conceivable in the period of the later kings. Those who attempt to clarify the import of the story by literary analysis still do not sufficiently take into account the interconnections of this story within the cycle. It is surely connected to the opening chapter of the first part of the cycle (12:1ff.) and to the second part (chap. 15) by motif and form of expression; but it is here that the problems raised in the second part (chaps. 16–20), concerning the conception of the son, come to the fore. Abraham's *going* for the sake of the land (chaps. 12–14) takes place with little difficulty. In contrast to this, the second section describes a series of questionable events, beginning with Abraham's "hearkening to the voice of his wife" (16:2). This and the laughter about the conception of a child (17:17; 18:12), and especially the

---

* Translation of: "Omdat ge gehoord hebt naar mijn stem (Gen. 22)," *Amsterdamse Cahiers* 5 (1984) 41–60.

"*Gefährdung der Ahnfrau*" at the moment when she could become pregnant (chap. 20), lead to Genesis 22, where Abraham learns to "hearken to the voice of YHWH" (22:18). The appendage 22:15–18 forms an integral part of both the story and the cycle, and expresses the story's true tendency. The oath sworn by YHWH (because of this *going* of Abraham) forms the basis of the oath given to the fathers (specifically recorded in Deuteronomy). Abraham breaks with his natural past (12:1) and his natural future (22:2 as parallel). This last *going* consists in "hearkening to the voice" of YHWH and trusting in what God sees *ʾĕlōhîm yirʾeh* (22:8, see 22:14f.). For that reason he is a *yĕrēʾ ʾĕlōhîm* (22:12), a God-fearing man. The substitute-sacrifice motif contributes to this theme.

Genesis 22, the gripping and highly praised story of Abraham's sacrificial journey—praised[1] and appreciated as source of inspiration[2] —in Jewish tradition called "the binding of Isaac," may, with respect to its *Tendenz* and rhetoric, be understood only within the context of Gen 11:27–25:18.[3] To be sure, it may also function as an independent narrative; as such it has suggested profound interpretations, even though what must be regarded as obvious is hardly expressed. One might expect that professional exegetes would be modest in applying their literary and traditio-historical insights to a composition that presents itself as a unit, and that they would critically test their hypotheses on that unit. However, the supposed results of scholarly investigation would seem to function powerfully and dogmatically.[4]

---

[1] Frequently in accord with the first chapter in Erich Auerbach, *Mimesis. The Representation of Reality in Western Literature* (Garden City: Doubleday, 1957).

[2] Particularly also in connection with Jewish-Christian dialogue. In addition to, e.g., the correspondence of Rosenzweig-Rosenstock, see Franz Rosenzweig, *Der Mensch und sein Werk. Gesammelte Schriften. 1. Briefe und Tagebücher, 1. Band* 1900–1918 (Reprint: The Hague: Nijhoff, 1979) 189–91; and also recently Willem Zuidema, Albert van der Heide, et al., *Het offer van Isaak en de holocaust. Betekenis en verwerking* [The Sacrifice of Isaac and the Holocaust. Significance and Application] (Baarn: Ten Have, 1982).

[3] For the compositional division of Genesis, see F. H. Breukelman, *Bijbelse Theologie, I: Schriftlezing* (Kampen: Kok, 1980) 127, 128.

[4] Claus Westermann, *Genesis 12–36. A Commentary* (London: SPCK, 1985) does not see unity in the literary context but in the *Motivfolge*: "Childlessness of the father/the mother—Lament of the Childless—Promise of a Son—Promise of the Son— (Endangering of this Promise)—Birth of the Son—Endangering of the Son—Continuation of the Generations through this Son" (143). In spite of this redactional unity there remains a series of individual tales, a conclusion that affects exegesis. Regarding the original individual tale of Genesis 22, possibly at a presupposed pre-literary stage of oral tradition, one has various options, e.g., a joining of two stories concerning an itinerary plus an aetiological foundation of the substitute offer (R. Kilian,

Yet, previously accepted viewpoints on or developed approaches to Genesis 22 have foundered of late.[5] Westermann remarks precisely of this narrative "that the interpretation that moves from hearing to telling, wants to lead back to hearing."[6] Every exegete will gladly confirm that, but every exegete also knows that between *coming from hearing* and *leading back to hearing* many different things happen to various interpreters. Are the steps *Form-Ort-Wort* adequate? In characterizing *Form* one runs the risk of letting generalities dominate the interpretation of a unique text, which the reader of a commentary gets to hear, then, only third-hand.[7] Under the heading *Ort* Westermann feels impelled to refer *in this case* to a specific interpretation and concludes that *this* story must stem from the late royal period.[8] Indeed, *this* case might be particularly

---

Isaaks Opferung. Zur Überlieferungsgeschichte von Gen. 22 [SBS, 44; Stuttgart: Kohlhammer, 1970], or the reconstruction of a folkloristic tale with the rescued son as its central figure (H. Graf Reventlow, *Opfere deinen Sohn. Eine Auslegung von Genesis 22* [BibS(N) 53; Neukirchen/Vluyn: Neukirchener Verlag, 1968]), or an initiation legend concerning a dying child who rises as a grown young man (Hugh C. White, "The Initiation Legend of Isaac," *ZAW* 91[1979] 1–30). It is tempting to think of scholarly arbitrariness.

5 E.g., the question of whether this story must be assigned to J or to E becomes irrelevant. The "fear" of God was deemed characteristic by Friedemann W. Golka, who believes that we have in Genesis 22 the "locus classicus" of the Elohistic theology; "Die theologischen Erzählungen im Abrahamkreis," *ZAW* 90 (1978) 192; but see the *Exkurse* in Westermann, *Genesis* 435, 436, and 443.

6 Westermann, *Genesis*. Graf Reventlow, *Opfere deinen Sohn*, on the other hand, wishes to go back to the story as he has reconstructed it. The "monotone Geschlossenheit...bestätigt die Richtigkeit der...vorgenommenen Scheidungen" (32). He deletes, e.g., the splitting of the wood (22:3). "The final redactor...was pedantic" (49); not so, Graf Reventlow.

7 In disputation with Van Seters and Coats, Westermann claims that this is a story of testing. With that he immediately gives us a scheme: a command to the tested, the execution of the command, and the determination of whether he has passed the test or not. The obvious result is the division of the text, Gen 22:1b–2, 3–10, according to the scheme, 11–12a revocation of the command and 12b the statement that the test has been passed. Vv. 13 and 14 fit in with the revocation, v. 19 is the conclusion, and vv. 15–18 appear to fall outside the scheme, so that one may conclude that they are an addition (Westermann, *Genesis*). But it may be questioned whether the story (except for vv. 15–18) corresponds completely to the scheme, in other words, whether the characterization of the *Form* is not much too general and functions in a manner too abstracted from the context of the Abraham cycle. It might turn out that in context vv. 15–18 are a necessary "addition" in connection with this *special* test (thus also G. W. Coats, "Abraham's Sacrifice of Faith: A Form-Critical Study of Genesis 22," *Int* 27 [1973] 389–400).

instructive for the exegetical application of Karl Barth's saying: *Latet periculum in generalibus.*[9]

> It happened after these events
> that God tested Abraham (22:1a).

By means of a formula and compact background information using the perfect form of *nsh*,[10] "to test," the author indicates a relatively new beginning and calls attention to his theme. The reader knows what the main actor in the story does not know. The tension within the narration lies not in the unraveling but in the act and word of Abraham. The reader has gotten to know him, particularly in chaps. 16–21, as a questionable figure.[11] "It happened after these events." Untold events or words between Isaac and Ishmael,[12] such as we have in the midrash, remain outside the exegesis. The formula adds emphasis, presupposes connections, and orders thematically, framing the narrative here (22:20) and giving it a weight of its own. In 15:1 the formula leads from the stories that stress the *land* theme to the introductory chapter of the series on the generation of the *son*. It is those events that God's testing follows.[13]

> He said to him:
> Abraham!
> He said:
> Here I am!
> He said:
> Take your son, your only one, whom you love, Isaac,
> and go to the land of Moriah

---

[8] Westermann is thereby not unfaithful to his general view of these stories, which is that they are a family history. An older story must be the basis of the "son threatened by death" (Westermann, *Genesis*).

[9] *Kirchliche Dogmatik* (Zurich: Zollikon, 1946) 2/2: 51.

[10] See Wolfgang Schneider, *Grammatik des Biblischen Hebräisch* (Munich: Claudius, 1974) 48:2.3, 48:6.1.4.

[11] This is particularly relevant to the central theme of these chapters, the generation and birth of the son: in Genesis 16 the emergency solution, listening to his wife; in Genesis 17 the laughing; and, as nadir, Genesis 20, allowing the "threatening of the ancestress" to happen, when she could become pregnant. See K. A. Deurloo, "Die Gefährdung der Ahnfrau (Gen 20)" [The Threatened Ancestress], *Dielheimer Blätter zum Alten Testament* 25 (1988) 17–27.

[12] E.g. *Gen. Rab.* 55:4.

[13] For the meaningful alternation here, *God* in the dark beginning and messenger of YHWH at the denouement in 22:11, see B. Jacob, *Das erste Buch der Tora. Genesis*, (Berlin: Schocken, 1934) 491–93.

and make him there go up as a burnt offering[14]
on one of the mountains which I will tell you (22:1b–2).

A call and a confrontation, which afterwards appears to have been at night (v. 3), tersely lay the basis for two others: vis-à-vis the son (v. 7) and the messenger of YHWH (vv. 11, 12). In "here I am," "here I am, my son," "here I am," the high tension of the entire event becomes audible: the two characteristics of Abraham's actions are described as love (v. 2) for the son and the fear of God (v. 12).[15]

The climax: "your son, your only one, whom you love, Isaac," reminds in its rhythm of Gen 12:1, which is underlined by the fact that the only other ethical dative with the verb "to go" in Genesis appears there: "Go (you) out of your land, out of your 'family,' out of the house of your father."

That command stands at the beginning of the stories concerning the land; it indicates a break with the "natural" past. It also stands at the end of the stories of the generation of a son and indicates a break with the "natural" future, which rests on that son.[16] Abram had to go to see, i.e., "to the land that I will *show* you"; here, "to the land of *Moriah*." With the LXX one can hear in it an assonance: the land of the "seeing." The verb rʾh, "to see," which plays such an important role in the first series of stories,[17] is also the most important motif word in Genesis 22.

Isaac is the "only one"; in him the progress of the ongoing history is concentrated, he is *the son*. The "only one," *yāḥîd*, recurs regularly, with consonant "together," *yaḥdāyw*, in striking ways: only (2), together (6), together (8), only (12), only (16), together (19).[18] This consonance of "the only" with "together" says something thematically as a part within the whole. The place, the land of Moriah, is very puzzling apart from its

---

[14] Notable and telling, the word *lî*, "for me," is lacking. The preposition *lĕ* before "burnt offering" hides an ambiguity, leading to the translation: "make him then go up (on that mountain) toward (for the) sacrificial journey" in connection with v. 13. See W. van der Spek, "Abraham en zijn jongens" [Abraham and His Boys] in: *Vlegels op de dorsvloer* (Festschrift, Thomas Naastepad; C. Elshout, et al., eds.; Kampen: Kok, 1981) 191, 194.

[15] See Gregoire Rouiller, "Le sacrifice d'Isaac," second lecture in: *Exegesis. Problèmes de méthode et exercises de lecture*, ed. François Bovon & Grégoire Rouiller (Neuchatel/Paris: Delachaux et Niestle, 1975) 282, 283.

[16] Breukelman, *Bijbelse Theologie* 127.

[17] Gen 12:1, 7; 13:10–14.

[18] A primary reason not to judge vv. 15–18 too hastily as a *later* addition that does not belong to the story.

assonance-connection with Genesis 12 in view of the last line of the command: "one of the mountains which I will tell you"; "the place which God had told him" (3), "saw that place from afar" (4), "we go there" (5), "they came to the place that God had told him." There Abraham "built the altar" (9), after which the puzzle finds a solution in the naming of that place, reinforced by a (different) aetiological formula (14) in which the word "mountain," from the command of God, returns. No other mountain than Zion can be intended here.[19] Doesn't the expression "the place which God had told him" remind us, precisely through its repetition, of the stereotyped reference in Deuteronomy to Jerusalem—the name which is avoided in all of the Torah? "The place, which YHWH, your God, shall choose."[20] That is the place for burnt offerings and tithes (Deut 12:5, 6). Abram brought tithes in the last chapter of the stories concerning the land, where the place, hardly concealed, is called Salem (14:18ff.). Here he has sacrificed a ram, in the final and decisive story about the son.[21]

The three imperatives, *take, go, sacrifice* were already heightened in the command as building blocks of the story. When they are repeated in vv. 3–10, they remain in tension with v. 2 until this is resolved in v. 13, where the words recur briefly and powerfully: Abraham went, took, caused to go up as burnt offering. Thus they draw a circle around the central event, within which other circles are drawn that indicate the decisive center of the story.

> Abraham arose early in the morning
> saddled his ass,
> took two of his servants with him,
> and Isaac his son.
> He split the wood for the burnt offering
> he arose and went to the place that God had told him (22:3).

The three words are repeated in this sequence with a variation in word order. The order of the actions has occasioned surprise, however.[22]

---

[19] See also the oldest "interpretation" of Moriah in 2 Chron 3:1.

[20] Deut 12:5, etc. In Josh 9:27 resistance to using the name Jerusalem is repeated, but it is named in Josh 10:1.

[21] Westermann (*Genesis*) recognizes child sacrifice as a *narrative motif* and points correctly to its connection with the offering of the firstborn (Exod 22:19; 34:10). Polemic against this is still found in Ezekiel.

[22] The Dutch *Groot Nieuws Bijbel* (comparable to the *Good News Bible* [—Ed.]) "improves" the text: "Early in the morning Abraham arose, split the wood for the

Yet, precisely that sequence produces a certain emphasis. The first and last sentences frame the way Abraham hearkens to God's voice, which said: go, and he *went*. But what about "take?" He *took* (as if it were written down by mere coincidence) "two of his servants," but then: "and Isaac his son!" Following directly on the mention of Isaac, illogically and thus with greater effect: "wood for the *burnt offering*." Saddling the ass and taking along the two servants are not mentioned just to add color to Abraham's *going* or effect to his *taking* Isaac; they will have a function later on. This is all the more true for the wood that is split for the burnt offering. The departure before the offering-journey has been expressed broadly by means of the three words in the command, which resound as imperatives. On the other hand, a sequence that might have followed, the itinerary,[23] is omitted. The journey or the route traveled apparently do not matter in this story, only the place of which God had told him.

> On the third day Abraham raised his eyes
> and saw the place from afar.
> Abraham said to his servants:
> You remain here with the ass.
> I and the boy, we go there,
> then we bow down (worship)
> and return to you (22:4, 5).

"On the third day"—i.e., the day on which an important event was to happen, inaugurating a new era[24] —Abraham "saw the place from afar." The significance of this seeing is marked by the words: "he lifted up his eyes." The same words introduced seeing the land (13:14) that God would let him see (12:1). With the special seeing in 22:13, they form another framing. In both cases the seeing is suggested by God himself.

The place is still far away; a goodly distance needs to be traveled by Abraham and his son. To create a division, v. 2 mentions the ass and the two servants so that their going could be tersely sketched. The author takes advantage of Abraham's leaving the others behind to draw *him* in direct speech, not only as someone who conceals this matter from out-

---

sacrifice, saddled his ass and got underway with his son Isaac, to the place which God had mentioned to him. He also took two of his servants along." This demonstrates a lack of understanding. Westermann (*Genesis*) sees a doublet and mentions the possibility that two *Erzählungsgänge* are joined together. "But this assumption is not necessary." Indeed it isn't!

[23] To Kilian, *Isaaks Opferung*, it is the fundamental datum of one of the earlier stages.

[24] H. Jagersma, *Ten derden dage* (Kampen: Kok, 1976) 28–30.

siders[25] but as one who audibly communicates confidence to the reader. Abraham says emphatically: "I and the boy"—not "my son," for he speaks to his "boys,"[26] his servants—"we...return." The distance within "you here...we there" is not undone till v. 19: "Abraham returned to his servants. They arose and went together...." In the previous section, especially in vv. 15–18, it becomes clear why the boy Isaac is not expressly named here, but is only implicitly ("together") present.

> Abraham took the wood for the burnt offering
> and laid it on Isaac his son.
> He took in his hand the fire and the knife.
> Thus the two went together (22:6).

The final sentence forms the conclusion of v. 8, the second sentence the framing of the conversation, the center of the story. The three imperatives in v. 2 and their echo in v. 3 together with the conclusion of v. 13 form the outer *inclusio*, whereas vv. 4 and 13a correspond, referring to Abraham's special "seeing." The word to the servants (v. 5) precedes acts of preparation (v. 6); the word of the messenger (vv. 11, 12) follows acts of preparation (vv. 9, 10).[27]

The preparation in v. 3—"took...and Isaac his son. He split wood for the burnt offering"—is continued more intensely: "Abraham *took* the wood and laid it on Isaac his son," reaching a (mirrored) climax in v. 9: "bound Isaac his son and laid him...on the wood." The second *taking* refers to Abraham's *hand*. On Isaac the fate, for Abraham the act.[28] Another climax follows in v. 10: "Abraham stretched out his *hand* and *took* the knife...." This attribute is sensitively omitted by Isaac, who mentions only fire and wood (v. 7). Thus Abraham goes, with his *yāhîd*, his

---

[25] See Rouiller, *Sacrifice*, first lecture, 22.

[26] See also the alternation "son," "child," and "boy" in Gen 21:9–11. White, "Initiation Legend" 14, relates to this the theory of initiation to adulthood in a two-fold tradition. The two servants in Genesis 22 are witnesses belonging to the "class of young, recently initiated men." In v. 19, Isaac has also become such a "boy" during the ritual. Van der Spek ("Abraham en zijn jongens..." 199) claims (also with reference to Genesis 21) that the "servants" refer to the "freeman," the *liberi*. But in Numbers 22–24, which is reminiscent of several aspects of the Abraham story (for example, the blessings and curses in the oracles, and Gen 12:1, 2), Balaam also has two of his "servants" with him, in addition to his ass (Num 22:22).

[27] See the concentric structure which Lack sketches on the basis of the vocabulary; R. Lack, "Le sacrifice d'Isaac," *Bib* 56 (1975) 1–12.

[28] Hermann Gunkel, *Genesis, übersetzt und erklärt* (5th ed.; Göttingen: Vandenhoeck & Ruprecht, 1922) 237.

only one. Thus they go, *yaḥdāyw*, together. The road they travel is not described, but is made real audibly in their dialogue:

> Thus the two went together.
> Isaac said to Abraham his father, he said:
> My father!
> He said:
> Here I am, my son.
> He said:
> Here are the fire and the wood,
> but where is the lamb for the burnt offering?
> Abraham said:
> God himself will see to the lamb for the burnt offering,
> my son,
> Thus the two went together (22:6e–8).

The reader has arrived at the holy of holies of the story and holds one's breath. The son who, since Gen 12:2 and particularly Genesis 15, has been the focus of the story, says: "My father." The father who has said to God: "Here I am," says: "Here I am, my son." Fire and wood, but where is what is destined *lĕʿōlāh*,[29] *for the burnt offering* (vv. 2, 13)? Framed by the pharse "the lamb for the burnt offering," Abraham speaks the words: "God *will see* for himself." It might be called Abraham's confession of faith, prepared by his word to the two servants (v. 5), confirmed by the proclamation of the name of the place: "YHWH will see" (v. 14). In the land of Moriah, "sight," Abraham only sees what God lets him see and trusts in what God sees, what he has in mind, by listening to his voice. In this story he does what was lacking in Genesis 16–21. The one who says: *ʾĕlōhîm yirʾeh* will be called (as by assonance) a *yĕrēʾ ʾĕlōhîm*,[30] a God-fearer (v. 12). Abraham's answer to the son he loves is implicitly the answer that is expected from the God-fearer when tested. This answer is the decisive center of the story and is emphatically confirmed in the sequel to the act.

> They came to the place which God had told him.
> There Abraham built the altar,
> he arranged the wood,
> bound Isaac his son,
> and laid him on the altar, on the wood.

---

[29] "Lamb," see Isa 43:23; in v. 13 the more regular "ram," see Lev 1:10, etc.
[30] See Rouiller, *Sacrifice*, first lecture, 20.

Abraham stretched out his hand
and took the knife to slaughter his son (22:9, 10).

With painful precision, in quasi-cultic terms,[31] while retarding his tale, the author takes the reader along via the "slowest take:" stretched out his hand, took the knife, to the sinister word "slaughter." It happened in *that* place that Abraham had to build his only altar for his son—Isaac's name is not heard anymore from here on (cf. Genesis 12). This journey of Abraham is the break with the future which he envisaged for Isaac who bears the name of his "laughter" about the promise (17:12), trusting the God "who sees." The dark call of the beginning, repeated twice, "from heaven," now turns brilliant:

Then the messenger of YHWH called from heaven:
and said
    Abraham, Abraham!
He said:
    Here I am!
He said:
    Do not stretch out your hand to the boy!
    Do nothing to him!
    For now I know that you are God-fearing.
    You have not withheld from me your son, your only one (22:11, 12).

The scene is stopped, as it were, when Abraham stretches out his *hand*. The deed that confirms his word is the central event in the story. Isaac the son is present only to provide background for Abraham. He no longer plays a "present" role in the story,[32] for he represents the seed of Abraham. The "only one" he has, he has only as a God-fearer, who yields the son to the God who sees.[33] This is the secret of Israel's existence.

Abraham lifted up his eyes
and saw, see! A ram was back there[34] with his horns,

---

[31] See Westermann, *Genesis* 441 and A. van Selms, *Genesis deel II: De prediking van het Oude Testament* (Nijkerk: Callenbach, 1967) 23.

[32] According to the Midrash, Isaac was removed by angels to learn Torah at the school of Shem; *Gen. Rab.* 56:11 et al.

[33] See also the preparatory story in Genesis 21, esp. v. 19 and its parallel Genesis 16, esp. vv. 13, 14. The *Groot Nieuws Bijbel* is completely erroneous when it "translates": "Now I know that you have respect for God, because you were even prepared to sacrifice your only son to me."

[34] Or, according the emendation based on textual witnesses, "*a ram*" (ʾeḥad). See Van Selms, *Genesis* 24 and a different view by Kilian, *Isaaks Opferung* 57.

caught in the thicket.
Abraham went,
took the ram
and made him go up as burnt offering instead of his son.

With these inclusive phrases the circles are, soberly, closed around the central narrative. The place he saw from afar is the place where the words *to go, to take* and *burnt offering* refer to the ram instead of the son, as prescribed in the Torah for the firstborn (cf. Exod 13:15). One might say: all sacrifices look to Abraham's sacrificial journey.

The author deems two "additions" necessary before he closes the story with v. 19:

Abraham called as the name of that place
YHWH will see!
As today is (still) said:
On the mountain of YHWH it will be seen (22:14).

What Abraham confessed in the center of the story is indicated as the central point. The tetragrammaton is named (called)[35] and an irregular[36] actualizing aetiological formula is connected to the "seeing" of God. Today we know that place, that mountain in the land "Moriah." There "one appears," one lets oneself be seen *coram Deo*; there "is seen," one receives sight; there "he appears," one lets himself be seen.[37] The formula underscores the weight of this story as the decisive Abraham story, as a similar actualizing formula does that in the decisive story in the following cycle (Gen 25:19–37:1), where the name Israel is sounded for the first time. Then the sons of Israel are already present *in* the story (Gen 32:32).[38]

The indication of the fundamental character of this story demands a second "addition," which is introduced as such even more explicitly. The author did not want to burden the real story with this information but saved the import of the narration for a speech by the messenger:

The messenger of YHWH called to Abraham
for the second time from heaven,

---

35 See 12:8.
36 I. Fichtner, "Die etymologische Analogie in den Namengebungen der geschicht-lichen Bücher des AT," *VT* 6 (1956) 372–96.
37 Three possible translations. See 12:7, Exod 23:15, etc.
38 See K. A. Deurloo, "De naam en de namen (Genesis 32:23–33)" [The Name and the Names], *Amsterdamse Cahiers* 2 (1981) 38.

he said:
> By myself I swear
> —saying of YHWH—
> Truly, because you have done this
> you have not withheld your son, your only one,
> therefore bless, indeed I bless you,
> I will make your seed much, as much
> as the stars of heaven,
> as the sand on the shore of the sea.
> Your seed inherits the gate of its enemies.
> Then in your seed will be blessed
> all the peoples of the earth
> because you have hearkened to my voice (22:15–18).

A meaningful redundance, which receives extra emphasis through the prophetic formula "saying of YHWH," which is hardly found in narrative texts, insures a solemn ending to this story and to the actual cycle of Abraham stories.[39] As the beginning of Genesis 22 calls to mind words from Gen 12:1, thus also the conclusion. They may be read as parallels:

> With you all the generations of the earth will bless themselves (12:3).
> With your seed all the peoples of the earth will be blessed (22:18).

"With you," "with your seed" *both* return in the typical Abrahamic blessing in Gen 28:13, 14,[40] where both texts are presupposed.

The expression "stars of heaven"—strengthened by "the sand of the sea" (see Gen 32:12)—points back to the opening chapter of the stories of the son (15:5); blessing and making great revert to 12:1. The notable phrase,"Your seed inherits the gate of its enemies," parallels the blessing of Isaac's wife Rebekah (Gen 24:60). The unique formulation seems to stem from the sphere of royal justice. But is that not also the case with the words of blessing themselves (see Ps 72:17)? The royal blessing is democratized in the seed of Abraham.[41] *Seed* is the central word in this speech. In Isaac the seed of Abraham was at stake. Because of his *deed* in this

---

[39] After this follow "the death of the matriarch," with the theme of *land*, and "the going out of her land to the land of the new matriarch," with the theme of *son*; Gen 23:24. See K. A. Deurloo, "Het graf van Sara" [The Grave of Sarah]; *Amsterdamse Cahiers* 1 (1980) 22–32.

[40] See J. P. Fokkelman, *Narrative Art in Genesis* (Assen: Van Gorcum, 1975) 55–57.

[41] J. Van Seters, *Abraham in History and Tradition*, (New Haven/London: Yale University Press, 1975) 237.

story the seed, the people of the future, will be there. The entire speech is therefore framed by:

—because you have done this
—because you have hearkened to my voice.

This is the *dābār* of Abraham par excellence. As in 15:1, the formula "after these words/events" marks a transition from chaps. 12–14 to chaps. 15–21, and from 22:1 to this chapter in the context of the previous stories, thus the formula marks this *dābār* that Abraham has done through the transition to 22:20–24. This *dābār* is explained through the framing as a listening to God's voice in contrast to listening to the woman's voice (16:3). For the story of Abraham is told through the relationship "humankind: man and woman," as the Jacob story is told through the relationship "humankind: man and brother," corresponding respectively with Genesis 3 and Genesis 4.[42] The latter is concerned with one's meeting face to face with God and with one's brother (Gen 32:33; see 4:5,6); the former—beside the central theme of *father* and son—is concerned with one's hearkening to God or to a woman (see Gen 3:17).[43]

With Abraham history begins anew because twice he has hearkened to the imperative: go! (12:1 and 22:1). The whole of the second cycle of the book of Genesis culminates in the sacrificial *journey* of Abraham. Correcting what went on before, this testing was necessary to learn how to deal with his son as he did with the land. *"Because you have done this* dābār, *because you have hearkened to my voice"* sums up the significance of Genesis 22. Here a new history begins; here the son needs to step back to point to the seed. For this reason he is not personally named in the final sentence:

Abraham returned to his servants.
They arose
and they went together to Beersheba
and Abraham remained in Beersheba (22:19).

---

[42] See Breukelman, *Bijbelse Theologie* 127.

[43] The theme returns in reverse and corrected order in 21:12. Partly because of this verse, Maria de Groot was inspired to compose a beautiful song about Sarah, which, however, contains exegetically dubious lines: "The Lord has highly valued your word: In everything that she says, he will hear you" (*Mededelingen Prof. dr. G. van der Leeuwstichting*, Aflevering 58, 4866).

In *yaḥdāyw*, together, *yāḥîd*, the only one, which is the "germ" of the abundant "seed" (vv. 16, 17) is incorporated.

They go to Beersheba. That place may also have been thought of as a point of departure,[44] but at the beginning it is ignored in order to give the name Beersheba, mentioned twice, a function in the play with "oath swearing" besides that in 21:23ff. They go to the "Well of the Oath" under the sign of the oath that God swore by himself (v. 16). In the present form of the Torah this oath is the basis for the oath to the fathers, drawing a line to the widely used formula in Deuteronomy.[45]

Before the Sarah and Rebekah stories, which are thematically connected with the whole of the cycle, are told, there is first a meaningful introduction with the formula: "and it happened after these events," a genealogy reminiscent of 11:7–32. Particularly with the names of Nahor and Milcah, genealogy frames the real corpus of this cycle, which moves from 12:1–3 to 22:1, 15–18. The list 22:20–24 points beyond the pericope of Sarah's death to the advent of the new matriarch in Genesis 23. By the surprising variation of a woman among "sons and brothers," her way is prepared (v. 23). But the list also has its function vis-à-vis the preceding! "See, Milcah, she too bore sons to Nahor your brother," thus sounds the report. There are eight. But the concubine, "she also bore"—four, for a total of twelve, the number of the sons of Israel in the following cycle, in contrast to Abraham's only one. The report comes at the right time, for has he not for the first time received his son as son of the promise, as his seed, in Genesis 22, because he hearkened to God's voice? Does the secret of Israel's origin among the nations not lie precisely in that?

A word, *dābār*, must be heard, must penetrate in the soul, *nepeš*, to move it to act according to that word, to a deed, *maʿăśeh*, in the confidence, *heʾĕmîn*, that the speaker of the word guarantees his word and promise. The hearer trusts, moving from *hearing*—and therefore, doing— to *seeing*. As to the first *lēk-lĕkā*, go! (12:19), it is true of Abram. Gen 15:6 may be applied to that. But the journey in which the promised land is

---

44 See 21:22–34 for Beersheba in connection with "seven" and "swearing an oath." Westermann notes that "an older form of the narrative with information of an itinerary began, which contained the name of Beersheba," *Genesis* 446, but the oath in vv. 15–18 he deletes from the story as a later addition.

45 As a part of the interwoven promises to the fathers. See J. Hoftijzer, *Die Verheissungen an die drie Erzväter* (Leiden: Brill, 1956). Note the Dtr. terminology in Gen 22:15–18, such as *ʿēqeb ʾăšer*, and see, e.g., Deut 28:62: "...you shall be left few in number, while you had been as numerous as the stars of heaven—because you did not hearken to the voice of YHWH your God" (see Deut 1:10; 10:22).

also *seen* is meaningless without the promise of the *seed* (13:4, 15). In the opening chapter of the second part of the cycle Abram therefore says: "See, I *go* 'childless'," with the connotation: the journey of my life ends, I die childless (see 25:32). The new *word* to the question concerning wages is therefore the promise of the son from Abram's body (15:4) and—deliberately unsaid but understood by the reader—from Sarai's infertile womb. It is her initiative, her word, by which the action continues. Formally it is not in conflict with the *Wortlaut* of the promise in Genesis 15, but in an alarmingly questionable turn of events, Abraham hearkens to her voice (16:3; 3:17).

The following narratives, especially Gen 17:17, confirm that. An all too human rivalry within the harem occasions God's sarcastic accommodation to Sarah, the "directress" (21:12). Isaac and Ishmael, the people, are separated (see 13:7ff.) to concentrate all attention on the one, the only one, the son of the promise. "For through Isaac *seed* will be for you, offspring will be named" (21:12).

That matter, that *dābār*, is at risk in Genesis 22. A second *lēk-lĕkā*, go!, is necessary as a test to make clear to Abraham and the reader that in this son a natural continuation of the genealogy is not envisaged but that a people enters history in a new perspective. The threatening loss of an only child is a general, human, and understandable grief. The narrator consciously avoids making something perceptible of it. He is concerned with something of much greater dimensions: will the voice of God be hearkened to, so that there may be a single one who stands among the nations in whom all will be blessed? The testing is not an arbitrary occasion, it is not intended to arouse admiration for Abraham for passing the test, neither is it intended for commiserating with him in his need—possibly as consolation for the reader in comparable situations of one's own. The testing was intended to teach something. Isaac is the son who belongs to God; God has a plan for him. To omit 22:15–18 as a later addition is to leave out essential information.

The testing does not generate virtue or the fear of God. Abraham's fear of God has a different object, viz., the confession that *God sees*—Isaac and his seed in great numbers; his confessing is doing, hearkening to God's voice. Thus the fear of God is heightened by the testing of the people at Sinai (Exod 20:18b–21): not sinning but hearkening to the commandments. Testing by means of the remaining peoples in the land has as its purpose to *teach* the battle that Joshua fought (Judg 3:1–4). Abraham had learned—22:12 is deliberately repeated in 22:16—not to "withhold" his son from God (see Gen 39:9). Only thus is the only one there, together with him, the son of the promise, given freely to the God who sees.

The sacrificial journey of Abraham unveils the meaning of the sacrifice. Everyone who makes an offering includes oneself in the history begun with Abraham. For that reason the location of the story is of great importance. The author is not acting mysteriously when he first speaks so enigmatically about the land of Moriah, while continually reminding his readers of the question of the place in the story. Its meaning is that the Jerusalem cult is borne by the story of Abraham.

By claiming that the narrative says nothing about a historical event do we leave reality behind and place the center of gravity in the *Geistesgeschichtliche*? No, the believer in a general sense is not in sight. Von Rad says rightly in his polemic with Hesse: "The texts of the Old Testament aim at history and also originate in history."[46] But their historical roots do not need to lie in the narration or the time of the narrating. Israel also told fictional tales based on their experience in actual history, aiming at the real history which bore them. Indispensable for the impact of the story, therefore, are the words:

By myself I swear
—saying of YHWH—

as the introduction to the promise, framed by Abraham's doing and hearing. The beginning of the following cycle, 25:19–37:1, with its recapitulation of Abrahamic themes surrounding Isaac—now father of the *son*—quotes this oath verbatim (26:3): "because Abraham has hearkened to my voice" (26:5). The prophetic expression "saying of YHWH," which is unique in Genesis, is paired with a prophetic expression "by myself I swear" (Isa 45:13; Jer 22:5; 49:13; Amos 6:8) and is also made unforgettable by the repetition in Gen 26:3: "I will fulfill the oath which I swore to your father Abraham." Jacob will hear it implicitly: "I am YHWH, the God of your father Abraham…In you and your seed all the generations of the earth will bless themselves" (28:13, 14; see 22:1, 18) so that the book of Genesis can close with the naming of the triad in connection with the oath (50:24). Wherever the motifs of Genesis 22 may originate, they have been made to serve this *fundamental* narrative concerning the test that opened ears to the oath. When the people's future would seem to be ruined, the author of Exodus 32 lets Moses speak these poignant words of YHWH:

46 Gerhard von Rad, *Theology of the Old Testament* 2: 11, 12.

Remember
Abraham, Isaac, Israel, your servants,
what you *swore* to them *by yourself*
how you spoke to them:
Multiply will I your seed
as the stars of heaven
and all this land, of which I spoke
I will give it to your seed
that they may gain it forever (Exod 32:13).

The story about the *father* and his son that culminates the cycle Gen 11:27–25:18 is a story of and about Israel. Therein is its special *Ort*. Generalities about *family history* may be interesting, but they must be subordinated to the analysis of the given text; otherwise they tend to lead interpreters on erroneous tracks. We *know* nothing about earlier stages of the story. It is purely hypothetical to claim that in an oral tradition there was a story preceding this one.[47] Westermann barely maintains his hypothesis concerning a threatened child in the family even though he says: "This older narrative may go back to patriarchal times."[48] However, for him this point plays no greater role than that of a motif. In view of Jeremiah's and Ezekiel's polemics against child sacrifice and the sacrifice of substitutes, such a story need not be so ancient.

For Westermann the fear of the Lord is decisive as a "theological" aspect of the testing. Through that the story is elevated *into a more general* religio-historical context and *out of* its *particular* context. He sees the testing of the individual—for that, in his opinion, is what this chapter is dealing with—as a development subsequent to the testing of the people in the late royal era. The participating reader sees oneself involved in the of suffering of *one* heavily tested father. From the general, familiar human situation in a religio-historical setting Westermann then makes a leap to Paul (Rom 8:22), saying, in the context of the suffering of Christ: "God has suffered, because he had to give his son for the salvation of humankind. In this sentence God becomes human."[49] Deep thoughts and contexts! The *Aqedah* motif surely plays a role with Paul and in other parts of the New Testament; but doesn't Westermann flee under the heading "Ziel" *nota bene* in connection with this *text*, toward a facile "Christian" sermon? "It is essential that this narrative live on." Here

---

47 Apart from the fact that doubt is justified concerning the reliability of oral tradition outside of the official tradition-circles in temple and court.

48 Westermann, *Genesis*.

49 Ibid.

impracticality vis-à-vis the given text in its traditio-historical context seems to go hand in hand with impracticality in the dogmatic and homiletic aspects.[50]

The *vitium originis* lies in the fact that the text itself is not taken seriously in its given "historicity." Westermann empathizes as a "participant" in "the suffering and heavily tested father"—who as such is absent in the text—to save himself from such generalities through Paul.

One might expect something else from scholarly exegesis and practical biblical theology, precisely with such a pregnant text as Genesis 22 as well as elsewhere. This is not to say that the historical and technical questions dealt with in introductions are inconsequential. However, they are not prescriptive for exegesis; they should perform modest auxiliary services for interpretation. If Genesis 22 is dated "late" (correctly in my opinion), that judgment needs to be made of the entire Abraham cycle. The stories are thematically much too related and presuppose each other in details. Undoubtedly, the material has come together from various corners; the "author of the text" has many styles and must hide within himself different circles of writers. Doesn't the text suggest that the writer "P" knows the writer "J," but by the same token that "P is not a stranger to "J?" "Late royal era," says Westermann, and in the time of Jeremiah there is indeed a swarm of writers. The climate of crisis during and after the life of this prophet, which is not presupposed by the Abraham story, is not unthinkable as the cradle of such a cycle. Late writers knew pious semi-nomads from their own experience (Jeremiah 35), the motif of child sacrifice was not foreign to them (Jer 7:29–31), and the mountain of YHWH for them was "the place." However, possibly traditional motifs were no more than material for a cycle of stories that had taken on their own life. The living story, which has its particular tension and eloquence within the literary context in which it is placed and to which it points, must be heard. What existed before may by virtue of its information be useful at best for that hearing. "That the narrative live on," according to what it has to *say*—that is the goal the exegete hopes to serve.

---

[50] The conclusion of von Rad's *Theology of the Old Testament* opens "Christian" escape routes vis-à-vis the *Tanakh*. Through such traditio-historical considerations the relationship of the "testaments" is kept within a traditional ecclesiastical approach. It may be questioned whether the church and theology are really served by this.

—∾ **C** ∾—

Other Hebrew Bible Studies

—◦৩ 9 ৩◦—

THE PLACE WHERE
YHWH SHOWED HIMSELF TO MOSES

A STUDY OF THE COMPOSITION OF EXODUS 3[*]

Aleida G. Van Daalen

ABSTRACT

Professor Beek's claim, "this word has a proclaiming function," serves as a motto for this paper and has been a guide for my reading and attempting to understand the text of the Old Testament. Against that background, this study is offered as an illustration of narrative technique: how information is introduced, varied, worked out, and mutually related.

Part I (vv. 1–6) allows the reader to understand through both direct route and observations and statements by the actors. Various items of information suggest how the study will develop and that a confrontation with a super-human figure is about to take place.

In Part II (vv. 7–12) the thrust of the confrontation is revealed; vv. 7 and 9 narrate YHWH's motivation, vv. 8 and 10 the action he plans. Pharaoh is introduced in the actual commission (v. 10) and in Moses' words.

---

[*] This article is a slightly adapted translation of: "De plaats waar *JHWH* Elohim zich aan Mozes liet zien. Een onderzoek naar de compositie van Exodus 3" [The Place where YHWH Showed Himself to Moses. A Study of the Composition of Exodus 3] in: *Verkenningen in een stroomgebied. Proeven van oudtestamentisch onderzoek* (Festschrift for Prof. Dr. M. A. Beek on the occasion of his retirement from the University of Amsterdam; ed. M. Boertien et al.; Amsterdam: Universiteit van Amsterdam, 1974) 30–40.

Part III (vv. 13–15) deals with the name of God Moses is to communicate to the people of Israel. The first answer is the bare statement *ᵓehyeh ᵓăšer ᵓehyeh*: followed by two commands "Thus you shall say...": the first referring to *ᵓehyeh* (v. 14), the second identifying him as YHWH the Elohim of the patriarchs (v. 15).

In Part IV (vv. 16–17) the stress falls on the deeds of YHWH Elohim. The elders are to join Moses in his approach to the king of Egypt.

The story needs to be read on two levels. Questions confront both Moses and the reader. Moses' questioning of himself is pointed toward God who will be worshipped on this mountain. The other questions are answered and used to inform the reader of the purpose of the narrative: the commissioning of Moses and the news that the purpose of YHWH, the Elohim of the patriarchs, is to save his people from oppression.

The story of Exodus 3 was written for the sons of Israel, to proclaim to them that calling on the name of YHWH means that "our Elohim" is one, who is there, who is with them, and that serving him means: to be led from oppression to a good and broad land, a land flowing with milk and honey.

My teacher, the late Professor M. A. Beek, to whose memory I dedicate this article, has emphasized in word and writing[1] that the words of the Hebrew Bible have a proclaiming function. The biblical word has been shaped by proclamation, and this function is quite evident in ancient Israel.[2]

---

[1] M. A. Beek, "Verzadigingspunten en onvoltooide lijnen in het onderzoek van de oudtestamentische literatuur," *Vox Theologica* 38 (1968) 6. This article is translated as chap. 2 above.

[2] "Verzadigingspunten" 6–14, in which Beek suggests that the literary approach of Old Testament texts may open one's eyes to its unique character, and offers the insight that it is premature at least to atomize the text according to Western criteria, to speak at the outset of historical stratification, and to look for hypothetical traditions. In his dissertation *Kain en Abel* (Amsterdam: Ten Have, 1967), K. A. Deurloo offers a methodology in which he has most consistently executed a literary approach to Old Testament texts. The introductory chapter of this dissertation is translated as chap. 3 above. W. Richter, *Exegese als Literaturwissenschaft, Entwurf einer Alttestamentlichen Literaturtheorie und Methodologie* (Göttingen: Vandenhoeck & Ruprecht, 1971) and G. Fohrer et al., *Exegese des Alten Testaments. Einführung in die Methodik* (Heidelberg: Quelle & Meyer, 1973) also apply achievements of literary criticism, but only after the text is fragmented according to the methods of literary-historical criticism, so that we miss the interpretation of stories in their totality. See Richter's treatment of Exodus 3 in the above cited study, 53–55, and in more detail in his "Literaturwissenschaftliche Studie," *Die sogenannten vorprophetischen Berufungsberichte* (Göttingen: Vandenhoeck & Ruprecht, 1970) 57–59.

This view is my starting point for this article, which offers a study of the composition of Exodus 3, as well as an investigation[3] of the manner in which information is introduced, varied, worked out, and mutually related.[4] With the investigation of composition, what is in the foreground is not the question of what is happening, but the question of what is to be expressed, heard, and proclaimed in the event.[5] The hearer must therefore listen to the story beyond the events, over the heads of the acting and speaking personalities.[6]

In the story, figures appear and allusions are made to themes and situations which are familiar from the context. The question of how far the context extends must be asked: "where does the pericope end?" From possible answers, conclusions may be drawn—conclusions relative to the question of the readers to whom both this text and this context, this verbalizing of proclamation, are directed. The limited extent of this paper demands that this question remain unanswered here. Nor can we pay much attention to contextual reading.[7]

Analyzing Exodus 3, the following parts may be indicated: (1) vv. 1–6, (2) vv. 7–12, (3) vv. 13–15, (4) vv. 16–17, and (5) vv. 18–22. Each part is a section of the text; the division can never be absolute since each part contains elements of what follows; the sequences dovetail.

A translation of the text of Exod 3:1–18 follows. Our investigation is thus limited, even though parts of vv. 19, 10 and 21, 22 each develop references found in v. 18.

---

3 The literary analysis in this essay can only be by way of an outline, offering only a single aspect of the possible literary approaches.

4 The neutral word "information" (Dutch: *gegeven*) has been chosen; the difference between concepts such as theme, motif, etc., in the above cited study by Fohrer, 99–116, was influenced by presuppositions concerning historical stratification of the text to such a degree, that the use of these terms may only create confusion.

5 This word was chosen because it is less charged than the word "structure."

6 Discussions with my colleague Drs. F. J. Hoogewoud were very helpful in this study.

7 Examples of the treatment of stories in their totality, in their place in context: B. Jacob, "Mose am Dornbusch," *MGWJ* 66 (1922) 11–33, 116–37, 180–200; see also "Gott und Pharaoh," ibid. 68 (1924) 118–26 and 202–11. Also M. Buber, "Moses," in *Schriften zur Bibel. Werke* (Munich: Kösel, 1964) 2: 9–230, particularly "Der brennende Dornbusch," 47–66; and U. Cassuto, *A Commentary on the Book of Exodus* (Jerusalem: Magnes, 1967) 30–32. The factors that have influenced their treatment of the text cannot be discussed here.

PART I

1   Moses was grazing the cattle of his father-in-law Jethro, priest of
    Midian;
    he led the cattle behind the wilderness
    and he came to the Elohim-mountain, to Horeb.

2   YHWH's messenger was seen by him
    in the flame of fire, from the midst of the *sĕneh* (blackberry bush).
    He saw:
    see, the *sĕneh* burned in the fire, but the *sĕneh* was not consumed!

3   And Moses said:
    Let me turn aside
    and see this great sight:
    why the *sĕneh* does not burn up.

4   YHWH saw
    that he had turned aside to see
    and Elohim called to him from the midst of the *sĕneh*
    and said:
    Moses! Moses!
    And he said:
    Here I am!

5   He said:
    Do not come closer;
    take off your sandals from your feet
    for the place on which you are standing is holy ground!

6   He said:
    I am the Elohim of your father,
    the Elohim of Abraham,
    the Elohim of Isaac,
    and the Elohim of Jacob.
    And Moses hid his face
    for he was afraid to look at Elohim.

PART II

7   YHWH said:
    I have seen, indeed seen, the oppression of my people in Egypt
    and their cry (for help) I have heard, because of their slave-drivers;
    indeed, I know their sorrows!

8   Therefore I have come down
    to deliver them from the hand of Egypt
    and to bring them up out of that land
    to a land, good and broad,

to a land, flowing with milk and honey,
to the place of the Canaanite and the Hittite,
the Amorite and the Perizzite, the Hivite, and the Jebusite.

9 Now, see, the cry (for help) of the sons of Israel has come to me,
   I have also seen the oppression whereby Egypt oppresses them.

10 And now, go,
   I send you to Pharaoh;
   Bring my people, the sons of Israel, out of Egypt!

11 Moses said to Elohim:
   Who am I
   that I should go to Pharaoh,
   and should bring the sons of Israel out of Egypt?

12 He said:
   kî-ᵓehyeh (for I am indeed!) with you,
   and this is the sign that I (myself) send you:
   When you bring the people out of Egypt
   you will serve Elohim on this mountain.

PART III

13 Moses said to Elohim:
   See, I come to the sons of Israel
   and I will say to them:
   The Elohim of your fathers has sent me to you,
   and they say to me:
   What is his name?
   What shall I say to them?

14 Elohim said to Moses:
   ᵓehyeh, that is "I will be there."
   And he said:
   Thus you shall say to the sons of Israel:
   ᵓehyeh has sent me to you.

15 And Elohim said moreover to Moses:
   Thus you shall say to the sons of Israel:
   YHWH,   the Elohim of your fathers,
            the Elohim of Abraham,
            the Elohim of Isaac,
            and the Elohim of Jacob has sent me to you.
   This is my name forever,
   and thus must I be called upon from generation to generation.

PART IV

16 Go,
    and gather the elders of Israel
    and say to them:
    YHWH the Elohim of your fathers was seen by me,
    the Elohim of Abraham, Isaac, and Jacob, saying:
    I have concerned myself, concerned about you,
    and about what has been done to you in Egypt.

17 And I said:
    I will bring you up from the affliction of Egypt,
    to the land of the Canaanite and the Hittite,
    the Amorite and the Perizzite, the Hivite and the Jebusite
    to a land flowing with milk and honey.

PART V

18 They will hearken to your voice
    and you will come
    you and the elders of Israel, to the king of Egypt,
    and you will say to him:
    YHWH, the Elohim of the Hebrews, has appeared to us,
    and now, please let us go a journey of three days in the wilderness
    and to sacrifice to YHWH our Elohim.

With the reading of this story, different levels need to be kept in view. The reader takes cognizance of what is told, both by a direct route as by means of observations and pronouncements of the acting figures. The reader is therefore from the beginning better informed than Moses. Thus the reader knows from the information in v. 2 that the messenger of YHWH shows himself to Moses in a flame of fire; that the miraculous appearance might have something to do with YHWH, Moses will perceive eventually.

First, let us consider part I, vv. 1–6. Apart from the context in the narrower and broader sense and from the notions which an Old Testament reader might have on hearing the word Elohim or when seeing a figure appear as shepherd or as messenger of YHWH, there is sufficient information in the text itself that points to the direction in which the story will develop. When after noting the place "behind the desert" the mountain of Elohim Horeb arises, the word Elohim, which belongs to the category by which superhuman figures are indicated, is a signal for a confrontation with such a figure at this place.

When v. 2 tells us that YHWH's messenger shows himself to him (Moses) in a flame of fire, from the midst of the *sĕneh*, further that Moses sees the burning-but-not-burning-up of the *sĕneh* and says (v. 3) that he will go to see how that can be, then the reader knows that YHWH's messenger is a more than human figure. And in v. 4 (YHWH sees Moses' intention, Elohim calls to him from the midst of the *sĕneh*) the reader understands that YHWH's messenger, YHWH, and Elohim refer to the same (divine) figure, that the word *sĕneh* expresses something special, and that the place—"behind the desert," the "Elohim-mountain of Horeb," and the "*sĕneh*"—have everything to do with each other, but also with YHWH's messenger, YHWH, and Elohim. The two notices, "do not come near…for the place on which you stand is holy ground" and "I am the Elohim of your father, the Elohim of Abraham, the Elohim of Isaac, the Elohim of Jacob," underscore this. Moses' reaction points to his awareness of the connection between place and divine appearance and at the same time lets the reader share in the experience of the *mysterium tremendum*. What the reader knows, but Moses does not yet know, is that this Elohim is at the same time YHWH.

In part II the reader retains this advantage (v. 7: YHWH said…; v. 11: Moses said to Elohim…). This sequence (vv. 7–12) may be subdivided into vv. 7–10 and vv. 11–12; and vv. 7–10 into vv. 7–8 and 9–10.

In vv. 7–8 YHWH says to Moses why he shows himself here: YHWH has become aware of what the people in Egypt had to undergo; therefore he has come (has descended) to save the people, to make them go up (another move) from this land…to a land…, to the place….

In vv. 9 and 10 he explains why he showed himself to Moses here. Both verses, each of which begins with *wĕ-ʿattāh* ("now"), summarize vv. 7 and 8 to some degree and heighten them. V. 9 corresponds with v. 7 and v. 10 with v. 8. However, v. 10 points to Moses with a double commandment which places in his hands the execution of the deliverance, and the going up:

Now go,
I send you to Pharaoh
lead out my people, the sons of Israel, out of Egypt.

In vv. 11–12 a series of dialogues between Moses and Elohim begins, which continue in Exodus 4 (there between Moses and YHWH). Moses' question to Elohim in v. 11 omits "I send you" from YHWH's words and places all emphasis on "I":

Who am I
that I should go to Pharaoh
and should lead the sons of Israel out of Egypt?

In the answer the accent returns to the "I" of the one who sends, both by the "for I am with you" and by the connection, laid between Moses' leading them out of Egypt and "you will serve Elohim on this mountain" (v. 12):

he said
kî-ʾehyeh (for I am) with you
and this is to you the sign that I send you:
when you lead the people out of Egypt
you will serve Elohim on this mountain.

To the reader who knows that Elohim is also YHWH, *kî-ʾehyeh* might be a wordplay, an indication of a possible revelation.

The Pharaoh is not mentioned anymore in Elohim's answer to Moses "...that I send you...." The sending obtains a different direction in the following part, namely, to the sons of Israel. These are the object of deliverance in vv. 7–12, together with "people." The grouping of the words "people" with "sons of Israel" in these verses is concentric: my people (7), the sons of Israel (9), my people, the sons of Israel (10), the sons of Israel (11), the people (12).[8]

In part III (vv. 13–15), Moses mentions in his second reaction to Elohim's commission, that he would go to the sons of Israel and say: "the Elohim of your fathers has sent me to you"; the reference to v. 7 reveals—within the story—that Abraham, Isaac, and Jacob are the fathers of the children of Israel. Hypothetically Moses has the children of Israel, too, ask about the name, and he asks directly: what must I answer them then?

Elohim's answer is in three phases. In the final two it is introduced with: "thus you shall say to the sons of Israel," in the first the answer is only: *ʾehyeh ʾăšer ʾehyeh*. What this means may be derived from what follows. In the second answer Moses is to say to the sons of Israel: "*ʾehyeh* has sent me to you," and in the third: "YHWH, the Elohim of your fathers, the Elohim of Abraham...has sent me to you; that is my name forever, thus I am to be called upon from generation to generation." The name is thus YHWH. Parallel to the third answer, the second has *ʾehyeh*, in the

---

[8] Though Moses' first question (v. 11) is a turning point in the story, vv. 7–12 belong too much together to see v. 11 already as the beginning of a new part.

same place in the sentence as YHWH in the third answer; the word is indicated as subject and named: it functions here as a name. However, at the same time *ehyeh* refers to v. 12 in which YHWH in the construction *kî-*ehyeh* had another function. In Elohim's first answer, these two functions are juxtaposed with the word *ʾăšer*, which interprets the name *ehyeh*, between them[9]: *ehyeh*, that is, "I am present." This word is therefore indeed a real answer to the question about the name.

In the third answer, the name of YHWH is paired with the notion "I am present," "I am with you." The reader may suspect, where in this connection we read as a parallel to YHWH: "the Elohim of your fathers, the Elohim of Abraham, of Isaac, and of Jacob," that in this story the "I am present," might refer to Abraham-Isaac-Jacob. With "forever" and "from generation to generation" the reader knows that for the descendants also "I am present," "I am with you" is valid.

Thus the name of YHWH is revealed: hypothetically in the answer that Moses would have to give to the sons of Israel, and therefore to Moses himself. Moreover the significance of the name has been given again hypothetically to the sons of Israel and thereby to Moses, and moreover to the reader of this story, who admittedly already knew the name YHWH, but to whom the meaning of the name had not yet been explained in this manner.

If the sons of Israel appeared as possible partners in conversation in a dialogue between Elohim and Moses, in part IV (vv. 16–17) the elders of Israel who are to be approached and informed by Moses by order of Elohim, as follows: to me (Moses) YHWH the Elohim of your fathers has appeared, the Elohim of Abraham, Isaac, and Jacob, and (in his own words) why this happened: because of the distress (summarized from the information in v. 7) and because of the notice that I (YHWH Elohim) "will cause you to go up…" (variant of v. 8). In this sequence the emphasis also falls on the deeds of YHWH Elohim.

In part V (vv. 18–22) the elders of Israel, "when they hear your voice," are given a second role in the commission of YHWH Elohim to Moses. Together they must go with Moses to the king of Egypt (variant of Pharaoh, vv. 10 and 11) and say to him: YHWH the Elohim of the

---

9   For a discussion of the usage of *ʾăšer*, See Paul Joüon, S. J., *Grammaire de l'hébreu biblique* (3d ed.; Rome: Institut Biblique Pontifical, 1965) §§ 158–59, and L. Koehler & W. Baumgartner, *Hebräisches und aramäisches Lexikon zum alten Testament* (3d ed.; Leiden: Brill, 1967–). K. Marti, *Geschichte der Israelitischen Religion* (5th ed.; Strassburg: Bull, 1907) suggests the translation of *ehyeh*: "ich bin," with the explanation: "der Seiende" (72).

Hebrews (variant of the fathers) has appeared (variant of "let himself see," v. 2) to us and to ask permission "to go" on a journey of three days in the desert (v. 1) and bring sacrifices "to YHWH our Elohim." The word "to go" is expanded in vv. 19–22, particularly in vv. 19 and 20 with the refusal "to let go," the result of which is striking with a miraculous sign and in vv. 21 and 22 with the word "not go empty."

The last two parts show agreement with the first two parts, which speak of letting himself see, respectively, the appearing of YHWH Elohim, referring to the first sequence (vv. 2–6), while the combination of the second half of both parts (resp. v. 17 and the conclusion of v. 18) reminds one of the conclusion of v. 12: "when you lead the people out of Egypt, you will serve Elohim on this mountain," whereby "you lead out" is "I will cause to go up," "serve": "to bring sacrifices"[10] and "this mountain": "the desert" (see v. 1).

Now that the story has been opened up, the data has been uncovered in their differentiated presentation, elaboration, and coherence; in short, an analysis has been made. The question concerning composition follows. Because vv. 19–22 (as we saw, elaborations of "going") may be regarded as an extension, we limit our investigation of the composition to vv. 1–18.

We have already seen that we need to read on two levels. The reader does not only make direct observations but also learns from the words and observations of the actors. At a certain point in the story Moses asks questions in reaction to YHWH Elohim's words to him; but at the same time the reader is confronted with information which demands elaboration, and in this sense one might say that there are questions:

1. After YHWH's announcement in v. 6: Is Moses also told that Elohim is named YHWH and how does that happen?
2. After v. 12: Does ʾehyeh have anything to do with YHWH?
3. After v. 10: What is Moses to do with Pharaoh?
4. How is Moses to lead the sons of Israel out of Egypt?

Each one of these questions is answered in the progress of the story, the direction of which is determined by Moses' questions and the answers to them.

Moses' first question is not so much related to the execution of his orders, but points to itself: who am I…. The answer is: kî-ʾehyeh with you,

---

[10] In the following chapters of Exodus, "serving" is used alternately with "sacrificing"; see Exod 8:21–23 and 9:1.

and: the sign that I send you is: when you lead the people out of Egypt, you will serve Elohim on this mountain. Both answers lead away from Moses to the one who sends and thereby give a partial answer to the reader's fourth question.

Moses' second question, concerning the name, causes a new turn in the story: the sons of Israel, the object of deliverance, become the object of approach (when I come to the sons of Israel…) and of mission (…has sent me to you), so that the Pharaoh disappears from sight for the time being. Using the answer to Moses' first question, the answer also reveals the significance of the name, and at the same time answers the reader's first and second questions. Thus the name which in v. 6 had to remain incomplete, may now be pronounced completely: YHWH the Elohim of….

After v. 15 the question concerning the commandment (the reader's third and fourth questions) demands elaboration. We remember that this command: go…lead out… closed the declaration of YHWH (vv. 7–10) of why he showed himself to Moses and in which the "distress" in the first phase concluded with an act of YHWH himself: to make (the people) go up out of …. to…. Again Elohim commands Moses to go to the Pharaoh; however, in preparation, as representative of the sons of Israel, he must first approach the elders of Israel and inform them of the fact that YHWH, the Elohim…has shown himself to them, with his declaration concerning the "distress," and the pronouncement to make "you" go up out of…to….

Now there appears what Moses must do with Pharaoh: declare the appearance of YHWH the Elohim of the Hebrews "to us," and consequently to pronounce the wish flowing from that "to go" on a three day journey in the desert and to sacrifice "to YHWH our Elohim." Thus can happen the reason that YHWH has let himself be seen at the holy place: to go up from the oppression of Egypt…to a land, flowing of milk and honey and as YHWH Elohim said to Moses: thus it will happen: when you lead the people out of Egypt, you will serve Elohim on this mountain—that is the sign that I am the one who sends you.

The manner by which the story is composed is to be found by investigating which information, introduced in the first part of the story, needed to be further elaborated. The turning point is Moses' first question, which provided both "ᵓehyeh with you" and the indication that there was a connection between serving Elohim at the holy place and the leading out of Egypt. This connection—the sign that YHWH Elohim is the one who sends Moses—is underlined at the conclusion: in the combination of the information that Moses is to share with the elders of Israel and, together with them, to the king of Egypt. The appearance of YHWH Elohim (on account of the distress, to make the people go up from the oppression of Egypt to a land…flowing with milk and honey) has to lead to a "going" in the desert, to sacrifice "to YHWH our Elohim." The double command to Moses served that purpose:

> Now go,
> I send you to Pharaoh.
> Lead my people out, the sons of Israel, out of Egypt.

Not all questions which this story elicits can be answered here. For much of the information, contextual reading is necessary. One such item is the *sĕneh*. It is the place of an appearance of fire. This, together with the frequent repetition of the word, might lead one to suspect that this word for "a bush" is not chosen arbitrarily.[11] Whatever conclusions may be drawn, the question concerning the relationship between Deuteronomy 33 and Exodus 3 is decisive. If one supposes that "the one inhabiting the *sĕneh*" was a familiar epithet for YHWH Elohim (Deut 33:16), then the author of Exodus 3 may have chosen the word *sĕneh* in view of that; in that case there would be no connection between *sĕneh* and Sinai.[12] If one judges it possible that the poetic expression in Deut 33:16 refers to Exodus 12, then the word *sĕneh* may have been chosen because it points to Sinai. *Sĕneh* is reminiscent of Sinai. Regardless, *sĕneh* indicates the place where YHWH appears to Moses, the place where he wished to be served.

The story of Exodus 3 was written for the sons of Israel, to declare to them that invoking the name of YHWH means that "our Elohim" is one who is, who is with them, and that serving him means: to be led out of oppression to a good and broad land, a land, flowing with milk and honey.

---

[11] M. A. Beek, "Der Dornbusch als Wohnsitz Gottes (Deut. XXXIII,16)," *OTS* 14 (1965) 155–61.

[12] Not only to Exodus 3, but all of Exodus; see also Exod 24:16–18. A possible connection with YHWH's living on (Mount) Zion (see passages like Isa 8:18; Joel 4:17, 21; Ps 74:12) is beyond the scope of this paper.

—∽ **10** ∾—

JOSHUA THE SAVIOR[*]

M. A. Beek

ABSTRACT

In a systematic inquiry into the name of Joshua bin Nun and the part he plays in the book of Joshua, all texts following the beginning of Judges that contain his name have been subjected to exegetical research. Neh 8:14–18, 1 Kgs 16:34 and 1 Chron 7:20–27, by their mutual reference to themes like the Feast of Tabernacles, Passover, Jericho, and the crossing of the Jordan, justify the conclusion that the figure of Joshua was meant to express the ideal savior. The book of Joshua was hereby not only given the function of bridging the gap between Torah and Former Prophets, but it could also prepare the hearers for the history of salvation that was introduced anew in the book of Judges. Literary criticism leads to the conclusion that the book of Judges originated in a period during which the scriptures were rearranged according to new principles. One may consider the time after the Babylonian exile as such a period. It was Joshua, the ideal savior, who assembled *all* the people in *one* country around *one* Torah.

In addition to the Hexateuch and the beginning of the book of Judges, the name of Joshua bin Nun only occurs in Neh 8:14–18, 1 Kgs 16:34 and 1 Chron 7:20–27. The exegesis of the texts cited is important not

---

[*] Translated from: "Josua und Retterideal," *Near Eastern Studies in Honor of William Foxwell Albright*, ed. Hans Goedicke (Baltimore: Johns Hopkins Press, 1971) 35–42.

only for the study of the Book of Joshua but also to determine the role this book plays in Israel's salvation history. Where possible, the exegesis of these texts should be done in a manner by which they will illumine one another.

I

Neh 8:14–18 offers a lively description of the Feast of Booths. This feast was celebrated after instructions as to its date (the seventh month) and rituals were found in the Torah. The text undoubtedly speaks of Joshua bin Nun, though he is notably named here Jeshua. It has been proposed to drop "bin Nun" in order that we might identify this Joshua with Joshua the high priest (a contemporary of Zerubbabel). This proposal is not convincing, however.

The text says emphatically that the Feast of Booths had not been celebrated thus since the days of Joshua bin Nun, "to this day," i.e., the day on which Ezra read from the book of the Torah. These prescriptions were found in the Torah that YHWH had given through Moses. As represented in the Book of Nehemiah, these prescriptions go back to Moses, and the correct celebration of the Feast of Booths had only begun in the days of Joshua. It was not celebrated in this manner any longer thereafter till Ezra read the book of the Torah of Moses in the seventh month on the square before the Water Gate. One might ask therefore whether there was anything comparable to the celebration described in the book of Nehemiah in the days of Joshua or the period shortly thereafter.

The summary of the rituals according to Neh 8:15 does not give a satisfactory answer. The material for the construction of the booths had to be obtained in the hill country. The words used agree in content with Lev 23:40. They emphasize joy as the hallmark of this festival. The author of the book of Nehemiah did not feel obligated to give us a verbatim account of the familiar law of the Torah. This difference, however, does not give us a solution to the problem.

Nor do the other texts relating to the Feast of Booths explain why the festival, after the appearance of Ezra, would have been different from what was customary in the days of Joshua (see Deut 16:13–17; Exod 23:16; 34:22; Num 29:13–34). If the differences and deviations do not lie, therefore, in the rituals concerning which Nehemiah gives scant information, it seems useful to attend to the circumstances in which the festival was celebrated.

As to those circumstances, Neh 8:17 reports that the festival was celebrated by the *entire* congregation of those who had returned from exile. The word "entire" receives much emphasis in Nehemiah 8; *kol-hāᶜām* is mentioned eleven times, besides *běkol- ᶜārêhem* and *kol-qāhāl*.

The word *kōl* is also a motif word in the Book of Joshua. Joshua stresses that an "entire" people is ushered into the only land that yhwh had promised and then granted them (1:2). According to Josh 24:1 Joshua gathers *kol-šibṭê yiśrāʾēl*, "*all* the tribes of Israel," and he speaks *ᶜal-kol-hāᶜām*, "to the *entire* people" (24:2). He does the same once more when the large stone is erected (24:27). In the same manner Nehemiah 8 speaks of an *entire* people that has returned as a single congregation from exile.

The same people were gathered by Joshua around the Torah which Moses had commanded and which had been written in a book (1:3,8; 8:31,32,34; 23:6 and 24:26). Precisely the same expressions with the same nuances occur in Neh 8:1, 2, 3, 7, 8, 9, 13, 14, and 18. Both Nehemiah 8 and Joshua speak of an *entire* people that has returned from exile and is committing itself to obedience to the book of the Torah of Moses or God.

While the parallelism of Joshua and the entry into the land on the one hand and the appearance of Nehemiah on the other hand is obvious, it remains unclear why Joshua is named in Nehemiah 8 in connection with the Feast of Booths. The word *sūkkôt* does not occur in the book of Joshua and, with the exception of Nehemiah 8, no hint is given of a connection between Joshua and this festival. The Book of Joshua has an account of a Passover that was celebrated after completing the circumcision near Gilgal *běᶜarbôt yěrīḥô* (5:10). Obviously Passover has precisely here obtained a significant place. The circumcision followed the crossing of the Jordan and this crossing is described as a repetition of the crossing of the Sea of Reeds. When the ark was carried through the Jordan, the waters of the Jordan were "cut off" (4:7).

2 Kgs 23:21ff. offers a text that is stylistically related to Neh 8:18. Josiah commanded that the Passover be celebrated again. The king had commanded that *kol hāᶜām* act in accordance with the prescriptions in the Book of the Covenant. The feast had not been celebrated in this manner since the days of the judges. If we assume that the restoration of Passover must be viewed in the context of Josiah's reform, as an event which is centralized in Jerusalem, then the expression "since the days of the judges" is unintelligible, for only in the days of David had Jerusalem become a political and religious center.

This difficulty may also be observed in Nehemiah 8. In the description of Nehemiah 8, the festival in Jerusalem is emphasized above all: the booths are built in the courts of the temple, on the square before the Water Gate and on the square of the Gate of Ephraim. But neither could

Israel celebrate its Passover in Jerusalem in the days of Joshua. 2 Chron 30:26 reports that in Hezekiah's days a Passover festival was celebrated such as had not been done since Solomon. This text, however, does not give us the same problem as do Nehemiah 8 and 2 Chronicles 23.

The problem can be solved only if we note the historicized significance of the Feast of Booths. The Feast of Booths may then be seen as a second Feast of Passover in the autumn.

According to Lev 23:42–43 *kol-hā^ʾezraḥ bĕyiśrā^ʾēl* is obligated to reside in booths, as it is explained: "…that your generations may know that I made the people of Israel dwell in booths when I brought them out of Egypt." But that is not correct either because nomads are accustomed to live in tents and not in booths. The commentator did not care to point to visible booths but to the invisible protection of God of which the booth is the symbol, as the psalm poet sings: "…thou holdest them safe under thy shelter (booth) from the strife of tongues" (Ps 31:21b; see Isa 4:6a).

The conclusion of the book of Jonah stresses the relative worth of a booth that a man has built. God had grown a miraculous tree which was better than the booth that Jonah built. After the miraculous tree withered, the booth no longer played a role. The silent *ḥamsīn* stung the head of Jonah and, in spite of his booth, the prophet longed for death.

According to the historicizing interpretation, the Feast of Booths is a recollection of divine protection that Israel experienced during the exodus and the passing through the wilderness. The Feast of the Gathering (Exod 23:16 and 34:22) was celebrated after the olive and grape harvest; that festival borrowed its ritual from the annually returning nature festival. But this ritual could only be celebrated as a second Passover, after the *entire* people was living in the promised land. In a second phase the rituals were moved from the land to the city of Jerusalem, where it had not originally belonged. Both festivals, Booths and Passover, are called *ḥag-yhwh*. Appealing to such a feast, Moses asked the Pharaoh for permission to leave (Exod 10:9). Judg 21:19 mentions a festival in the autumn in which girls dance rounds in the vineyards and the text calls it a *ḥag-yhwh*. Hos 9:5 uses the same expression of an autumn festival, which can only be identified as the Feast of Booths; Lev 23:41 emphasizes it with the words *wĕḥaggōtem ^ʾōtô ḥag layhwh*. According to the biblical writer, both festivals obtained their essential significance and form after the *entire* people was brought into the land under the protection of the one God.

II

The second text that requires our attention is 1 Kgs 16:34. These words conclude some reports concerning the appearance of Ahab and introduce the Elijah and Elisha narratives in so far as they occur in Jericho (2 Kgs 2:4ff; 19–22). 1 Kgs 16:34 functions in a manner comparable to 1 Kgs 16:25, which contains the report of Samaria's founding by Omri. In Samaria, too, important events in which Elijah and Elisha played their great roles are subsequently localized (1 Kgs 20:22; 2 Kgs 2:25; 6:24–7:20).

The question of whether 1 Kgs 16:34 goes back to the curse of Jericho by Joshua (Jos 6:26) or vice versa, can hardly be answered. Noth characterized 1 Kgs 16:34 as an original datum. The text of Joshua would then have to be regarded as an addition based on historical or legendary narratives concerning Hiel and his two sons Abiram and Segub. We can only say with certainty that the narrator of the Elijah and Elisha cycles has connected the name of Joshua bin Nun with the curse of Jericho. This curse was supposed to have been fulfilled in a catastrophic event in which the sons of Hiel perished, or, as was formerly thought, were offered as a building sacrifice.

What role did Jericho play in the salvation history of Israel? In view of very limited information the answer can be simple. With the exception of Joshua and 2 Kings 2, Jericho is no more than a geographical point of contact. Thus the expression *bĕ'arbôt mô'āb mē'ēber lĕyardēn yĕrīḥô* occurs eight times in Numbers (see also Jer 39:5 = 52:8; 2 Sam 10:5 = 1 Chron 19:5). Ezra 2:34 = Neh 7:36 mentions men of Jericho who had assisted in the rebuilding of Jerusalem. In 2 Kings 2 Jericho becomes more important as domicile of the sons of the prophets. Moreover, the city of Jericho is near the Jordan. In this river the miraculous crossing is repeated: the mantle of Elijah was the means enabling Elisha to cross the Jordan dryshod.

In the Book of Joshua Jericho is mentioned 27 times, mainly in connection with the conquest of the city. The story of the miraculous collapse of the city walls has distracted many exegetes from the essence of the proclamation. Abel[1] appropriately has pointed out that the story of the conquest of Jericho was intended as an illustration of Israel's concept of the "ban." In connection with the *ḥērem*, three groups may be distinguished: the families of Rahab and of Achan, and the Gibeonites.

---

[1] F.-M. Abel, "L'Anathème de Jéricho et la maison de Rahab," *RB* 64 (1957) 321–330. C. H. W. Brekelmans, *De Herem in het Oude Testament* (Nijmegen: Centrale Drukkerij, 1959) emphasizes the theological significance of the *ḥērem*.

Rahab may be compared with Abigail. Just as Abigail foresaw the kingship of David and made her decision in anticipation of it, so Rahab saw the victory of the people of God and acted accordingly. The family of Rahab escaped the ban even though she did not belong to Israel. Achan violated banned goods and perished with his family even though he was an Israelite. The Gibeonites withdrew themselves from the ban by stealth and thus landed in a dependent position.

In the narrative of the conquest of Jericho, the city is to be regarded as a *pars pro toto*. To scout Jericho means scouting the land, to conquer the city means conquering the entire land.

The mysterious pericope Josh 5:13–15 must be explained in the same manner. In a dream vision Joshua found himself in Jericho, where he saw opposite him a man with a drawn sword, who introduced himself as *śar-ṣĕbāʾ yhwh*, "an officer of YHWH's army." He commanded that Joshua take off his shoes because the ground on which he was standing was holy. The intermezzo ends when Joshua did as he was told. To tell more would have been superfluous. The territory of Jericho is sacred; it belongs to the people of YHWH. Very soon even Rahab's family must live outside the camp (Josh 6:23).

1 Kgs 16:34 anticipates the Elijah-Elisha cycle and connects these tales in a meaningful way with Joshua bin Nun and with the city of Jericho in the vicinity of the Jordan.

The manna stopped raining from the sky. Unleavened cakes were baked from the harvest of the land; thus the way was paved for the Feast of Booths.

The name of Joshua was included in the genealogies of 1 Chronicles 7. According to 7:20–27 he is a descendant of Ephraim in the fourteenth generation. Appropriately the *ICC* comments: "This is the only record of Joshua's line of descent, and its late and artificial character reveals itself at once."

Rudolph expresses the same embarrassment in his commentary,[2] when he speaks about "the glueing together of two separate genealogies" to produce an ideal genealogy. The genealogy relates striking things about Ephraim, whose sons Ezer and Elead were killed by men from Gath, and about a certain Beriah and a daughter Sheerah. But about Joshua and his father Nun, nothing was apparently worth mentioning. It cannot even be said that the content of the Book of Joshua was presupposed to be familiar.

---

[2] W. Rudolph, *Chronikbücher* (HAT 21; Tübingen: Mohr, 1955).

III

In the books of Ezra, Nehemiah, Haggai, and Zechariah, Joshua occurs 21 times as a proper name and in the short form *yšwᶜ* another 20 times. 1 Sam 6:14 and 18 mention a man from Beth Shemesh, and 2 Kgs 23:8 a *śar hāᶜîr* who bears this name. The name *hôšēaᶜ*, which according to Num 13:8,16 and Deut 32:44 was a second name of Joshua, is also the name of the last king of the Northern Kingdom (2 Kings 15–18) as well as the name of a prophet who around the middle of the eighth century preached in the Northern Kingdom. Though the name is related to the verb *yšᶜ*, "to save," it is never expressly said that a deeper connection was suspected between Joshua and "salvation." There is an exception; in Sir 46:1 it is said of Ιεσους Ναυη: "who was, in accordance with his name, great in the salvation of his elect." The Hebrew text reads here *bĕyāmāyw* instead of the more obvious *kišmô*, yet the Hebrew text has made the Greek translation possible where it says that *yĕhôšûaᶜ* has brought *tĕšûᶜāh*.

Yet it remains possible that a certain Joshua, son of a father with a unique and mysterious name (Nun = fish?), has because of that name received the characteristic function which he assumes in the salvation history of Israel. It is indeed striking that the *hiphil* of *yšᶜ* occurs so frequently in the book of Judges. This motif word is given is 12:18a: YHWH raises up a judge. He is with the judge and saves his people from the hand of its enemies all the days of the judges.

Again and again YHWH raises up a judge: Othniel (3:9), Shamgar (3:31), Gideon (6:14, 15, 36, 37; 7:2, 7; 8:22), Tolah (10:1). About Samson it says *wĕhûʾ yāḥēl lĕhôšîaᶜ ʾet-yiśrāʾēl miyyad pĕlištîm*. YHWH himself acts as a *môšîaᶜ* (10:12f.).

Sawyer recently subjected the meaning of *môšîaᶜ* to a thorough investigation; his conclusion was that "there was a place in ancient Israel for an advocate or a witness for the defence and also a witness for the prosecution."[3] He believes that we can assume a "forensic root" for the stem *yšᶜ* and suggests a development "from a definite office within a definite sphere of life, and from there to a title of God in any general context." His arguments are convincing when he appeals to passages like Deut 22:27; 1 Sam 25:26, 31, 33; 2 Sam 17:4; and 2 Kgs 6:26. Also, his thesis, that "the meaning of advocate or witness for the defence fits well and adds something to the passage" has its exegetical value for the background of Isa 43:3,11 and 45:2–4. However, his other thesis that "there are no other

---

3 J. Sawyer, "What was a *môšîaᶜ*?" *VT* 15 (1965) 475–86.

cases in the *OT* where a forensic meaning is impossible," is contradicted by the exegesis of relevant passages in the Book of Judges.

In the Book of Judges, the word *môšîaᶜ* has a theological significance. The judges saved Israel, but they were only able to do so with the help of YHWH. This is expressed most clearly in the story of Gideon, where Israel must not be able to say: *yādî hôšîᶜāh lî* (Judg 7:2). An application of this fundamental confession may be found in 1 Sam 14:6, 23, 39 and 17:47.

Thus, in the Book of Joshua the name of the leading figure is a program that bridges the gap between the Torah and the book of Judges. The name of Joshua proclaims that salvation may only be expected by the power of YHWH, and Joshua acts in consonance with his name. Initiatives come always from YHWH, and Joshua is the model of obedience. He carries out commands or fulfills divine commissions (Josh 1:1ff; 3:7; 4:1b, 15–17; 5:2, 9, 14–16; 6:2–6; 7:10–15; 8:1–3, 18; 9:14; 10:8; 11:6; 13:1b; 20:1; 24:2). When he is obedient, his undertakings are successful; when he refrains from consulting YHWH in a difficult situation, failure results. This is illustrated with the successful ruse of the Gibeonites. The author of the Book of Joshua provides a picture of the true savior, and in doing so the function of the book is given. It not only bridges a gap but also prepares for a narrative of salvation history that makes a new beginning with the Book of Judges.

Questions concerning historicity, historical background, or the relations between aetiological tales and historicity, we may leave aside as we attempt to determine how the image of Joshua functions in salvation history.[4] Eissfeldt says that the stories surrounding Joshua are "largely *sagenhaftiger Art* which can only be evaluated historically by careful, critical investigation." Yet he drops phrases like "dependable memories," "historical figures," and "statements which are at least fundamentally historical."[5] In doing so he must allude to the kind of investigation in

---

[4] G. E. Mendenhall, "The Hebrew Conquest of Palestine," *BA* 25 (1962) 66–87, has justifiably questioned the traditional representation of the conquest and convincingly defended the thesis: "In summary, there was no real conquest of Palestine at all; what happened instead may be termed, from the point of view of the secular historian interested only in socio-political process, a peasants' revolt against the network of interlocking Canaanite city states." See also M. Weippert, *Die Landnahme der israelitischen Stämme in der neueren wissenschaftlichen Diskussion. Ein kritischer Bericht* (FRLANT 92; Göttingen: Vandenhoeck & Ruprecht, 1967).

[5] O. Eissfeldt, "Israels Führer in der Zeit vom Auszug bis zur Landnahme," *Studia Biblica et Semitica Theodoro Christiano Vriezen… dedicata* (Th. C. Vriezen Festschrift; ed. W. C. van Unnik et al.; Wageningen: Veenman, 1966) 62–70.

which intuition rather than facts have paved the way, while archeological material cannot furnish convincing proofs.

Segal has concluded that the Book of Joshua was never an integral part of the Pentateuch.[6] In this he is correct; yet there is reason to speak of the Hexateuch. The names of Moses and Joshua, which outside of the Hexateuch occur only sporadically, are themselves a plea for the literary unity of the Hexateuch. With the redacting of Joshua, a new beginning was made, and the book was assigned to the Former Prophets. It is likely that the Torah in its first draft was already finished before the Book of Joshua was composed. Segal thought he could locate its origin in a period of political stability and prosperity, such as the one during the reign of the Omrides in the Northern Kingdom.

What we have found, points to a late origin in a period in which the literature was ordered in relation to a new beginning.[7] At that time, after the exile, when the time was ripe for a model of the ideal *môšíaᶜ*, projected in the person of Joshua, this idea developed. He was the one who gathered the entire people in one land around one Torah, which he was able to do with the help of YHWH and in obedience to him.

---

[6] M. Segal, "YHWH and Elohim in the Book of Joshua," *The Pentateuch. Its Authorship and Composition and Other Biblical Studies* (Jerusalem: Magnes, 1967) 117–19.

[7] J. G. Vink, "The Date and Origin of the Priestly Code in the Old Testament," *OTS* 15 (1969) 63–80 has correctly seen the connection between the text of Joshua and the actions of Ezra and Nehemiah. As to Josh 8:30–35, he arrives at a late date via a source-critical method.

— 11 —

DAVID AND ABSALOM*
A HEBREW TRAGEDY IN PROSE?

M. A. Beek

ABSTRACT

Though some superb examples of Old Testament writing have been drama-
tized, we have no evidence that any plays were ever performed in ancient
Israel. The story of David and Absalom is not an eyewitness report. The
historical framing, set in David's court, suggests various lines of opposition
to the king, which eventually coalesced in Absalom. The tragic tale begins
with Amnon, son of David, raping Absalom's sister Tamar, who then lived
alone, violated. David ignored the episode, but Absalom revenged his sister
by killing Amnon. Soon after Absalom was recalled through Joab's efforts,
he prepared cunningly for his rebellion: "he stole the heart of all the men of
Israel."

   During the rebellion, the drama heightens with the contest between two
reputable royal counselors, Hushai and Ahithophel. David's prayer that
Ahithophel's counsel be frustrated is heard: Absalom accepts Hushai's ut-
terly senseless scenario—the turning point in the story. In the battle between
the armies of David and Absalom, Joab kills David's rebellious son. In
David's reaction to Absalom's death, protecting his son seemed more
important to him than protecting his throne. David surrenders to his grief. If

---

*   This lecture was presented on the occasion of the 340th anniversary (*dies natalis*)
of the University of Amsterdam, on January 10, 1972.

this is not a tragedy, the fate of the *dramatis personae* is tragic. Crime and punishment are clearly linked, there are no accidental circumstances. The king bore his burden of guilt, repentance and suffering. The author wrote well, but he wrote to be heard, not to be praised.

Old Testament stories have furnished rich material for dramatization and ample use has been made of that fact. Some stories may be made into tragedies, although a tragic feeling of life is strange to the Old Testament.[1] We do not have a single report from which we might be able to conclude that a play, comparable to Greek tragedy was performed in ancient Israel. There are no references to a dramatization of narrative, e.g., within the framework of the temple liturgy. Authors whose names have remained unfamiliar created stories, which may without exaggeration be counted among the high marks of ancient Oriental literature. The stories were not told gratuitously; they have their own message, which is best understood through literary analysis. They have their typical function within the framework of Israel's history, which concluded with the humiliation of Jerusalem and the deportation into Babylonian exile. Such a story, of which the content could effortlessly be made into a tragedy, is that of king David and his son Absalom.

I emphasize at the outset that we are dealing with a narrative and not with an eyewitness report, though such a suggestion has been raised.[2] The narrator has observed his fellow humans both gently and realistically. They are possessed by uncontrollable passions, driven by a desire for lust and power. Destroying others, they destroyed themselves and were finally delivered to an infamous death. No illusions are aroused concerning the nobility of humanity. Everyone, king David included, has horrible potentialities and uses them. The dramatic personages are not heroes; they act, with a single exception, in their weakness. No miracle

---

[1] Th. C. Vriezen, *De overwinning van het tragisch levensgevoel in Israel. Kernmomenten der antieke beschaving en haar moderne beleving* [The Conquest of the Tragic Sense of Life in Israel. Highlights of Ancient Civilization and Its Modern Experience] (Leiden: Brill, 1947) 33–48.

[2] Influenced by an article written by Th. C. Vriezen, " De Compositie van de Samuel-boeken," *Orientalia Neerlandica* (Leiden: Brill, 1948) 167–89, the present author thought for a long time that we are dealing in 2 Samuel at least with a report from close circles, if not with the report of an eyewitness (Vriezen thought of Zabud, the son of Nathan). Observing the literary shape made me conclude otherwise. I have no opinion concerning the dating of the author; I do not consider an exilic date impossible.

occurs, no God acts noticeably, the events apparently take their fateful course within human possibilities.

There is a historical setting by which we are placed in the court of King David in Jerusalem. The progenitor of the Messiah had overcome resistance and provoked resistance. The family of the rejected King Saul still had its supporters and might speculate on increasing discontent. It is clear that the still novel experiment with the monarchy in Israel has disturbed the harmony of an agrarian society. The army, but particularly the bureaucratic apparatus, created unforeseen differences between poor and rich.3 Between the lines of the eulogy on David's fame we also read of activities undermining authority by the so-called "men of Belial."4 Brief reports in between the stories explain how with seeming surprise a rebellious movement could spread and chase David temporarily out of Jerusalem. The leader of the movement was Absalom, son of the king and pretender to the throne. He wanted to take advantage of the situation and push his father from the throne. The attack failed, the father triumphed, and the son was killed. This is the historical background of the David-Absalom drama.

Quite consciously has the narrator made Absalom, the son of David, the principal character of a narrative which includes 2 Samuel 13–19. Thus, the beginning reads: "Absalom, the son of David, had a beautiful sister, named Tamar, and Amnon, the son of David, was in love with her" (13:1). With that the reader or hearer is prepared for a series of disastrous, fatal events. Amnon is sick with desire and his half sister Tamar is inaccessible to him. A clever plan, devised by cousin Jonadab, plays the unsuspecting maiden into the hands of Amnon. Amnon violates his half-sister. It is typical of the stylistic technique of the narrator to recall the deed in a few verbs: "he overpowered her, he humbled her, he lay with her" (13:14).

After Amnon has surrendered to his burst of lust, he is disgusted with the woman whom he has deflowered. The text says: "Then Amnon hated her a very great hatred; greater was the hatred with which he hated her, than the desire with which he had desired her." He has a man-servant throw her on to the street and bolt the door behind her. Tamar

---

3 A. Alt, "Der Anteil des Königtums an der sozialen Entwicklung in den Reichen Israel und Juda," *Kleine Schriften zur Geschichte des Volkes Israel* (Munich: Beck, 1959) 3: 348–72 has dealt with this in great detail.

4 See, e.g., 2 Samuel 20, the rebellion of Sheba, a prelude to the defection of the ten Northern tribes. See G. Fohrer, "Der Vertrag zwischen König und Volk in Israel," *ZAW* 71 (1959) 1–22.

said plenty in protest but the words of Amnon were limited to two short commands: "Come, lie with me"—"arise, be gone." The narrator does not add disapproving commentary; his sober report of facts suffices. He lets Tamar go away crying, with her ornate dress torn. She takes up residence in the house of her full brother Absalom and lives as a lonely, violated person. We learn nothing further of her. Father David heard about the matter, became angry, and did nothing. Absalom came to dislike Amnon but hid his feelings. He awaited his turn; meanwhile the first steps had been taken on the road which inevitably led to Amnon's and Absalom's destruction. One evil elicits another.

After two years, during a sheep shearing festival, Amnon was murdered by the servants of Absalom. Absalom had cunningly prepared the fatal attack, he bore the responsibility, which he also openly assumed. One might question the reason that the narrator lets the brother of the dishonored Tamar act instead of her father. Hoftijzer, in a valuable article, has demonstrated that a fratriarchal motif is brought into play to make both the passivity of David and the activism of Absalom acceptable.[5] Absalom was the brother who was expected to avenge his sister, so he had to control himself. David did not need to hide his anger, for he was not expected to do anything. Indeed, this so-called fratriarchal behavior is also attested in the Book of Genesis, where the sons of Jacob revenged the shame done to their sister Dinah on the Shechemites, while father Jacob shook his head, pondering the results.

Shortly after the murder of Amnon a rumor circulated in Jerusalem that Absalom had killed all of David's sons. The shrewd Jonadab knew how to quiet the shocked king: he understood the situation, he had seen it coming, it could be read on Absalom's face. This was Jonadab's last activity for he, too, disappeared from the scene. Of the five *dramatis personae*, two remained: father and son, and all attention is concentrated on their relationship.

---

5 J. Hoftijzer, "Absalom and Tamar: A Case of Fratriarchy?" in *Schrift en Uitleg. Studies aangeboden aan W. H. Gispen* [Scripture and Interpretation. Studies Offered to W. H. Gispen;] (Kampen: Kok, 1970) 54–61. In my opinion the history which is told in Genesis 34 was formative for this segment of the Absalom story. That the narrator let David watch idly is no proof that he knew fratriarchy in the sense of Hoftijzer and C. H. Gordon, "Fratriarchy in the Old Testament," *JBL* 54 (1935) 223–31. In any case, the institution of fratriarchy did not leave Absalom unpunished, for he needed to seek asylum abroad. One also gains the impression that the narrator wanted to portray David as a man who was weak in judging his sons, which caused grief.

David mourned, and the narrator purposely leaves it to his listeners to discern for whom he mourned. He mourned for his son, but which son? Amnon, who was murdered, or Absalom who fled abroad? Three years later, Joab, the army commander concluded that David had comforted himself over Amnon but was weighed down by Absalom's absence. David was a father but also a judge; justice forbade him to accept the murderer in mercy. Joab sought a way to help his king out of the impasse and engaged the wise woman of Tekoa. The narrator takes a certain pleasure in confronting Joab the broadsword with a wise woman who accomplished through good counsel what the violence of weapons could not.[6]

The wise woman played before the king the role of a widow with two sons. They had fought, one was killed, the other had fled, and the family demanded blood vengeance. The widow made an appeal to the king to intervene, for, she said, "they want to extinguish the glowing coal which remains to me."[7] The king promised to take the murderer under his protection, he enforced his promise with an oath and thereby created a precedent in casuistic jurisprudence, characteristic for ancient Oriental justice. Thus far the wise woman of Tekoa had played the game that Joab had prompted and staged. Then, suddenly she uttered an admonition beyond Joab and the king. She said: "Why do you then harbor such thoughts against the people of God? For since the king has spoken this word, he has become guilty himself, since the king has not allowed to return the one he has banished. We must all die and we are like water spilt on the ground, which cannot be gathered up again. But God will not take away life, but seeks ways that one who is banished does not remain disowned by him."

She then returned to her role of a poor widow, a slave who had made bold to speak to the king.[8] "For the king is an angel of God in hearing good and evil." Then David saw through the matter: Joab must be involved in this! Indeed, "my lord is an angel of God, he is wise, and aware of everything going on in the land."

Joab got his way, and David got what he wanted: Absalom was allowed to return to Jerusalem; he was not permitted to appear at court,

---

6 See 2 Sam 20:16–22, the wise woman of Abel of Beth-maacah.

7 J. Hoftijzer, "David and the Tekoite woman," *VT* 20 (1970) 419–44. He correctly stresses the intention of the wise woman: to confront David with the consequences of his sentence, also for his people.

8 M. Buber, "Weisheit und Tat der Frauen", in *Kampf um Israel. Reden und Schriften, 1921–1932* (Berlin: Schocken, 1933) 107–14.

but he needed fear no punishment. In another two years he managed to force his return to the palace. The text says:

> The king called Absalom,
> he came to the king,
> he bowed with his face to the ground before the king,
> the king kissed Absalom (14:33).

This scene was painted by Rembrandt in 1642 with motifs reminiscent of the return of the Prodigal Son, yet also as an expression of "a complicated moment of reconciliation."[9]

To the listener it has become clear that this is not the end of the story. Absalom's aspirations reached further. He could make use of his charm. He is described as a handsome man with a flawless body. The hair of his head was one part of his beauty, once a year he had it cut; his cut hair was weighed and found to weigh more than three kilograms. Goslinga in his commentary on 2 Samuel speaks with a slight understatement of a "very luxuriant growth of hair."[10] The heavy-haired young man was also audacious and bold. When Joab did not come to him immediately, he had his barley harvest put to flames with the desired effect. In addition, he was the heir apparent who was not planning to wait for the death of his father. What is announced without expressing it, will now appear in actions.

The heir apparent impressed the population by outward display. He rode in a wagon with horses, while David and the other princes still used donkeys. He undermined the authority of his father as supreme judge. On the way from the gate he caught people who had not found the justice they desired from the lower judges and wished to appeal to the king. He abused their frustrations, agreed with them all in advance, and predicted that they would not get justice from the king. Before citizens could show him obeisance, he took them by the hand and kissed them. The new Dutch translation of 1951 reads: "Thus did Absalom with all Israelites who came to the king for justice and thus Absalom stole the heart of all the men of Israel." The expression "to steal the heart" has a hidden meaning in Hebrew: it also means "to deceive." People who sought justice fell into the hands of a man seeking power. Four years he

---

9 G. Knuttel Wzn., *Rembrandt. De Meester en zijn werk* [The Master and his Work] (Amsterdam: Ploegsma, 1956) 144. The painting (Br. 511) is found in the Hermitage in Leningrad [St. Petersburg].

10 *Commentaar op het Oude Testament. Het tweede boek Samuel* (Kampen: Kok, 1962) 265.

bided his time; then the net of conspiracy was spread and the time was ripe. Absalom had himself acclaimed king in Hebron.

David immediately perceived the danger of his situation and left Jerusalem with his supporters; weeping, he crossed the valley of Kidron en route to Transjordan. There were meetings with admirers and enemies, moving episodes, and bitter incidents on his escape route. The kernel of the story, in which its message becomes clear, now requires full attention. Two new figures appear on the scene, both advisors of David. One of them, Ahithophel, had gone over to the party of Absalom; the other, Hushai, remained faithful to his king.

It suits the intention of the narrator that he nowhere allows David to be frightened as much as he is because of Ahithophel's desertion. David was more afraid of the advice this shrewdest of counselors might give, than of the army that his rebel son might be able to field. The only prayer that David directed to God on his flight consists of a few words: "Turn the counsel of Ahithophel into folly." In the context of the story it is a brief, but revealing, prayer.

It is also the introduction to the most exciting part of the story; everything now turns on the hour of the decision which will occur not on the field of battle but in the meeting of counselors. Hushai was charged to act as Ahithophel's foil. David sent him back to Jerusalem: in the army he could not be useful, but in the gathering of counselors he could. All appearances were against him. He had joined David as a deeply saddened friend with a torn garment. Now he entered the city gate at the same time as Absalom and was greeted with understandable distrust. The dialogue is as follows (16:15–19):

> *Hushai*: Long live the king! Long live the king!
> *Absalom*: Is this your loyalty to your friend?[11]
> Why did you not go with your friend?
> *Hushai*: No, the one whom the Lord and this people of Israel
> have unanimously chosen, I will belong to.
> With him I will stay.
> Moreover, whom shall I serve?
> Is it not his son?
> As I served your father, so I will serve you.

---

[11] "Friend" is here to be understood as a title of one of the highest officials at the royal court. The advisors of the Seleucid kings are also called "friends" (*philoi*). E. Bickerman, *Institutions des Seleucides* (Paris: Geuther, 1938) 40–50.

All distrust is not removed thereby, but Hushai has made an impression. For the time being Absalom trusted Ahithophel. He counseled that Absalom should enter the harem of his father in public. This meant that everyone might see how complete the breach was and that reconciliation would be excluded.[12] Moreover, he insisted on quick action. David and his people must immediately be destroyed in their flight. They must not have any time to organize their defense. Absalom and the counsel of the elders found Ahithophel's advice entirely agreeable.

Then there was a strange turn in the course of events in that Absalom also wanted to hear Hushai's advice. Hushai did not need to push himself, he was called. His task was not easy. The narrator has assured his listeners that the counsel of Ahithophel weighed as heavily as a word from God, "so was all the counsel of Ahithophel esteemed, both by David and by Absalom" (16:23).

How could Hushai defeat counsel which was good, which all had accepted, which was spoken by such a prestigious man? Hushai is told what Ahithophel said.

Hushai: The counsel which Ahithophel has given is not good this time.

Between the lines one reads amazement and a brief pause. Hushai continued:

> You know that your father and his men are mighty men
> enraged like a bear robbed of her cubs in the field.
> Besides, your father is expert in war; he will not let the
> people spend the night. Even now he has hidden himself in
> one of the caves. When he will launch an attack soon, and
> people hear of it, they will say: the people who follow
> Absalom have suffered defeat. Then even the valiant man,
> whose heart is like the heart of a lion, will utterly melt
> with fear, for all Israel knows that your father is a mighty
> man, and that those who are with him are valiant men.
> Therefore my counsel is: gather all of Israel from Dan to
> Beersheba, numerous as the sand of the sea. Then you must
> enter the battle yourself. So we shall come upon him in
> some place where he is to be found, we shall light upon him as

---

[12] The motif occurs again when we are told that Adonijah asks to marry Abishag of Shunam, the young woman who was added to the royal harem at the end of David's life (1 Kgs 2:13–25), which resulted in his death sentence, pronounced by Solomon.

the dew falls on the ground.
Of him and all the men with him not one will be left. And if
he should withdraw into some city, then all Israel will bring ropes
to that city, and we shall drag it into the valley, until
not even a pebble is to be found there.

Hushai did his best with a piece of sheer nonsense and he knew it. Attentive listeners to the story knew it, too. They noticed that Hushai used a strange and impressive word[13] that he once needed to scrape his throat, got stuck, and lapsed in a trivial phrase.[14] The unreality was as plain as the nose on your face, but the narrator does not comment on this demagoguery. He did not need to. His irony reaches a high point in the simple addition: "Then said Absalom and all the men of Israel: The counsel of Hushai the Archite is better than the one by Ahithophel." There is only one who had seen through the deceit of Hushai and drawn its consequences. Ahithophel understood that the Absalom affair, together with his own, was lost. The narrator is silent on Ahithophel's feelings but offers an inimitable close-up with a few verbs: "When Ahithophel saw that his counsel was not followed, he saddled his donkey, went on his way, went to his house, to his city, put his affairs in order, and hanged himself. Thus he died, and was buried in the grave of his father."[15] It is clear that we are dealing with literature here. The narrator was not an eye-witness to David's flight and the emotions that it elicited among his faithful ones, anymore than Aeschylus was witness to the uproar at the court of Xerxes when he returned from Greece defeated; he did not hear the speech of Hushai anymore than Shakespeare heard the speech of Mark Antony at the forum of Rome after the murder of Julius Caesar. Historical motifs are perceptible in the background, but above all else what we hear is essentially what narrators and tragic poets are telling us.

Our narrator wants to make clear at which moment Absalom's fate was decided. The military qualities of Joab and David, the bravery of their men, the terrain of operations in the forests of Transjordan—their influence on the outcome is slight compared to the confusion that Hushai succeeded in creating with his nonsensical speech. He achieved what David needed: delay, an opportunity to place himself in an advantageous position, hesitation and apprehension in the opponent. Hushai is

---

[13] *Paḥat* (cave) in v. 9, and the last word ṣĕrôr in v. 13 (pebble) occur very infrequently.

[14] Near the end of v. 9a.

[15] Other examples of similarly revealing close-ups: Gen 37:24 and Esth 3:15 as utterances of indifference when faced by suffering done to fellow humans.

not called a wise man in so many words; he is only a "counselor," and what he achieves answers to the insights of ancient Israelite wisdom. Ecclesiastes has summarized it briefly: "Wisdom is good above violence" and "wisdom is good above weapons of war" (9:16,18), and "good" also refers to efficiency.

Meanwhile our narrator shares in the audience's amazement over the blinding of Absalom and his cohort. How is it possible that all of them, with a single exception, were bamboozled by a shrewd speaker? An explanation is given as an enigmatic aside: "For the Lord had ordained to defeat the good counsel of Ahithophel, so that the Lord might bring evil upon Absalom" (17:14).

The motif of David's prayer is borrowed here. A third power must have been in the game. What happened in the counseling sessions of the usurper was too strange to ascribe the outcome only to human factors , such as a lack of critical sense. No matter how brilliantly Hushai had presented his nonsensical oration, he would not have accomplished anything were it not that, apart from him, the fate of Absalom had been decided.

Many commentators regard the aside about the Lord's decree as a pious notation, added later in a report of events, in which nothing was said *expressis verbis* that a deity was in control of things. A copyist would then later have added the religious interpretation to the text because he could not explain that strange and decisive turn on the basis of human responses. I am not so sure that we are dealing with a gloss. In any case, the verse summarizes briefly and tersely the narrator's message, which offers the typical biblical data of double causality.[16]
Ecclesiastes says:

> I have also seen this example of wisdom under the sun and it has made
> a deep impression on me: There was a little city with few inhabitants and
> a great king marched against it and surrounded it and built great siegeworks
> against it. And in that city was found a poor wise man and he by his
> wisdom delivered the city. But no one remembered that poor man. Then I
> said: good is wisdom above might, but the poor man's wisdom is depised,
> and one does not listen to his words (9:13–18).

---

[16] I. L. Seeligmann, "Menschliches Heldentum und Gottliche Hilfe", TZ 19 (1963) 385–411; L. Schmidt, *Menschlicher Erfolg und Jahwes Initiative, Studien zu Tradition, Interpretation und Historie in Überlieferungen von Gideon, Saul und David* (Neukirchen/ Vluyn: Neukirchener Verlag, 1970).

The force of this statement is confirmed in Absalom's council session. Hushai, in the light of wisdom, craftily abused the impression that verbiage can make even on those who are out of the ordinary. He would not have been able to succeed if David's prayer had not been heard. Thus, there are two sides, a human and a more-than-human. That is the secret of double causality, the final decision lies not in the power of the advisor, still less in that of the general, but advisor and general must appear in action to realize the decision. Hushai may now leave the scene; he accomplished what David asked of him: to frustrate good counsel and with bad counsel thwart Absalom. He leaves us with the question: was all honor due to Hushai?

The conclusion of the drama is now certain, but the narrator still has an element of surprise left. He calls full attention to the reactions of father David, who appeared to love his rebellious son in an almost unimaginable manner. He wanted to save his throne, but he also wanted to protect his son. Thus he is inwardly torn. It is a secret to no one that he ordered that the young man Absalom be treated "gently" (18:5). The battle in the forest of Ephraim deteriorated into a horrible, man-killing slaughter. The foot soldiers of Absalom found their death in the forests: "the forest devoured that day more of the people than the sword had devoured."

Absalom was encountered on a donkey; when it came under the dense branches of a large terebinth, Absalom's head got stuck, the donkey ran away from him, and he remained hanging helplessly between heaven and earth. According to a popular Sunday School representation, which is iconographically very old, he was left hanging with his hair in the branches. The story does not say this in so many words, and thus no actualizing sermon may be based on it concerning the dangers of long locks in warfare and the incompatability of luxurious hair and battle dress.

Joab made short shrift of the crown prince; his corpse was thrown in a ditch. The war was over, but the story was not finished. The narrator set a more difficult task for himself than a happy ending would have been. His most difficult task awaits. He must evoke the emotions of David who is anxiously waiting, not for the outcome of the battle but for the report about his son. He tried to reason away anxious premonitions.

The king, by Joab' request, had not gone along in battle. He sat at the gate of Mahanaim, and from the roof the watchman looked down the road in the direction of where a courier might be expected. A runner came hurriedly, and the watchman announced him. There then followed a revealing dialogue in which the expression "good news" was repeatedly sounded, to suppress the bad news that the king was afraid to hear.

The king:	If he is alone, he brings good news.
The watchman:	There comes yet another man running.
The king:	He also brings good news.
The watchman:	If I can see the running of the first man, he appears to be Ahimaaz the son of Zadok.
Ahimaaz:	Peace! Blessed be the Lord your God, who has delivered up the rebels against my lord the king!
The king:	Is it well with the young man Absalom?
Ahimaaz:	I saw a great crowd when Joab sent your servant, but I do not know what it was.
The king:	Turn aside.

An Ethiopian arrived. Joab had given him orders to tell the truth, a message that might endanger the messenger's life. But he is black, a foreigner, he may be risked.

The Ethiopian:	Good news for my lord the king, for the Lord granted you justice this day against all who have risen against you.
The king:	Is it well with the young man, with Absalom?
The Ethiopian:	May the enemies of my lord the king, and all who have risen up against you to do evil, be like that young man.

After slow preparation the truth is said without saying the worst. David did not control his sorrow. He went to the upper room of the gate, and while he was running back and forth, weeping, he called out: "My son Absalom, my son, my son Absalom. Would that I had died instead of you, O Absalom, my son, my son." By repeating simple words David's grief is conveyed without mentioning the word "grief." The narrator does not need to.

The trials of the king were not thereby over. Joab and his men were completely at a loss. The soldiers entered the city gate stealthily, as if they had fled from the battle. And David kept on wailing.

Again it was Joab who pitilessly acted and powerfully verbalized to the king that the soldiers had not risked their lives so that he might wail. It looked as if the king hated those who loved him and loved those who hated him, as if he would rather see Absalom alive and his supporters dead. Joab put the loyalty of himself and his men on the table; the throne of David was now really in danger. "Then the king arose, and took his seat in the gate. The people were told, Behold, the king is sitting in the gate. And all the people came before the king" (19:8).

Thus is the drama essentially ended. There is no fanfare of victory but rather a depressed mood. David played the game that was forced upon him. He was, as Prov 25:20 says, as one "who sings songs with a heavy heart," and that is, says the sage, "like one who takes off a garment on a cold day, and like vinegar on lye."

In the victory that was gained for him, David lost all except his throne. He then returned to Jerusalem, which was unrolled like a film in reverse. There were humorous and difficult meetings on the way back but they do not contribute to the essence of the story. That story was finished with David's mourning for the death of the son who had threatened his own life.

Looking back to the beginning, when Amnon unleashed a series of fatal, related, and overlapping events, we can draw up the balance of misery. Tamar was violated for life, Amnon was murdered, Absalom fell dishonorably, Ahithophel committed suicide, innocent people were killed in battle, fighting for a senseless purpose.

The narrator has shown people as they are; no one is a caricature, no one is idealized. He has shown human behavior and let nothing happen that is impossible within the bounds of human conduct. No *deus ex machina* appears, no ghost from the dead is needed to interpret or predict.

Only mortal humans played a role in a drama of delight and suffering, and what they did, they did with a view toward death. This theme of biblical wisdom was expressed by the wise woman of Tekoa: "We must surely die, and become as water spilt on the ground which cannot be gathered up again" (2 Sam 14:14). In the face of the death that awaits all, the wise woman asked for mercy, which is the reflection of God's patient compassion "who seeks ways so that one who is rejected should remain rejected." David went the way of mercy in his love for a disloyal son. He thereby entered a way of suffering which was almost too heavy for him. In the end he was a broken man.

May we speak of a Hebrew tragedy?[17] Following common linguistic usage, we may call the fatal path of the *dramatis personae* tragic. However,

---

[17] The characteristics which B. A. van Groningen, *De boodschap der Griekse tragedie over Hellas en Hellenen* [The Message of Greek Tragedy concerning Hellas and Hellenes] (Amsterdam: Meulenhoff, 1964) 101–15) has given, may be partly recognized in the story of David and Absalom: portrayal of human life, life arm in arm with

no one escaped responsibility. Crime and punishment are linked; no one is a victim of an accidental conjunction of circumstances.

What then about David? With this question we must not forget that the Absalom story is the second part of a trilogy which began with the murder of Uriah that David had orchestrated, because the king had fathered a child by Uriah's wife Bathsheba. Therefore, Vondel in his Dutch drama *Koning David in Ballingschap* [King David in Exile] lets the ghost of Uriah appear as accuser from the underworld. David also bears his burden of guilt, repentance, and suffering.[18]

Moreover, he is the king, the embodiment of his people, God's people. The wise woman of Tekoa reminded the king of that: the king who did not allow the banished to return, harbored thoughts against God's people. This statement anticipated the outcome, not only of David's life but of his dynasty, when his people were banished to Babylonian exile. The historian who wondered what the cause of this humiliation might be, had already been answered by the prophet Jeremiah: the causality of guilt and punishment was also realized in the fate of the people. An unknown author wrote his story of human weakness and passion—an episode in the history of God's people—in light of causality and retribution, but also realizing that human repentance and divine compassion can break the fatal chain of cause and effect. At the conclusion of my Bible story hour I am not permitted to say that the author wrote well or that he mastered his style in a grand manner, for he wrote to be heard, not to be praised.

---

death, the concept that suffering is punishment for guilt, and that the way of humans is determined by more than human power. There are also great differences: no positive meaning is assigned to death in the Old Testament, not all suffering is penance: it may also be temptation. But the most important difference is that in the context of the Old Testament, human fate appears in a different light than in Greek tragedy: it is very closely related to the fate of God's people in their course through history from exodus to exile and from exile to return.

[18] Opening of the second act, where Uriah's ghost appears in David's harem: "God's vengeance casts off him, who has cast off Uriah, removed from his faithfulness...."